BANNOCKBURN

Now retired after a 29-year career in the army, **Peter Reese** is a leading military historian and writer. His abiding love for Scotland ensures frequent visits north from his home in Surrey.

PETER REESE

BANNOCKBURN

Scotland's Greatest Victory

CANONGATE
Edinburgh · London

To my son, Martin

Published in Great Britain in 2000 by Canongate Books Ltd,
14 High Street, Edinburgh EH1 1TE

This new edition published in 2014

www.canongate.tv

1

Illustrations © as credited
Maps based on Ordnance Survey Pathfinder 1:25,000 series maps by
permission of Ordnance Survey on behalf of the controller of Her
Majesty's Stationery Office
© Crown Copyright MC 00100012896
Maps produced by Paul Vickers and The Wheel

British Library Cataloguing-in-Publication Data
A catalogue record for this book is available on
request from the British Library

ISBN 978 1 78211 176 4

Typeset by Palimpsest Book Production Ltd, Falkirk, Stirlingshire
Printed and bound in Great Britain by Clays Ltd, St Ives plc

CONTENTS

LIST OF MAPS AND BATTLE PLANS

INTRODUCTION TO THE 700TH ANNIVERSARY EDITION

I needed no persuading to write this book for, whatever Bannock-burn's qualities as a battle – and it scores highly in this regard – it also marks the greatest victory ever gained by the Scots over the English. William Wallace's success at Stirling Bridge seventeen years earlier was also fought against superior forces who, with their heavy cavalry and famed bowmen, enjoyed technological superiority. At Stirling Bridge however, Wallace merely prevailed over an army led by Edward I's representative, John Warenne, Earl of Surrey, whereas at Bannockburn Robert the Bruce utterly defeated the English Army led by its monarch, Edward II. Following Wallace's victory it was predictable that the redoubt-able Edward I (the so-called Hammer of the Scots) would respond by leading another army into Scotland to hunt Wallace down and complete his process of subjugation. Bruce's success, however, released him from having to appeal for peace from Edward II. He had done so in 1310,[1] attempting to gain the moral high ground along with more time to gather his military strength. His victory at Bannockburn gave him new opportunities to continue with his own diplomatic and military initiatives to free his country from English domination. In 1320, the Declar-ation of Arbroath justified Scotland's independence and fourteen years later, with the Treaty of Northampton, the English parlia-ment recognised Scotland as a sovereign state and Robert Bruce as its legitimate king. Without Bannockburn he could never have succeeded, thus enabling Scotland's representatives to voluntarily enter into a process of union with England almost 400 years later.

In light of the battle's pivotal importance it is surprising that relatively few accounts had been written about it until recently.

It is also curious that despite the presence of a singular contemporary source – on the Scottish side at least – there should be such divergence about where the battle occurred – a debate that continues to the present day.

When this book first appeared in 2000 it was believed to be the first dedicated analysis of the battle for some seventy-five years. Since then interest in Scottish history and the country's most successful battle has grown, and with Bannockburn's 700th Anniversary approaching more books on the subject have emerged. Despite predictable differences in interpretation, without major new archaeological discoveries or the emergence of any hitherto unknown sources about the battle, all writers – like their predecessors – depend largely on the four contemporary narratives used in this book. These sources recount a largely similar sequence of events. Foremost is the graphic verse account *The Bruce* by Archdeacon John Barbour of Aberdeen, written some sixty years after the battle. It is in the style of other fourteenth-century romances rather than a blow–by-blow account of events, but Barbour did have access to contemporary chronicles and talked with the descendants of men who fought in the battle. While an undoubted work of art, the general accuracy of *The Bruce* has also been acknowledged by several subsequent writers.

Although far shorter, there are contrasting commentaries representing the English side. There is the *Scalacronica* – the so-called 'ladder chronicle' due to its author's desire to survey events from a detached position – written by Sir Thomas Grey, the younger, whose father was taken prisoner at Bannockburn.[2] His soldier's account was completed in 1355–1356 and drew freely on his father's experiences. The second, *Vita Edwardi Secundi* (Life of Edward II) is not strictly a chronicle but a journal about the King's reign, probably written in 1326 by the well-connected John Walwayn, agent to the Earl of Hereford. A fragment of the *Chronicle of Lanercost* constitutes the third account and was written by an Augustinian monk – or a succession of monks – from the Priory at Lanercost. The Priory was the target of repeated Scottish raids and unsurprisingly the account shows strong English prejudices.

Invaluable as such sources are for studying the battle, their failure to give a clear indication about where the main engagement occurred has led to remarkable consequences. Initially it was thought to be in the locality of Bruce's Borestone (in which he placed his standard) where the Rotunda Memorial, Pilkington Jackson's equestrian statue of Robert the Bruce, and the Bannockburn Heritage Centre stand today. However, in 1913 a book by William MacKay MacKenzie conclusively disproved this site as the location of the battle, although MacKenzie's suggested alternative to the east, close to the River Forth, has also been conclusively rejected. Contemporary writers have further limited the site but still differ over whether the battle occurred on Carse Land near Balquhiderock or within corn land nearby, with some still unwilling to commit themselves either way. Both sites however, lie over one-and-a-quarter miles from the Heritage Centre.

While researching this book and walking the battlefield to help me determine the location of the main clash of arms, I resolved to examine the conflict by assessing the opposing leaders' military experience and capabilities (together with those of their subordinate commanders). I also considered the characteristics of both armies including their weaponry, favoured tactics and their reported use of the ground. As a result, I concluded that the most likely location is on Carse land enclosed by the two water courses, the Bannockburn and the Pelstream Burn adjoining the dry field of Balquhiderock. However on 24 June 2014 when the Battle's 700th anniversary celebrations take place they are to be held on the Borestone site which has been newly landscaped. The Rotunda Memorial and equestrian statue of Robert the Bruce have been refurbished and a new visitor centre created. Here visitors will be able to experience a virtual recreation of the two-day battle.

While this undoubtedly represents a massive advance over previous facilities, fundamental questions remain about the actual site of the battle. To date no archaeological survey has been commissioned for the most favoured area (and therefore no mass graves have been discovered) and more serious still no preservation methods have been put in place to protect this site. Unlike the Heritage Centre which enjoys the protection of the National Trust, the most likely true site of the battle remains vulnerable to further urban development, if not eventual obliteration. To help avoid such a tragedy I believe that a ban should be placed on further building and that steps be undertaken to purchase all available ground for the Scottish nation.

In the meantime a battlefield trail should be designed for those visitors wishing to explore the most likely site of the conflict. Without such initiatives, and in spite of all the admirable work recently carried out in the vicinity of the Borestone site, the commemoration of Scotland's greatest victory remains wanting. With such expectations in mind, this book's essential purpose is to give an accurate, balanced and graphic account of the epic military confrontation that occurred on the Carse during the 23rd and 24th June in the lea of Stirling's great castle. At present the opportunity for visitors to appreciate it fully is incomplete. For those with limited time or physical abilities the virtual experiences at the visitor centre, and a written account such as this might suffice, but the majority should also have the opportunity of retracing the actual movements of both armies across the field of battle. Such additional facilities will give all visitors a genuine opportunity to appreciate the remarkable events that took place there. At Bannockburn, a lesser army under its outstanding warrior king – who had previously served the formidable English monarch Edward I, and was considered a usurper by many of his own countrymen – maintained a unity of purpose to overcome a disunited English force and enabled Scotland to regain its national voice.

Whatever people's knowledge of the battle, its 700th anniversary gives them the chance to make judgements about it. Contemporary observers involved in the current debate on Scottish independence, for instance, are likely to reach conclusions that favour their cause, with those championing independence believing that the Scottish victory at Bannockburn, owing much to patriotic fervour and loyalty, can provide fresh inspiration today. Those favouring continued union might well point to the subsequent series of defeats suffered by equally patriotic Scottish

armies and look to the continuing pattern of Scottish achievements within the wider canvas of the United Kingdom.

Whatever such reactions, this book sets out to portray, faithfully, a singular and notable engagement which, like so many
others, experienced a 'grinding phase' when things could have
gone either way. At Bannockburn there were moments when
luck played a significant part, but there were other moments – as
there were in many other battles between determined men – when
insight, belief and the spark of inspired leadership counted most.

Peter Reese
Ash Vale
November 2013

INTRODUCTION AND ACKNOWLEDGEMENTS

THE BATTLE OF BANNOCKBURN was the greatest victory ever gained by the Scots over the English. As such it gave Scotland new confidence to continue with the series of military and diplomatic initiatives that enabled the country to regain its freedom from English domination. Yet apart from the action's significance, both to the Scottish nation and to the fortunes of Scotland's warrior king, Robert Bruce, Bannockburn stands comparison with other western battles of the time in the tactical skills and masterly control shown by its victorious commander. It was also an heroic and, by medieval standards, a prolonged encounter.

Unlike many other battles during this period, Bannockburn is well documented. Foremost among its chroniclers is Archdeacon John Barbour of Aberdeen. Although he wrote his magisterial work *The Bruce* sixty years after the battle he interviewed a good number of those who actually took part and mentioned many by name. From his post in Aberdeen Barbour was able to keep in touch with eminent men from the Scottish court and ordinary people alike, and he also listened to the songs and traditional stories associated with the great battle. As a result the comprehensive work of this Scottish Chaucer, written in graphic verse using metre and rhyme and running to 13,000 lines, represents not only a powerful romantic story in the genre of other chivalric romances of the fourteenth century such as *The Romance of Fierabras*, but it gives a thorough-going and authoritative account of the conflict. It also happens to be the most detailed life of any medieval king in the west. Read in the prose translation of George Eyre-Todd its accuracy has, for instance, been acknowledged by people as far apart as Barbour's contemporary, Andrew of Wyntown, in his *Orygynale Cronykil of Scotland*, and by that demanding and pertinacious writer of comparatively modern times, John E Morris. In his book on Bannockburn, Morris was initially determined to be highly critical of Barbour but ended up acknowledging the accuracy of *The Bruce*.

While there is nothing on the English side to compare with *The Bruce* for detail, three accounts are of particular use. There is the *Scalacronica* – the so-called 'ladder chronicle' because of its author's desire to survey events from a detached, lofty position – written by Sir Thomas Grey the younger, of Heton, whose father was taken prisoner at Bannockburn before being subsequently released.[1] Thomas Grey was himself captured by the Scots in 1355 when, as constable of Norham Castle, south of Berwick, he made an unsuccessful sally against superior numbers. While confined for two years in Edinburgh Castle he had the run of its considerable library. There Grey wrote his *Scalacronica*, including an account of Bannockburn which would have inevitably drawn on his father's experiences.

Another English authority of particular interest is a comprehensive account called *Vita Edwardi Secundi*, the Life of Edward II. The authorship of this is uncertain, but it was obviously written by a highly educated layman of mature years who was an authority on civil law; evidence points here to it being John Walwayn, who was the Earl of Hereford's agent in both England and Scotland. The account is written with flair and outspokenness and it ends abruptly in 1326, the year in which Walwayn died. It is, therefore, highly probable that it was written no more than twelve years after the actual battle, and is all the more valuable for that.

The third 'southern' account was the work of an Augustinian monk, or succession of monks, most probably from the priory of Lanercost near Carlisle, and shows strong English prejudices – unsurprising from a cleric whose religious house was an inevitable target for successive Scottish raids. The writer claimed he was told about the battle 'by somebody worthy to be believed who was present there himself and saw it'.[2] Although the Lanercost account is quite short, it is invaluable both for its

English perspective and for being a relatively contemporary description.

Other contemporary chronicles and documents, together with later commentaries, are acknowledged at the end of the book. Of the later authorities four men and one woman deserve particular acknowledgement. They are Professor Geoffrey Barrow, whose truly authoritative book on Robert Bruce (1998) is essential for anyone examining the king's path to power as well as his greatest battle, Ronald McNair Scott (1993) for his graphic biography of the Scottish king, and Caroline Bingham (1998) for her own elegantly written account of the king's life. With regard to the two writers on the battle itself, John Morris' *Bannockburn* (1913) is both an acute and distinctive commentary, while William Mackay MacKenzie's *Battle of Bannockburn* (1913) changed radically all previous thinking about its location.

Since the two latter books published almost ninety years ago – and Mackay MacKenzie's is a comparatively short work – no comprehensive account of Bannockburn has appeared. This is despite the fact that during the interim, and especially in recent years, renewed attention has been paid to the early Wars of Independence and to Scotland's premier battlefield success. During the last quarter century, for instance, the numbers of visitors to the Scottish Heritage Centre at Bannockburn have increased markedly.

In such circumstances, particularly when one considers that not all observers are even agreed upon its actual site, some further consideration about the great confrontation that took place near Stirling Castle during the two days of 23 and 24 June 1314 seems long overdue.

The most notable analysis of the battle in relatively recent years is by General Sir Philip Christison whose findings, since 1964, are contained in a booklet produced by Scottish National Heritage. However, in spite of General Christison's work and further descriptions of the battle that occur in books on the Wars of Independence, such as Peter Traquair's *Freedom's Sword* or Raymond Campbell Paterson's *For the Lion*, the present book is the first full length account to appear since before World War One. In it I go somewhat further than MacKenzie and Morris in attempting to trace how the conflict stands in relation to Bruce's overall plans to recover Scotland. More attention is also paid to the individuals involved, not just the two kings but their chief subordinates, together with the two sides' contrasting military doctrines.

With respect to my researches, I owe an immense debt to the staff of the National Library of Scotland, both in its main building on George IV Bridge in Edinburgh and when in its temporary base at Causewayside, for giving me an opportunity to consult the early chronicles and contemporary documents held there.

Other libraries which have given valuable support are: the Edinburgh Central Library, Edinburgh University Library, the Royal Military Academy Library, Sandhurst, the Services' Central Library and the Prince Consort's Library, Aldershot, where the greater part of the writing has taken place.

For illustrations and maps I acknowledge the collections in the National Portrait Gallery, the Scottish National Portrait Gallery and the Scottish Map Library. The detailed battle maps have been produced by Mr Paul Vickers, the British Army's technical librarian, who has both walked and measured the battlefield with me, pored over Ordnance Survey maps and considered the different interpretations of the battlefield made by other writers.

The draft manuscript was produced by Mrs Christine Batten with her 'sparkling' word processor and most valuable preliminary observations on it have been made by Mrs Jennifer Prophet and Dr Leslie Wayper. Mrs Prophet and her son Charles also produced the index.

With regard to Canongate Books which is, of course, of crucial importance, the project would not have commenced without the proposal from Hugh Andrew, continued without the ever present support from Jamie Byng and Neville Moir, and come to publication without the sensitive, acute and constructive editorial work of Donald Reid.

Despite such remarkable support, as in the past I could not think of such a project without Barbara, my wife and mainstay.

Any errors are, of course, the author's responsibility alone.

PROLOGUE

AT DAWN ON 22 JULY 1298 the peremptory shouts of drill sergeants followed by their soldiers' shorter acknowledgements interrupted the regular birdcalls and the sloughing of the wind on a peaceful hillock adjoining Mumrills Brae just east of Falkirk. The Scottish army was preparing to take up its battle stations on the hill's crest. It was by no means the first time military commands had been heard there; some eleven centuries before, Mumrills had carried one of nineteen forts standing on the Roman wall that straddled the narrow waist of Scotland between the two great inlets of the rivers Firth and Clyde. Within fifty years the Romans had abandoned their northernmost wall and fallen back to the much longer one built by the Emperor Hadrian on what was to become the Scoto-English border.

The soldiers on their way up to Mumrills' flat crest were not peering northwards for marauding tribesmen, however. Instead, the Scottish host assembled by William Wallace, who, at twenty-six years of age had already proved himself a brilliant natural soldier and determined guardian of his country on behalf of its deposed king, John Balliol, was looking east for sight of a formidable army under the veteran English king, Edward I, approaching along the old Roman road from Linlithgow. The English column had reached Linlithgow the day before and as the Scottish spearmen left their bivouacs in nearby Torwood to form up, Wallace's scouts had already provided him with a steady commentary on Edward's progress westwards. In fact, the English were ahead of time following an injury to their king inflicted by his own war horse. Like other chargers it had remained bitted and saddled while being kept close to its rider who could then quickly mount in the event of any surprise

Scottish attack. As Edward lay resting on the ground his charger became excited and trampled on him, apparently breaking two of his ribs. Reports about his injuries soon spread and multiplied and a sense of near panic arose in the English camp. But Edward I had never lacked courage nor resolve and although it was still dark, the fifty-nine-year-old monarch immediately mounted his horse and resumed the advance. The king halted his army close to Mumrills before the grey morning sky gave way to full daylight where he ordered them to hear mass on this, the feast day of St Mary Magdalene. While tired from their wearisome pursuit and the shortest of rests during the previous night the English had strong cause to feel confident about the outcome. They had finally run to earth the one Scottish leader who had succeeded in thwarting their battle ranks. With their forces' marked superiority in archers, both long- and cross-bowmen, and their total dominance in heavy cavalry, they would surely soon overcome him.

On the Scottish side Wallace relied largely on his schiltrons, novel formations of spearmen aligned into circular formations. As the schiltrons formed up Wallace's engineers arrived with carts full of wooden stakes sharpened at each end. Working in pairs with one man holding a stake and the other hammering it into the firm ground they erected a protective circle of spikes pointing outwards which they afterwards roped together to help withstand the fearsome charges of English armoured knights.

Wallace gave further protection to his spear circles by positioning his own short-bowmen between them while further detachments of archers covered his open flanks. The third element in Wallace's human redoubt was his cavalry, just an eighth of the English strength, dressed in lighter armour and riding smaller horses. Not only were the Scottish cavalry utterly outnumbered and outclassed but they had been sent by such nobles as John Comyn (the Red) and the earls of Atholl, Menteith, Lennox and Buchan, while a further contingent was likely to have come from Robert Bruce, Earl of Carrick. Such senior magnates were unlikely to allow their riders to come under Wallace's full control.

With his fewer numbers, Wallace had been forced to conclude he could not spare any part of his force to meet the attackers before they came to close range. Committed to their formations on the hilltop his bowmen and spearmen had no option but to await the forthcoming attacks. However, Wallace had good reason to expect the English horses which, like their soldiers, had lived on short rations and had been hard used during the pursuit, would become winded negotiating his covering obstacles. In the worst case, he knew he could move his army back into the extensive Torwood stretching round his rear where the English cavalry would itself become vulnerable.

Wallace's final contribution before the battle was the traditional address of encouragement to his assembled men. 'I have brought you to the ring,' he said, 'dance the best you can.'

The initial attacks were mounted by Edward's massed heavy cavalry, mounted on their massive shire horses. The first was led by Norfolk, the earl marshal, who set off towards the Scottish right-hand schiltron before disappearing from Wallace's sight as it encountered the band of heavy marsh bounding the West Quarter burn. While it was still hidden from the Scottish commander's view, the English second division, commanded by the Bishop of Durham, was ordered to begin its attack against the Scots' left.

Simultaneous assaults on both flanks supported by a frontal attack from the English main body was quite the worst scenario Wallace could have expected. However, while approaching fast, the main body under the king had yet to engage in the fighting. The initial Scottish response to the two flanking attacks was both determined and effective. The left hand spear ring fully justified Wallace's formation; they withstood all assaults made upon them and impaled many English horses on their massed spikes. Unfortunately for Wallace the brave conduct of his spearmen was not equalled by the cavalry, who fled the field without striking a blow. As a result the English cavalry, deprived of any mounted opponents, were able to turn from the spearmen to easier targets. Thundering between and around the schiltrons, the armoured juggernauts succeeded in riding the

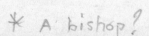
* A bishop?

Scottish archers down. As they attempted to stand their ground these were killed to a man, along with their commander, Sir John Stewart. With the flight of the Scottish cavalry other English horsemen were free to circle the rear of the hill and block Wallace's escape route. At this point the English king moved his third division forward. Instead of despatching his cavalry against the serried spears he ordered bowmen to loose volleys of arrows at point blank range into the beleaguered circles. From this short distance only the spearmen's wooden targes could successfully withstand such missiles. Taper-headed arrows tore through helmets and the plated armour of the day which in any case was only worn by a privileged few. The shafts had even less difficulty in penetrating chain mail. The defenders were under no illusions that if arrows entered their bodies, they were likely to die, while any limbs that were hit would need rapid amputation performed in the crude fashion of the time.

As medieval battles went Falkirk was both bitter and protracted. Despite alternate assaults on them by both cavalry and bowmen, the schiltrons showed amazing courage and continued to resist doggedly. But Wallace knew there could be only one outcome. With the schiltrons trapped the English king was in no hurry as he directed his bowmen's fire against each one in turn. Even when their shafts had been despatched the defenders gained little respite for the archers were ordered to pick up flints lying on the burn bed and on the hillside. Using slings or simply relying on their heavily muscled right arms, they were able to take deliberate aim at the faces or legs of the stationary Scots. As the rocks found their targets, bones fractured and cheeks reddened with blood; many spearmen went down joining those transfixed by arrows and the mail-clad cavalry began to break into the circles. Once inside, the heavy horses bowled over defenders before trampling them with their iron-clad hooves, while their riders' swords, maces and axes were used to terrible effect on those still struggling to keep their footing and point their lances outwards. Within the circles discipline loosened and the Welsh bowmen now gleefully joined in the hand-to-hand fighting that had become a slaughter. Of the Scottish nobles who fought dismounted, Wallace's great friend Sir John the Graham, together with MacDuff and his two sons and Andrew Moray of Bothwell, died where they stood.[1] About a third of the spearmen, many carrying serious wounds, reached whatever cover they could and Wallace rallied a group that turned savagely on the English who pursued them into Callendar Wood. During the engagement it was probably Wallace himself who killed Brother Brian de Jay, the master of the English Templars. But nothing could reverse the scale of the defeat. Many spearmen who found temporary hiding places in the open were subsequently killed as they attempted to flee north, run down by the rampaging cavalry as they searched desperately for opportunities to cross the slippery, treacherous banks of the river Carron.

Following the battle, Scottish patriots were bound to ask each other, 'Where can Scotland go now?' Wallace had assembled the best army his country could supply and after equipping and preparing it thoroughly he had not risked it in open battle until his English pursuers were half-starved and wearied due to a continuing lack of supplies. While his chosen defensive position on Mumrills Hill was undoubtedly not that impressive, it enjoyed protection on three sides from a burn and wet broken ground. And after the English had taxed their horses ascending it they came onto a flat top that favoured Wallace's formations quite as much as theirs.

The soldiers who survived the defeat and succeeded in returning to their townships would have left no one in any doubt about the stringent training they had undergone with Wallace, and they had good reasons to be proud of their own performance in the battle. Such survivors would have doubtless felt far differently about their cavalry – men who from childhood were trained in war but who fled the field at the very sight of the larger numbers of English knights. However, the plain fact was that in spite of the courage and tenacity shown by both the Scottish spearmen and their archers at Mumrills, they had been unable to counter overwhelming English arms.

Given England's superior military resources, Scottish fighting men, nobles and soldiers alike, had the strongest reasons to question how anyone could do better against such adverse odds.

Section One: *The Path to Battle*

CHAPTER ONE

≈

SCOTLAND UNDER SIEGE

(Edward I) 'decided with an oath that he would lay the whole of Scotland waste from sea to sea and force its people into submission.'

Chronicle Rishanger

IN THE LATE THIRTEENTH century Scotland faced a challenge to its continuing survival from a strong and acquisitive English king who as early as 1291 told his privy council that he had it in his mind 'to bring under his dominion the king and the realm of Scotland'.[1] While Scottish monarchs had always in some respects held subordinate positions compared with their more powerful English counterparts (the Pope, for instance, withheld their right to be anointed at their coronations) they had consistently rejected any suggestions that they could be considered vassals of the English crown. In accordance with this tradition, on 29 October 1278 King Alexander III stood before the Court of Westminster and denied that his brother-in-law Edward I had any degree of feudal superiority over him. '(Although) I become your man for the lands which I hold of you in the Kingdom of England for which I owe homage ... No one has a right to homage for my Kingdom of Scotland save God alone, and I hold it only of God.'[2]

Notwithstanding such close family ties and the generally friendly relations between the two countries, Edward, who by the 1280s had become the most respected monarch in Europe, became obsessed with extending his own claims of suzerainty over Scotland. Such a challenge could not be taken lightly for Edward was a monarch whose ambitions were matched by endless energy and single-minded ruthlessness. He had, for instance, already codified English law to his own pattern, justifying the changes by citing previous cases of corruption and miscarriages of justice, and had gone on to abrogate Welsh powers of jurisdiction in those parts of the principality brought under his control.

Whether a subtle-minded reformer or not (particularly when it was to his own advantage), this tall, commanding figure was essentially a warrior king who was quite prepared to achieve his objectives by mounting a military challenge to Scotland. However, with his on-going conquest of Wales, and almost continuous warfare with France, a third military front seemed very likely to place almost unbearable strains on the English exchequer.

Edward could never have doubted that Scotland, with its unbroken line of kings stretching back to before William the Conqueror and its geographical remoteness, represented a quite different and more difficult proposition than Wales. Apart from the amicable relations between the two crowns many of Edward's powerful and ambitious nobles, such as Balliol, Bruce and Umfraville, held lands on both sides of the border and their allegiance was therefore divided. Edward needed a strong pretext to involve himself in the affairs of Scotland and to justify despatching an English army into that country.

Such an opportunity presented itself through what many men in medieval times considered a stroke of fate. In March 1286 Alexander III met with a sudden and untimely death; on a storm-swept night he was hurrying to join Yolande, his new French wife, at Kinghorn by the Firth of Forth when in blizzard conditions he outdistanced his escort and his horse carried him over a steep crag along the foreshore. The role of the monarch was pivotal in the affairs of a medieval state and the tragedy for Scotland was that Alexander had no living male issue. A strong, wise king was succeeded by his four-year-old granddaughter, Margaret, the Maid of Norway, the only child of Alexander's daughter Margaret, who had died giving birth, and Eric II of Norway.

Alexander had shown himself well aware of the dangers that could come from internal unrest in the event of his death and he had arranged that prior to the Maid's enthronement, no fewer than six men should act as joint guardians of the kingdom made up from two representatives of the country's senior nobles, its earls, two representatives of the bishops and two representatives of the barons. The two most likely contenders for the Scottish throne, Robert Bruce, known as the Competitor, and John Balliol, were not included because the king foresaw a very real threat of civil war between their two factions. However, he had seen that support for Bruce and Balliol was evenly divided among the six guardians.

Bruce was much the older of the two men. By 1286, in spite of his continuing ambitions and still abundant energy, he was fully seventy-five years of age. Even in the event of his claim to the throne proving successful he was unlikely to have reigned for long. Fortunately for the Bruces their male line was well represented. The old Competitor's eldest son, another Robert Bruce, was Lord of Annandale, a vast estate in the Scottish southwest. Bruce of Annandale was forty years of age at this time and his eldest son also carried the family name of Robert Bruce. Although still a boy of twelve he was destined to become King Robert I. In 1286 John Balliol too, had a son, called Edward, from his marriage during 1281 to Isabel, daughter of John de Warenne, Earl of Surrey.

One of the guardians' first actions was to inform their seemingly friendly senior monarch, Edward I, of the plans being made to govern Scotland in the absence of the Maid. It is also likely they initiated the arrangements for a marriage to be negotiated between Edward Caernarvon, Edward I's heir, and Margaret, the Maid, for with Edward I acting as her guarantor the guardians could feel sure Margaret's succession would be implemented. Their concerns seemed justified for while their envoys were in England the Competitor and his son seized the two royal castles of Dumfries and Wigtown along with the Balliol fortress of Buittle in a bid to strengthen their position in the southwest against John Balliol. Through their concern for internal stability, however, the guardians seemed willing to ignore the even greater advantages of the union to the English king, including his use of it as a first step towards assimilating Scotland. Any such plans fell through when, in 1290, Margaret died as she made her way to Scotland.

With thirteen men possessing some sort of claim to the vacant Scottish throne the English king was given a fresh, and potentially more dangerous, opportunity to exert his control over the country. One of the guardians, Bishop William Fraser (Bishop of St Andrews and a Balliol supporter), fearing with some justification that the Bruces would make a full bid for the crown, wrote to Edward I asking him to come to the border to prevent bloodshed. In response, working on the assumption that he was their feudal superior, Edward issued a summons for the Scots to meet him – not in Scotland but at a parliament across the English border at Norham. While they had expected Edward to act as arbiter he came as overlord and judge demanding the claimants to recognise him as both their feudal superior and Lord Paramount of Scotland. To support his dictates he brought troops at his back calling up English levies from the northern counties to meet him at Norham on 3 June 1291. Nine of the claimants quickly acknowledged him as their feudal superior and on 11 June, avowedly to avoid internal unrest, Edward ordered all Scottish castles to be turned over to him until two months after the succession had been decided. He then proceeded to replace many Scottish officials with Englishmen.

Edward adopted a measured and unhurried approach to the so-called 'Great Cause' of deciding who had the best claims to the Scottish throne, and eighteen months passed in deliberation (during which Edward enjoyed considerable control over Scotland) before John Balliol was declared the strongest candidate. Unlike his main rival, the belligerent Competitor, Balliol was a younger son so probably destined for a church appointment and therefore unprepared for such elevation.[3] The Lanercost Chronicler for instance dismissed him as brainless.[4] While such seeming limitations did not debar him, he had fewer obvious interests in Scotland than the Competitor for, although Balliol had become Lord of Galloway on the death of his mother, he had estates in seventeen English counties and his main demesne was across the Channel, in Picardy.

Balliol was duly enthroned in November 1292 and during

the next month paid homage for his kingdom to the English monarch. Edward, giving Balliol no opportunity to establish himself as king, rapidly let it be known that authority to hear appeals from Balliol's courts lay with him and Balliol was, therefore, required to defend the judgements in his own courts by making the long journey from Scotland to London where he was also liable for any damages if the verdicts were amended.

Edward appeared determined to goad the Scottish king into rebellion, a situation which would, of course, allow him to seize Scotland as a forfeited fiefdom. The final insult came in June 1294 when he openly treated Scotland as his feudal property by summoning Balliol, together with ten earls and sixteen barons including Robert Bruce, the Competitor, to serve with him against France. In July 1295 a council of twelve leading figures assumed the direction of Scottish affairs from their timid king. They reasserted the rights of the northern kingdom by declaring forfeit the lands of English nobles in Scotland and followed this by making overtures to France for assistance; they also proposed that John Balliol's son, Edward, should marry King Philip's niece, Jeanne Valois, thus marking the formal beginning of the 'auld alliance'. At the same time summonses were put out across Scotland to raise an army in its defence to be led by a representative of the powerful Comyn family.

In February 1296, under Edward's command, a formidable English army, with a large component of armoured cavalry and stiffened by veterans from the Welsh and French wars, began a deliberate move towards the Scottish border, but on Easter Monday it was pre-empted by the Scottish feudal host that crossed into England. Their traditional means of recruitment had enabled the Scots to raise quickly a respectable army from able-bodied men aged between sixteen and sixty which in the main came from the country's earldoms north of the Forth. However, because their last encounter – no more than a skirmish – had been against the Norwegians at the Battle of Largs twenty-three years earlier, it was understandably inexperienced. Less excusably, its supporting equipment and level of discipline were also lacking. With the Comyn Earl of Buchan as the senior commander, the use made of what was predominantly an army of footsoldiers was also disappointing. Buchan was not much gifted militarily and, lacking siege equipment, he failed to capture the border fortress of Carlisle commanded for the English on this occasion by the Competitor's son, Robert Bruce, Lord of Annandale. In fact, the Scottish soldiers could do no better than ravage the countryside of Northumberland. In any case, their forces were weakened by the number of influential Scottish nobles who were out of sympathy with John Balliol and the Comyns and who remained loyal to the English king, including the earls of March and Angus, and the Bruces, both of Carrick and Annandale.

In contrast, the English army, with the king at its head, moved against the prime target of Berwick, Scotland's main port and the centre of its wool trade. The English soon pierced the town's long-neglected defences but, as it still refused to yield, the king granted his troops three days of pillage, rape and murder. It was said he did not finally give the order to stop until he saw a pregnant woman put to the sword and her dead infant sprawled beside her.[5] Chroniclers varied in their estimates of the dead, from 7000 by Hector Boece to 60,000 by Matthew of Westminster,[6] but corpses were piled high in the streets. Whatever the actual casualties, from his behaviour Scotland could have no illusions about Edward's intentions.

The first clash between the two main armies occurred at Dunbar, where the Earl of March had his castle. The opportunity came about due to the Scottish nobility's divided loyalties at this time. March was an English supporter but his wife, Marjorie Comyn, allowed the Scots to occupy the castle, thus prompting the English king to send one of his commanders, John Warenne, Earl of Surrey, together with a strong contingent of armoured knights, to retake it. The defenders appealed for help and the main Scottish army set out to relieve them. Warenne decided to meet the challenge by threatening the garrison with detachments of soldiers under his more junior commanders, while his veteran horsemen met the advancing Scottish army as it came over the crest of nearby Spottsmuir Hill. As the two sides closed with each other the English had to cross a steep valley intersected by the Spot burn, and when they disappeared from sight the Scots thought they were either withdrawing or had lost cohesion. Not for the first time their horsemen left a commanding position as, blowing wildly on their horns, they galloped down the hill in their anxiety to meet the enemy. Those with the strongest horses pulled their way to the front but by the time they came within striking distance, the English cavalry had regained their close formation. In the ensuing encounter they put the piecemeal Scottish attack to such flight that some of the cavalry did not stop until they reached Selkirk Forest, about forty miles away. Abandoned by their horse the unfortunate Scottish infantry were ridden down and suffered heavy casualties, which English sources put as high as 10,000 men. As a result of his conclusive victory Edward received the surrender of Dunbar Castle on the following day, together with that of three earls, Atholl, Ross and Menteith, as well as 130 knights and esquires.

Scotland's feudal host had proved wholly inadequate against the superior discipline and skilled leadership of the English; their defeat laid the country open to Edward's further conquest and he went on to occupy its central region without meeting more than token resistance. The formidable castle of Stirling, for instance, was deserted except for a porter who tamely handed its keys over to the invaders. On 21 June the English king reached Perth where he received two Franciscan friars sent by John Balliol to ask for peace. Their request was granted, although the price paid by Balliol was exorbitant. On 8 July at Montrose he was forced to surrender formally the Kingdom of Scotland and to acknowledge his errors 'through evil counsel and our own simplicity', followed by a humiliating public ceremony in which the arms of Scotland were ripped off his surcoat. Ever afterwards he was given the harsh soubriquet of 'Toom Tabard' – empty coat. This accomplished, Edward proceeded on a triumphal march northwards to the Moray Firth.

Having traversed the conquered kingdom, Edward left no one in any doubt about his respect for Scotland's independence when he had its sacred relics, the symbolic Stone of Destiny upon which the kings of Scots had traditionally been enthroned along with the fragment of the true cross bequeathed by Margaret, wife of Malcolm III, sent to Westminster Abbey. Edward also sent the Scottish royal records and plate to England, never to be seen again. At a parliament held in Berwick during August 1296 the English king endorsed his authority by requiring all substantial Scottish landowners to pay an oath of fealty to him as lord of Scotland. About 1500, including clergy, signed what became known as the Ragman's Roll – from the mass of tangled ribbons that carried their seals of authority – following which Edward issued his orders for garrisoning the country.

The short war was apparently over. In both its main engagements English leadership had proved markedly superior. Given their limitations in equipment the Scots could never have reasonably hoped to seize their chosen objective, the strong border fortress of Carlisle, and they were compelled to content themselves with the lesser one of burning and looting the surrounding countryside while the English experienced no such difficulty with their own chosen prize, the preeminent trading centre of Berwick. Similarly, at Dunbar, Warenne kept his military priorities clearly in mind. When it came to a choice between destroying the main Scottish army or relieving Dunbar Castle he much favoured meeting the army. He knew that if he could defeat the Scottish army they would have the greatest difficulty in retaining the castle. Warenne therefore attempted to prevent any sally from the castle's garrison against his rear by dividing his forces. However, in this he was careful to use his less-seasoned personnel to threaten the castle, keeping his experienced leaders and the bulk of his troops to face the advancing Scottish cavalry. One can only speculate about the possible outcome if the English and Scottish leadership had been equally competent but in their eagerness to exchange blows the Scots revealed startling naïveté and over-optimism, playing directly into Warenne's wily hands and allowing themselves to be caught at a massive disadvantage.

In September 1296 the English king crossed the Channel to conduct his war in Gascony. The country he now liked to think of as northernmost England seemed cowed; its nobility had sworn their loyalty to him and their disgraced king, John Balliol, was held securely in the Tower of London. The other main contender for the Scottish throne, Robert Bruce (his father, the Competitor, had died in the previous year), was being made to prove his loyalty as commander of Carlisle Castle while his son, the young Robert Bruce, was for the moment living quietly on his own estates.

In reality Scotland was far from cowed. Although large numbers of English troops, including armoured cavalry, were now garrisoned across the country, there was deep resentment against this English occupation from men of all classes, especially among senior members of the Scottish church, who supported two remarkable young leaders, William Wallace and Andrew Moray, in spearheading a new rebellion. Wallace was a squire and the younger son of Sir Malcolm Wallace of Elderslie near Paisley. Certainly no more than twenty-five years of age he was tall and extremely strong, and quickly demonstrated considerable powers of leadership when, in the spring of 1297, he began the fight-back by assassinating Edward's officials. His first target was Selby, the son of Dundee's English constable, and in May 1297 he followed it by killing William Heselrig, the English appointee as Sheriff of Lanark. Heselrig's death caused many men from southern and central Scotland to unite with the daring guerrilla fighter, including a nobleman and professional soldier, William Douglas, former commander of Berwick Castle. Together they planned to kill one of Edward's most senior officials, William Ormsby, his justiciar, who only narrowly escaped.

At this time another focus of revolt emerged headed by two senior figures, James Stewart, Wallace's feudal superior, and Robert Wishart, Bishop of Glasgow. Unlike Wallace, who kept to the great forests of Selkirk, they took the more conventional decision of openly raising their standard at Irvine in Ayrshire where they were joined by the twenty-three-year-old Robert Bruce, Earl of Carrick. In response an English cavalry force under Henry Percy, Yorkshire nobleman and grandson of Warenne, together with Robert Clifford, a major landowner and keen soldier from Westmorland, was rapidly despatched to attack them. Although its leaders were from the Scottish nobility, by far the largest proportion of the Scottish force at Irvine were infantry. In addition, the Scottish nobles, particularly Robert Bruce and the Balliol supporters, were unable to agree on their respective rights to command and on whose behalf they were fighting. It was a disastrous situation for any army and as a result Stewart and Douglas emerged from the Scottish lines to meet the advancing English and ask for surrender terms. These proved lenient enough although hostages were demanded to act as guarantors of the Scottish leaders' good faith. With this shameful capitulation the remaining hopes for resistance in southern Scotland depended on William Wallace and his growing numbers of followers. Although, with supreme confidence, Wallace ordered the Scottish nobles to join him, most remained unpersuaded of a modest squire's ability to meet the all-conquering English, and few answered his summons.

Meanwhile further north a second young man had raised his standard against the invaders. Andrew Moray, son of Sir Alexander Moray of Petty, came from one of Scotland's great Highland families. He started out with small bodies of men loyal to his family before being joined by a burgher from Inverness, Alexander Pilché, together with other citizens from the town. Initially he ambushed small English detachments but, as his numbers rose, he went on to attack and capture a number of northern castles, including the pivotal one at Inverness.

Further south Wallace knew the English were certain to seek him out and although, after Dunbar and Irvine, much the safest course would have been to continue with his guerrilla tactics, he took the amazingly courageous decision to meet the English in open battle – if strictly on his own terms – in an attempt to regain control of central Scotland. Wallace moved northwards to Dundee while the majority of his infantry continued to be trained in the forest of Selkirk. At Dundee he besieged the castle, which as Wallace had foreseen, provoked Edward's senior commander, Warenne, into leaving his safe haven at Berwick. Together with further military units under Hugh Cressingham, Edward's Scottish treasurer, he decided to seek out and destroy Wallace and his rebels.

On learning of their advance Wallace broke off his siege

and moved towards Stirling where anyone intending to move northwards would have to cross the River Forth. Shortly before this Wallace and Moray had met and agreed that they would work together and, equally importantly, that Moray would serve under Wallace's command. Their joint forces, together with Wallace's infantry from Selkirk forest, converged on Stirling where Wallace's conduct was to mark him, despite his youth and lack of formal experience, as a gifted military commander.

The battle of Stirling Bridge was a David and Goliath contest. Wallace and Moray's forces totalled 10,000 men at the most, against more than three times as many English. Although mainly footsoldiers, the Scots included a small cavalry element under the separate control of nobles such as Malcolm, Earl of Lennox, and James Stewart, whose earlier behaviour at Irvine had been less than heroic. The infantry, drawn from widely different backgrounds, had been together for less than a month and their experience so far was limited to irregular operations. In contrast the English footsoldiers were not only numerically superior but they included a company of the famed Welsh bowmen.[7] Most importantly, the comparatively large numbers of English heavy cavalry completely outmatched its few Scottish counterparts. In the Scots' favour their two young leaders were determined to win back their country's freedom and they had also both enjoyed a string of successes, albeit in small-scale operations. Crucially they were given the chance to choose the battlefield.

As for the English commanders, in the absence of the king, command devolved on John Warenne, Earl of Surrey, in poor health and older than the combined ages of the two young Scottish commanders. His experience of war, however, was immeasurably greater than theirs, even though most had been gained on the battlefield thirty years before. His ability had been clearly evident at Dunbar, but such a contest had been sufficiently undemanding to give him a dangerous measure of over-confidence. Nor was Warenne on good terms with Hugh Cressingham, his vanguard commander, whose own troops despised him for being both a bastard and a vain, self-opinionated individual.

Wallace positioned his men on Abbey Craig, an isolated

volcanic eminence rising a hundred feet from the flat and marshy plain where the River Forth meandered in great bends below it (see map). Abbey Craig overlooked the main road northwards at the point where it crossed the River Forth by a long and narrow wooden bridge. Despite some qualms on Warenne's part Cressingham accepted the option of crossing by the bridge under Wallace's full gaze, even when there were other fords downstream which could have been used to outflank the Scots' position.

Wallace had chosen a battle site with many advantages: fronted by wet and rough water meadows it gave the approaching English no opportunity to use their cavalry effectively; equally important for Wallace's smaller force, movement across such a narrow bridge onto the meadows was bound to be slow and would allow the Scots the opportunity of taking the offensive themselves before the English had brought a significant portion of their troops over it. Finally, it offered a good line of withdrawal if required.

However, to succeed against such superior forces required uncommon powers of leadership. Wallace needed cool nerves and sound judgement together with the ability to keep a tight control over his irregulars. For at least two hours the English cavalry and infantry clattered across the bridge and formed up on its further side within a loop of the river. Then with a blast on Wallace's horn the Scots came running down the steep slopes in tight formation, leaping across the turf hummocks to close with the English. Their speed of movement gave their opponents no time to draw up their battle lines nor bring their bowmen into action, while the English cavalry experienced major difficulties in holding their footing on the wet and broken carseland. As the Scots crashed into their packed ranks the English gave way and being unable to fight properly they started to panic. Wallace had appointed a dedicated group of soldiers to block the bridge and Warenne was forced to watch both the destruction of his vanguard and the killing of Cressingham before he turned and fled to Berwick, leaving his army to the mercy of the Scots as it sought to follow him.

Stirling Bridge was a great victory for William Wallace and

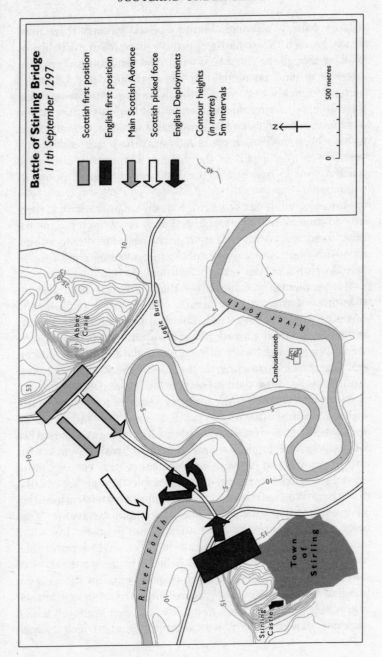

Battle of Stirling Bridge
11th September 1297

Scottish first position

English first position

Main Scottish Advance

Scottish picked force

English Deployments

Contour heights
(in metres)
5m intervals

0   500 metres

Andrew Moray, although Moray received wounds there from which he died. They had trapped as many of the English as Wallace thought he could beat within the bend of an impassable river on ground unsuitable for heavy cavalry, and he joined battle so quickly that the English were prevented from using their archers in their normal deadly fashion. His astute choice of ground avoided using his own weak and suspect cavalry, said to have been 'lurking in the woods near the hills',[8] although it went on to play a part in the pursuit. The victory also owed much to English over-confidence and fatal differences among its commanders.

However, while Stirling Bridge was a singular victory, there was no possibility that it would end the war. What it did, on the other hand, was to buy time for the Scottish leadership to rethink its possible response towards subsequent invading armies and to help develop a greater sense of national purpose.

During the next ten months Wallace did everything possible to gather together an army capable of meeting the English, who this time would be commanded by their king. Although initially retreating before the invaders and devastating the country as he went, Wallace eventually offered battle on a relatively modest hill near Falkirk, standing on the line of the Roman Antonine wall. Why he chose such a position has puzzled commentators not fully appreciative of the conditions needed for his spearmen, although several other important factors no doubt influenced his decision. He knew, for instance, that his delaying tactics had not only caused the English supply system to break down but the army's morale had fallen to an alarming degree. He might also have had his choices limited by the nobles among his cavalry, for whom Wallace's tactics of scorched earth and evasion were contrary to their chivalric codes of military behaviour. They might even have threatened to desert him if he did not stand and fight.[9] Such nobles, including the proud and powerful John Comyn (the Red Comyn, John Balliol's brother-in-law), were virtually certain to have chafed against being overborne by a modest squire, however skilled he might have shown himself the year before. With the Comyns the fact that Wallace's feudal superior, James Stewart, was a supporter and friend of their rivals, the Bruces, would not have helped either. Wallace could not risk their non-co-operation nor, worse still, their defection. Finally, he also had good grounds for doubting whether he could keep such a large army in being much longer and whether he could raise a similar one in the following year. Unless Wallace could beat the English decisively at Falkirk, Edward I's determination to subdue Scotland would keep him in the border regions with his household troops ready to resume operations over the next campaigning season when Wallace would be less well supported.

Although such factors undoubtedly played a significant part in persuading Wallace to fight at Falkirk it was his creation of schiltrons expressly designed to counter the English heavy cavalry that was likely to have weighed most heavily in his calculations. He placed his four detachments of spearmen numbering somewhat fewer than two thousand men each in a rough semi-circle on the forward edge of Mumrills' small rounded crest. These soldiers with their twelve-foot spears and wooden targes were aligned in circular formation at the edge of which men knelt shoulder to shoulder with the butts of their iron-tipped spears resting on the ground. Immediately in support were a further two ranks with their spears either grounded and pointing outwards or, more likely, lifted into a horizontal position to fend off attacking horsemen. Additional men waited in the redoubts ready to make good any gaps appearing as men fell.

The schiltrons, or shield rings as the chronicler Guisborough called them, were in some respects like traditional Greek phalanxes, although unlike the Greek formations they were static. In the Scottish phalanx its members' fighting qualities were enhanced by the contemporary practice whereby a proportion of knights chose to fight dismounted with their followers. Standing alongside their clan or household superiors such as MacDuff, the Earl of Fife, or Sir Nichol de Rutherford, who brought sixty followers with him, the spearmen would not have dared let their comrades down. The ordinary levies would also have been kept up to their task by Wallace's drill sergeants placed at strategic points within the ranks. These were given wide authority by a leader whose own determination was evident by the gallows which he ordered to be erected in every town 'on which all without a reasonable cause absenting themselves from the army under foreign pretexts should be hanged'.[10]

In theory if the spearmen held firm armoured cavalry would be unable to subdue them, being literally kept at spears' length. In practice, the cavalry enjoyed additional support from their own infantry, including the deadly longbowmen. To counter these opponents Wallace buttressed his schiltrons with Scotland's short bowmen. While their weapons' range and penetrative power were markedly inferior, once the English had moved onto the small hill to close with the spear circles the short bows could come fully into play.

By skilful use of ground Wallace had thereby countered the superior range of the English archers but he had no equivalent means of helping his other fighting component, the Scottish light cavalry, heavily outnumbered by their English opponents. He had tried the only way he knew how to make good this deficiency by requesting assistance from the French nobleman, Charles de Valois, along with his heavy horsemen, but this had been refused. Nonetheless while completely outmatched by the English heavy cavalry the few Scottish horsemen were still important to Wallace to help counter the English infantry and bowmen. Their presence alone prevented the English footsoldiers from ranging freely over the battlefield.

Whatever his concerns about the other arms, the essence of Wallace's army lay with his spearmen. There is little doubt he would have known about the earlier battle of Maes Moydog (1295) where the English had demonstrated how their skilful use of cavalry supported by bowmen could defeat a Welsh infantry army. Wallace knew he had to do better at Falkirk and therefore ensured his men would also be supported by bowmen as they stood on the forward edge of Mumrills hill. He knew that they awaited an army that was not only tired and weakened from lack of provisions but whose Welsh bowmen were mutinous. In such circumstances he had reason to hope the English would expend their energies against his resolute formations and that Scottish courage and determination would cause them to lose heart as had happened with the English main army at Stirling Bridge.

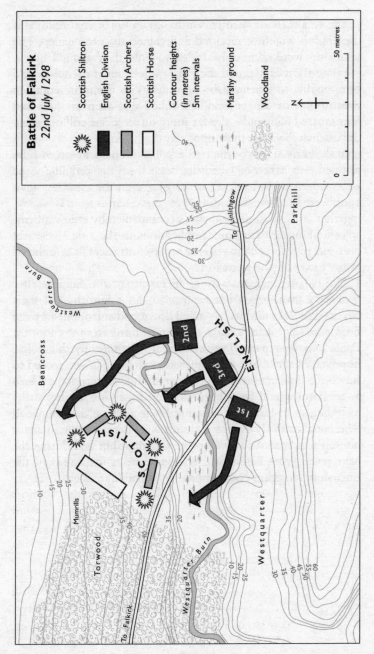

Battle of Falkirk
22nd July 1298

Scottish Shiltron

English Division

Scottish Archers

Scottish Horse

Contour heights
(in metres)
5m intervals

Marshy ground

Woodland

N

0   50 metres

To Linlithgow

Parkhill

Westquarter Burn

Beancross

ENGLISH

2nd

3rd

1st

SCOTTISH

Mumrills

Torwood

To Falkirk

Westquarter Burn

Westquarter

The weakness of such reasoning lay in his limited options if the English were not rebutted and gained the ascendancy. The schiltrons were admirably drilled to hold their ground but in the time allowed him and with his soldiers' inexperience he had been unable to extend their movements to the more complex ones of moving off the field in a cohesive fashion or – if it had ever crossed his mind – the far more difficult one still of taking the offensive against their opponents.

In the early stages of the battle Wallace's tactics seemed fully justified even when he faced the English cavalry totalling some 2400 riders formed into three divisions. Of these no less than 1300 were full-time (including some mercenaries from Gascony) together with 1100 nobles who, accompanied by their retinues, were honouring their feudal obligations to the king.[11] He not only succeeded in beating off the first two attacks but he inflicted heavy losses on the aggressors.

The balance began to move in favour of the English after Wallace's cavalry fled but even when his schiltrons lost their covering archers and were pinned down and surrounded by the English cavalry it took massed bowmen firing from the shortest range into their packed ranks to seal their fate. By this point, however, Wallace had no further alternatives. He was forced to watch the destruction of his army, and families across the whole of Scotland would be obliged to mourn men lost in the battle, including short bowmen who, until new archers had completed their comparatively lengthy training, were irreplaceable. Wallace himself was forced to give up the guardianship and during the next seven years before his terrible death at the hands of the English never again commanded any sizeable military force.

CHAPTER TWO

≈

DIVIDED LEADERSHIP

'For if the trumpet give an uncertain sound who
shall prepare himself to the battle?'

1 Corinthians 14:8

THE SEVEN YEARS OR so between Wallace's defeat at Falkirk
and Robert Bruce's final commitment to the nationalist
cause proved cruel ones for Scotland, despite the country's fleet-
ing diplomatic and military successes which delayed Edward's
programme of conquest and at one stage even promised to
unravel it. At no time did the Scottish forces feel themselves
capable of standing in battle against the main English armies. By
1304, when Edward extinguished the last remnants of Scottish
resistance by capturing Stirling Castle, prospects for Scotland's
survival as an independent kingdom seemed extremely poor. Its
former allies had disappeared like snow in springtime, with
France moving into the English camp and a papacy becoming
unsympathetic. Equally serious was the disunited nature of Scottish leadership during the period. With the absence of the lawful
king, John Balliol, attempts to rule through guardians acting
on his behalf were seriously hampered, largely because rivalry
between the Bruce and Comyn factions prevented them from
acting with the same authority and single-minded commitment
shown earlier by Wallace. The most notable result was that,
after taking part in the uneasy system of joint guardianship,
Robert Bruce, heir elect of his powerful family and a man with
the potential to become a genuine leader of the first rank, both
on and off the battlefield, had, by 1302, deserted the Scottish
national cause and made his peace with the English king.

It was a less surprising decision than might be considered today. While the Comyns had continued throughout to support John Balliol, for much of the time the Bruces offered their fealty to Edward I, the scourge of their countrymen, in the conviction that if Balliol were deposed Edward would support their own candidature for the Scottish kingship, even if he was likely to demand some restrictions on its power. Indeed, it was Edward's reneging on his promise to Bruce's father with regard to the Scottish throne and his attempt to incorporate Scotland within the English crown that in 1297 first led Robert Bruce, Earl of Carrick, to take the momentous decision of taking a contrary course to his father – who remained true to the English king – and join the opposition forces in Scotland.

At the time Edward I was still confident enough of both Bruces, father and son, for him to order Robert Bruce, Lord of Annandale and Governor of Carlisle, to charge his son with seizing the Douglas estates after Sir William Douglas had united with Wallace. Unexpectedly Bruce, who had only recently regained his lands from Comyn control following the English victory at Dunbar, made no more than a mock attack on Douglasdale and, after assembling his father's knights of Annandale, explained that his oath of fealty to the English king had been given under duress and as a consequence he had decided to move into the nationalist camp. He justified his decision by citing the loyalty he felt for his followers on the Carrick estate and to his country of Scotland. 'No man holds his own flesh and blood in hatred and I am no exception . . . I must join my own people (the men of Carrick) and the nation in which I was born.'[1] There seems no reason to doubt Robert Bruce's feelings for both his own followers and the land of his boyhood, those wide Carrick estates that he had ridden and hunted across with his brothers and sisters. Allied to this was the belief which had also fired his grandfather, that his family's royal blood gave them an undeniable right to occupy the throne of Scotland. It was this that became the very purpose of his life and with the removal of John Balliol he might well have considered that many Scottish patriots would now turn to him as the most likely contender for the Scottish throne. In the event most of the Annandale knights refused to join him since their own lord still took the part of the English king.

Robert Bruce, however, was not to be deflected and, after raising additional recruits from among his followers at Carrick, he took the dangerous step of moving to join James Stewart and Robert Wishart, Bishop of Glasgow, at Irvine. Following their tame surrender to the English, Bruce paid the price for his show of patriotism – and possible early bid for the Scottish throne – by being deprived of his lands once more. This time they were required by the English who also directed him to hand over his daughter Marjorie, as surety for his continuing good behaviour, a directive he managed to avoid.

It was as well Bruce did so for after Wallace's victory at Stirling Bridge in September 1297, he and his men of Carrick were out again. In March 1298 it was probably Bruce who knighted Wallace for his achievements and, although Bruce himself remained in the southwest of Scotland it is likely that he provided mounted elements for Wallace's army at the battle of Falkirk in July 1298. Having defeated Wallace at Falkirk, Edward I showed he recognised Bruce's ability and potential threat by attempting to go on and deal with him as well, but Bruce was too quick for him; after burning Ayr and destroying its castle he and his followers moved into the desolate hill regions of Carrick out of the king's reach.

When Wallace was compelled to surrender his sole guardianship of Scotland young Bruce became an obvious candidate to replace him in heading the opposition to the English king, the other outstanding contender being another young nobleman, John Comyn the Red, head of the senior branch of the Comyn family. Unlike Bruce, John Comyn had never wavered in supporting his kinsman John Balliol. In April 1296 he had accompanied the Scottish forces that crossed the English border during the first engagement of the Independence Wars, and he was not likely to forget that when the Scottish forces failed in their attempt to take Carlisle Castle it was being held on behalf of the English king by Robert Bruce, Lord of Annandale, Robert Bruce's father. Following the Scottish army's defeat at Dunbar and the fall of John Balliol, John Comyn had been one of the many Scottish nobles imprisoned in England, whereas Robert Bruce had been granted the return of his lands at Carrick which John Balliol had confiscated on behalf of the Comyns. Although the senior Scottish prelates and nobles appointed them as joint guardians to orchestrate resistance against the English, the chances of their success were not helped by the fact that, powerful figure as he was, Comyn entirely lacked Bruce's magnanimity and could never equal his powers of leadership. The intense rivalry between their two families did not augur well for a smooth working relationship and, in addition, by all accounts John Comyn was a most difficult man to deal with. Their uneasy relationship was first dissolved after an attempt was made in July 1299 to retake Roxburgh Castle in Lothian. The attack failed and as the disappointed party moved back into Peebles woods to reconsider their options a disagreement occurred over lands held by William Wallace, who, as Sir David Graham (a Comyn supporter) maintained, was leaving the kingdom without the guardians' permission and, therefore, should forfeit them. In the argument that followed John Comyn leapt upon Bruce and seized him by the throat. The quarrel was only patched up when Bishop William Lamberton agreed to be appointed senior guardian over them both.

In the light of such disunity it was as well for Scotland that the English king was experiencing serious difficulties with his own nobles over mounting another ruinously expensive expedition against Scotland. Due largely to Edward's inactivity the Scots were able to take the initiative. By the end of 1299 they succeeded in retaking Stirling Castle and plans were raised to bring the men of Galloway over to Scotland's national cause. The latter, however, brought additional strains on the Scottish leadership. The Gallovidians were not only traditional separatists but long-standing enemies of the Bruces, whose estates adjoined their territory. Bruce undoubtedly had other serious disagreements with John Comyn but the need to preserve his family's interests against the Gallovidians was the likely cause of his final resignation as joint guardian in early 1300. His place was taken by Sir Ingram Umfraville, a strong ally of the

Comyns, while Bruce returned to his estates in the southwest where over the next two years he continued to direct opposition against the English.

Edward I pre-empted all Scottish plans affecting Galloway, however, when, in the summer of 1300 after much lobbying with his senior nobles, he headed another army into Scotland with the intention of subduing the southwest, including Galloway. This force was almost as large as that which faced Wallace at Falkirk but because of incessant rain and the Scots' refusal to offer battle Edward had to be content with the capture of just one castle, that of Caerlaverock. On one occasion the guardians moved to prevent him crossing the River Cree in Galloway but at the approach of his heavy cavalry they thought better of it and fled into the hills. By the end of August Edward had returned to Sweetheart Abbey near Caerlaverock and while there, as a result of Scottish approaches to the Pope, he received a visit from Robert Winchelsey, Archbishop of Canterbury. Both countries had been protesting to the Pope about whether or not Edward's occupation of an independent Scotland was legal and, as the result of Scottish advocacy in Rome, the archbishop brought the English king a papal bull ordering him to cease inflicting injuries upon the Scots and to withdraw from their country. Infuriated as he was Edward recognised the need for a pause in his military operations to marshal his counter-arguments, and therefore agreed to the request from Philip of France for a truce until May 1301 and to the release of Robert Wishart, Bishop of Glasgow, from prison. However, it did not change his determination to conquer Scotland for, while his experts were composing his response to the Pope, Edward started preparing for his sixth invasion in the summer of 1301.

On the Scottish side, during the spring of that year Bishop Lamberton attempted to keep the Bruce and Comyn factions from breaking apart completely by persuading John Comyn and Ingram Umfraville to resign in favour of a single 'neutral' guardian. The proposed candidate was Sir John Soules, related by marriage to the Comyns but a close neighbour of the Bruces. Soules assumed his post in the spring of 1301 in time to meet the next English invasion. A strong indication that Soules was in fact a nominee of John Balliol came through the new procedure that was adopted for documents sent under the seal of Scotland. These were issued under the name of King John, or of Edward Balliol as his heir, with the guardian standing as witness.

For his 1301 campaign which again aimed at destroying Scottish resistance in the southwest Edward I split his invading forces in two. One detachment under his command was to advance from Berwick on the east coast towards Stirling, while his son, Edward Caernarvon, Prince of Wales, was to move along the western side of Scotland; the intention was to close the pincers near Stirling and catch the defenders in a great net. However the strategy failed, largely because Soules slowed the king by threatening his lines of communication, while in the west Robert Bruce, who had built up his forces in Carrick, succeeded in holding on to Turnberry Castle until September. As a result the Prince of Wales got no further than Whithorn on Galloway's southern coast and eventually returned to Carlisle before joining his father, who decided to spend the winter at Linlithgow.

Edward I chose Linlithgow as a convenient base in readiness for a further campaign during the spring of 1302 but in the face of French pressure he agreed to a nine-month truce which, in fact, meant there could be no further invasion of Scotland until early 1303. Throughout 1301 political events had swung in the Scots' favour: at the papal court their brilliant advocate, Master Baldred Bisset, effectively demolished Edward's arguments over his right to occupy Scotland and in the summer of the same year John Balliol was released from papal custody and allowed to return to his estates at Bailleul in Picardy. There was even talk of a French army being sent to reinstate him in Scotland.

These events were not to the liking of the English king nor Robert Bruce. While as a patriot he had demonstrated he would do everything possible to oppose English invasions, the restoration of John Balliol promised to bring Balliol's son, Edward, to Scotland who would effectively block Bruce's claim to the throne. In any case, while Bruce had fought for Scotland since 1297 he had arguably not exercised the influence in affairs he considered his position warranted. He had been unable to exercise his due powers as joint guardian through the hostility of his fellow titleholder towards him and his supporters. His Scottish estates had been devastated and the chance of John Balliol resuming power not only threatened his ambitions for the throne but endangered his chances of inheriting Annandale on the imminent death of his sick father. The prospect of the country being run by Comyns along with French forces committed to holding in trust any lands of nobles who, like himself, had opposed Edward I, was his worst nightmare. His best chance of securing his rightful estates lay with Edward I and because the Scottish patriots had turned to the Balliol family as their regal leaders, any chance Bruce might have with regard to the Scottish throne also seemed to lie in the hands of the English king. On the basis of such reasoning Bruce left the Scottish patriots and joined his father in the service of Edward I.

Despite their undoubted successes during 1301 the loss of Bruce, a leader of outstanding potential and de facto leader of his powerful family, was a major setback in Scotland's struggle for independence and a great bonus for Edward. The importance of Bruce's change of allegiance can be seen in the wording of the open memorandum drafted by the English king upon Bruce's submission. By it Bruce's titles and claims were acknowledged, including the key one to the Scottish crown – although how much Edward would have supported the latter in reality is open to question – '. . . (if) the Kingdom of Scotland may be removed from out of the King's hands (which God forbid!) and handed over to Sir John Balliol or to his son or that the right may be brought into dispute, or reversed and contradicted in a fresh judgement, the King grants Robert that he may pursue his right and the King will hear him fairly and hold him to justice in the King's court.'[2]

Along with Bruce's defection the Scots suffered other serious setbacks during 1302. On 11 July the French cavalry were defeated by Flemish peasant soldiers at Courtrai and the importance of France's support for Scotland was weakened proportionately. At about the same time relations between France and the papacy broke down and by August Pope Boniface was writing to the Scottish bishops ordering them to recognise Edward I as their legal ruler.

Notwithstanding, military resistance continued to be mounted against the English. In November 1302, immediately after the expiration of the truce between the two countries, the English king despatched a large reconnaissance force into the countryside southwest of Edinburgh to gather information for his projected expedition the next year. The Scots, under John Comyn and Simon Fraser, with William Wallace a likely addition to their ranks, fell upon the leading elements and at Roslin inflicted heavy casualties upon them. However, no such reverse could prevent Edward I's full-scale invasion in the following spring. In early 1303 the Scots took the field first and succeeded in capturing Selkirk Castle but the English appeared unstoppable; Edward was determined to conquer Scotland once and for all, whatever men and resources it required. Using prefabricated pontoon bridges (built at enormous expense) he moved across central Scotland and from there to Kinloss on the Moray Firth, which he reached in September. Returning to southern Scotland he stayed at Dunfermline Abbey while his forces were kept in the field until, on the 22 December, the Scots signalled they were willing to negotiate for peace.

On 19 January, 1304, terms were agreed between the two sides. The senior Scottish leaders were treated leniently but Edward summoned a parliament to meet at St Andrews to commence discussions on the full incorporation of the country. This time he determined to bring Scottish nobles into the process and in September 1305 ten Scottish representatives joined twenty-one English officials to draft a new constitution. In accordance with a new legal code, the land – no longer a realm – was to be ruled by a lieutenant appointed by the English king aided by a chancellor and chamberlain.

From the time of his submission early in 1302 Bruce was used by Edward I to help him conquer Scotland, but although Bruce was careful to convince the English king of his loyalty, in reality he offered little more than lip service and displayed scarcely anything of the military brilliance evident in his later years. He seemed determined to contribute nothing more than was absolutely necessary against his native country. For instance, in March 1302 he assured the monks of Melrose Abbey that he would not bring out his 'army of Carrick' again for his own purposes 'unless the whole realm is raised for its defence, when all inhabitants are bound to serve'. In other words he would not bring his men out in support of Edward I.[3] During Edward's twin-pronged invasion of Scotland in 1303 Bruce's role was limited to serving as Sheriff of Lanark and Ayr and acting as keeper of the castle there, hardly a demanding one for a gifted young leader.[4] During the spring of 1304, when the English king asked him to forward siege engines for Edward's planned assault on Stirling Castle he did so, but omitted to send a vital piece of machinery without which they could not function.[5] Following an order from the king to provide troops for the siege he wrote to him explaining his difficulties in doing so.[6]

In March 1304 Bruce, together with Sir John Seagrave, was ordered to lead a mounted raid on William Wallace and Simon Fraser in Selkirk forest, which was singularly unsuccessful, for while some of their followers were taken, both leaders were alerted to the raid and escaped. This earned Bruce a surprisingly gentle scolding from the king with the words, 'as the cloak is well made, also make the hood'.[7]

Shortly afterwards on 21 April Bruce's father died and there was now no question that the Bruce claims to the throne depended upon him. With his past record and strong ambitions he was playing a highly dangerous role but until late 1305 it appeared to be working. In spite of a secret compact to help Bruce gain the crown of Scotland made between him and Bishop William Lamberton at Cambuskenneth Abbey during the siege of Stirling Castle from May to July 1304, Bruce succeeded in remaining Edward's favoured son. The written part of the Cambuskenneth compact included the enigmatic clause, 'that neither of them should undertake any important business without the other of them'. This was accompanied by a spoken agreement that Bruce would assume the Scottish throne following Edward's death. Meanwhile Edward's grants to Bruce continued; he made him guardian to the young Earl of Mar, a concession that allowed Bruce effective control of the extensive

Mar estates along the Scottish northeast coast, together with the castle of Kildrummy. In March 1305, Bruce was granted the Umfraville lands in Carrick and enjoyed a leading role in advising Edward I on the feasibility of his proposals concerning the government of Scotland.

After October 1305 things changed markedly. While Edward I was seriously ill (and not expected to recover), according to the Scottish chroniclers Bruce made a daring proposal to his rival John Comyn. If John Comyn would be prepared to help Bruce become king of Scotland he would receive all Bruce's estates and if, on the other hand, Comyn gave Bruce *his* estates Bruce would undertake to support him for the crown. It is difficult to believe that Bruce would keep his word to help a man he disliked so heartily to gain the throne but Barbour – always sympathetic to Bruce – had Comyn opting for the additional estates rather than the crown and even signing an agreement between them to this effect.[8] On the other hand, although the English chronicler Walter of Guisborough also has Bruce contacting Comyn he maintained it was after Bruce had fled from the English court and followed the visit by Bruce's two brothers, Thomas and Neil (sometimes called Nigel), to Comyn's castle at Dalswinton with a request for Comyn to meet him at the Greyfriars Church, Dumfries, to discuss certain business, most likely the placing of Bruce on the Scottish throne.[9]

To everyone's surprise Edward I quickly recovered and, with the capture of Wallace, certain documents were found which, while not directly incriminating Bruce, served to confirm his ambitions for the crown of Scotland. Edward's attitude towards him cooled markedly and in September he ordered Bruce to place Kildrummy Castle into the hands of someone 'for whom he would be responsible', and Umfraville's lands were returned to their original owner.

Any trace of friendly relationship still remaining between the king and Bruce was destroyed when, according to the Scottish sources, John Comyn told Edward I of Bruce's plotting against him, even informing him about their mutual covenant concerning the throne of Scotland and undertook to produce the document signed and sealed by Bruce as proof.[10] Edward decided to wait until he had the evidence and took pains not to arouse Bruce's suspicions about the altered situation but, one evening when he had taken a large measure of wine, the king let slip he intended to arrest Bruce the next day and try him for treason. Among his guests was Raoul de Monthermer, Earl of Gloucester, a long-standing friend of the Bruces, who sent the keeper of his wardrobe to Bruce with twelve pence and a pair of spurs. The coins carried the king's head and no doubt implied being sold or betrayed while the spurs clearly indicated the need for haste.[11] The two men must have agreed on the signal beforehand for Bruce returned the twelve pence with his thanks and, after telling his staff he was not to be disturbed, took a squire for escort and leaving London, rode by day and night to Scotland. One Scottish chronicler, Fordun, even had them meeting a Scotsman travelling south to England whose suspicious conduct caused them to search him and find a letter from John Comyn enclosing the bond supporting Bruce's bid for the Scottish throne.

Five days after leaving the English court Bruce reached his family at Lochmaben and told them what had happened. By chance the local magnates, including John Comyn, were attending sessions held by English justiciars at neighbouring Dumfries and Bruce sent word for the Comyn to meet him in Greyfriars' Kirk there. There are conflicting versions of how their conversation went on 10 February 1306. The English chronicler Sir Thomas Grey said that after traditional words of greeting Bruce turned on Comyn and accused him of betraying him, while Guisborough – no lover of Bruce – has John Comyn refusing to listen to Bruce's planned treason against Edward I.

Whatever was said there was a quarrel, daggers were drawn and the Comyn fell wounded on the steps of the altar.[12] Comyn's uncle, Sir Robert Comyn, struck Bruce with his sword but Bruce's armour deflected it and Sir Robert was killed by Christopher Seton, Bruce's brother-in-law. As Bruce came out of the church there is a strong tradition that another of his followers, Roger Kirkpatrick, asked what had happened and, being told he returned to the church and made sure John Comyn was dead.

Whether or not Bruce killed, rather than wounded, the

Comyn is intriguing but not important. Responsibility for Roger Kirkpatrick's actions rested with his master. In any event the murder was most unlikely to have been pre-planned. In medieval times a strong contender for the throne would never deliberately commit both murder and sacrilege. Undoubtedly Bruce and Comyn hated each other and if Comyn had alerted Edward to Bruce's projected bid to be king and had caused him to flee from England these were even more reasons for a heated exchange to take place between them. Both were young, powerful and proud men and they had already come to blows over William Wallace.

Whatever the reasons the murder in the Greyfriars' church committed Bruce irrevocably to the Scottish patriotic camp and caused him to face the justifiable anger of a failing but still formidable English king along with the full enmity of the powerful Comyns and their followers, who with the exception of the southwest, controlled most of Scotland. At this time, before Bruce or the Comyns were able to come out on top, Scotland's leadership was more divided than ever.

Facing such terrible dangers Bruce needed above all to establish the legitimacy of his position, without which uncommitted men were unlikely to join him, while simultaneously securing a base from where he could build up his military forces. As his sister was Queen Dowager in Norway he could have moved away from his enemies and assembled a following with the object of returning to Scotland after Edward's death. In fact he opted for the more hazardous course of remaining in his country from the beginning. In Scotland he could call on the support of his family and their traditional adherents who together with their retinues of fighting men offered him the framework of an army, however poorly it might compare with the strength of his opponents.

Of equal importance was the question of his legitimacy. This received a powerful boost from the Scottish church where men like Bishop William Lamberton had already acknowledged him as the best hope to recover their country's independence. Bishop Wishart of Glasgow absolved him for his dual sin and in return Bruce agreed to respect the church's traditional liberties.

In his perilous situation it was Bruce's personal attributes that were likely to prove all-important. While he had already shown outstanding skills in the jousting field and before 1302 his activities as a guerrilla leader in the southwest had acted as a thorn in England's side, after joining the English king he had given little indication that he had the ability to become a genuine military commander. Energy and resilience were vital now and the hot-headedness that had characterised his conduct against John Comyn – and which had placed him and his whole family in such jeopardy – had to be curbed.

To survive at all Bruce needed practical and strategic awareness. John de Soules, as guardian, had already demonstrated the effectiveness of manoeuvre and evasion against the English. Conversely Wallace's victory at Stirling along with the initial achievements of Scottish spearmen at Falkirk showed that Bruce needed stand-up battles to win back Scotland from his Comyn enemies and hopefully eventually against the English too.

With so many powerful opponents and the strong likelihood of defeat and capture before him Bruce had little time for exhilaration at assuming what he had so long believed was his rightful role. Nor was there at this stage much opportunity to consider possible tactics before he knew the size or nature of the force he could raise. Decisions would have to be made in the saddle and longer-term thinking would be restricted to his short periods of rest. Whether the one-time self-seeking nobleman had the ability to take on the mantle and responsibilities of a warrior king was soon to become evident.

CHAPTER THREE

≈

WINNING A KINGDOM

'Potential is more than mass, decision and courage
of more value than numbers, and energy the deciding factor.'

Hilaire Belloc

B RUCE HAD GOOD REASON to believe that few other aspirants
to the Scottish crown had ever faced so many powerful
and implacable enemies. Consequently, during the six weeks
between 10 February 1306 when he killed John Comyn and
his coronation at Scone, his energy was never more marked.
This was essential for a man whom the English maintained had
murdered Comyn because he would not join Bruce in fighting
King Edward,[1] someone with the effrontery to declare himself
ruler of a country whose strongholds were all garrisoned by
the English and the large majority of whose nobles supported
the Comyns. As if this were not enough his sacrilegious act of
murder had put him at odds with the papacy and much of the
Scottish church. However tenuous his hold, Bruce's declared
heritage must also have seemed unpromising, for middle Scotland had been laid waste from ten years of war. In comparison,
although Edward I's Scottish campaigns had stretched England's
finances to breaking point, it remained a far more powerful and
influential country than its northern neighbour.

In these six weeks Bruce set out to strengthen his base in southwest Scotland with his family's estates at Carrick and Annandale
as its core. These were opposite the western approaches from
Ulster with whom the Bruces had traditional ties and from
where they could bring reinforcements. The MacDonalds of

the Western Isles were Bruce's allies and their galleys could either bring him more men from the Outer Isles or if everything failed, place him safely on one of the remote islands or in Ulster. Along with his followers Bruce succeeded in obtaining a string of castles among which were Ayr on the west coast, Dumfries, Dalswinton and Tibbers in Galloway, and the trio Inverkip, Rothesay and Dunaverty that commanded the Firth of Clyde. These he prudently stocked with provisions and supplies. In Glasgow Bruce ordered all men of military age to be on twenty-four hours notice of mobilisation as he sent a formal request to Edward I that he should be recognised as king of Scotland. Unsurprisingly, Edward replied by furiously demanding him to return the castles he had seized, to which Bruce responded that until Edward acknowledged him as king he 'would defend himself with the longest stick he had'.[2]

His next step was to adopt the revered mantle of kingship. Here Bruce received notable assistance from the one-time guardian of Scotland and staunchly nationalist Bishop of Glasgow, Robert Wishart, who after absolving him for his crime provided vestments for his coronation together with a royal banner carrying the lion and scarlet lilies that Wishart had long been saving for such an occasion. As yet there was no crown and urgent orders had to be sent out to make up the circlet of gold to be placed on Bruce's head.[3]

With so many enemies it was crucial that Bruce's coronation should be as dignified and heavily supported as possible. In the event the Scottish church was well represented not only by Robert Wishart but by Scotland's two other senior bishops, William Lamberton of St Andrews and David of Moray, while the bishops of Dunkeld and Brechin were probably in attendance, together with various abbots and other senior clergy. Foremost among the non-clerics were the four earls sympathetic to Bruce, Atholl, Lennox, Menteith and Mar, as well as Bruce's own kin. A hundred lesser nobles attended, including Robert Boyd, Reginald Crawford, Neil Campbell and the teenage James Douglas, disinherited by Edward from the Douglas estates, who was to become Bruce's foremost commander. As a ward of the English court the young Earl of Fife was unable to perform his hereditary office of crowning the new king but his aunt Isabel, married to the Earl of Buchan, who supported Edward I, seized her husband's best horses and rode to Scone to act on her nephew's behalf. She arrived a day late but on 25 March, forty-eight hours after the first inauguration placed the coronet upon Bruce's head in a second ceremony. Scotland might have a fighting king again but he was as yet so weak militarily that when his wife Elizabeth heard the news of his coronation she exclaimed 'Alas we are but King and Queen of the May'.

The chances of her fears being realised appeared all too likely when by 5 April the English king appointed Aymer de Valence, his own half-cousin and the Red Comyn's brother-in-law, as special lieutenant in Scotland, and armed him with the widest powers. Valence was authorised to ride under the dragon banner which released him from the few restraints on warfare at this time; knights supporting Bruce lost their privileges of ransom and were to be regarded as outlaws: a terrible end awaited any of Bruce's followers, or anyone found sheltering them. By June 1306 Valence had captured bishops Lamberton and Wishart who were only saved from hanging by their cloth, although this did not prevent them being despatched to England in chains. By 18 June Valence reached Perth, while Bruce was in the northeast raising support both from the Atholl and Mar estates and from among the followers of Bishop Moray. By such means Bruce managed to collect a sizeable military force of some 4500 men, although it was considerably smaller than Valence's and lacked his armoured cavalry.

Bruce moved his men across to Perth where, no doubt exhilarated by all he had achieved so far, he showed a degree of over-confidence about his chances of defeating Valence, a man whom he probably did not respect highly as a commander. In the chivalric tradition Bruce rode to Perth's city gates and challenged Valence either to come out and fight or to surrender, to which Valence replied that as it was late afternoon it was impossible to fight the same day, but that on the following morning he would accept the offer.[4] Bruce took him at his word and withdrew to Methven some six miles away to bivouac his troops for the night, neglecting in his confidence to set out pickets – an omission he came to regret. Working on the unprincipled advice given him by veteran Scottish commander, Ingram Umfraville, who now pledged himself to the English, Valence fell on Bruce's men during the night of 18/19 June when they were either sleeping or dispersed. Bruce's force was destroyed, although he and a group of knights managed to escape. Many of his bravest and devoted supporters were captured and under Edward's orders sixteen were executed without trial, of whom two were drawn and quartered. Of the senior men only Thomas Randolph, a close friend of Valence, was pardoned on condition he promised to fight for the English. This was not all: at the same time the Prince of Wales moved north from Carlisle, subjecting the southwest lowlands to a reign of terror that cowed the inhabitants in an area where Bruce might normally have expected considerable support. In less than three months as king, Bruce's army had been wiped out and many of his most notable followers killed or scattered. Yet worse was to come.

In early July 1306 Bruce sought refuge in Drumalban, the mountainous country between Perthshire and Argyll but, at a place near Tyndrum, Bruce's remaining detachment was again defeated, this time by the Comyn supporter, John MacDougall of Argyll. At this he sent off his womenfolk, including the queen and his daughter Marjorie, on the party's few remaining horses through the mountains towards Kildrummy Castle on Donside. Bruce appointed the Earl of Atholl, Neil Bruce (his brother), Alexander Lindsay and Robert Boyd as escorts to the party but on their way they learned the English were bringing up siege engines to invest the castle and decided therefore to move further north in the hope of taking ship to Orkney. It appeared to be a sensible decision for, although Kildrummy was an immensely strong fortress capable of withstanding a protracted siege, in early September 1306 the castle's blacksmith, Osborne, set fire to the grain store in its main hall, thus guaranteeing its early surrender. For his treachery the English subsequently rewarded him in gold – molten gold which was poured down his throat[5] – but with the fall of the castle Neil Bruce, Robert's younger brother was captured to be subsequently hanged and beheaded.

However, the women and their escorts fared little better, for they were captured at Tain on the Dornoch Firth while they were staying at St Duthac's shrine. At this time it must have seemed there was no escaping the English king for the Earl of Ross, who favoured the Comyns, broke the rules of sanctuary when he took them and handed them over to Valence.[6] Most of the men were hanged and beheaded at Berwick while the women were sent south to Edward I under escort. There they met his full anger and the Countess of Buchan and Bruce's sister, Mary, were confined in wooden cages jutting from the battlements of Berwick and Roxburgh castles, their only concession being the use of privies within the walls.[7] There they were to stay in solitary confinement for the next four years. A similar cage was prepared at the Tower of London for Bruce's twelve-year-old daughter, Marjorie, but the order was revoked and she was sent to a nunnery. Christina Bruce, whose husband Christopher Seton was hanged, drawn and quartered after being captured, was similarly lodged in a convent and Queen Elizabeth, wife of Robert Bruce but also daughter of Edward's powerful supporter the Earl of Ulster, was placed under house arrest in spartan conditions where she was to remain for the next eight years.

In the meanwhile Robert Bruce and his small group of fugitives made their way via Loch Lomond to Dunaverty Castle near the Mull of Kintyre, where they were welcomed by Bruce's friend, Angus Og ('the young') MacDonald of the Isles.[8] From Dunaverty it is likely Bruce and his companions went to the Isle of Rathlin off the coast of Ireland or alternatively to Islay, the centre of MacDonald territory. More improbably he could have continued to Ulster itself. Although Rathlin was just six and a half miles long by one and a half miles wide and there were enemies all around him he would certainly have been able to use Angus Og MacDonald's galleys to call on his estates for men and money in order to rebuild his strength. Wherever his winter base, by the spring of 1307 he had gathered enough strength to undertake a two-pronged attack on the mainland. Bruce himself with thirty-three small galleys went to Arran prior to making landfall on the Ayrshire coast while his two younger brothers, Thomas and Alexander, accompanied by Sir Reginald Crawford along with several hundred northern Irish recruits, made for Galloway, with the intention of creating a diversion to cover Bruce's more northerly attack. On landing, Crawford's party was ambushed and Crawford himself, together with Thomas and Alexander Bruce, were taken to Carlisle and hanged, drawn and quartered. The fact that Thomas Bruce had received serious wounds in the encounter did not save him from being spread-eagled on a hurdle and drawn by horses through the streets of Carlisle before being executed.

Meanwhile, Robert Bruce had arranged for a fire to be lit on the mainland coast if the local people were willing to join him. Seeing a fire his small band landed only to find it was not the work of his messenger, who appeared in a near frenzy telling them the nearby castle of Turnberry was garrisoned by 100 English under their commander, Henry Percy, while a further 200 were garrisoned in the adjoining village, and that Carrick was so thick with English soldiers no locals dared rise to assist Bruce. With so little to lose Bruce and his men opted to take the offensive. They surrounded the village and surprised its soldiers, killing them all except one man who alerted Henry Percy. Uncertain about the size of Bruce's force Percy remained in the castle while Bruce captured much-needed supplies, including war horses, before moving into the Carrick hills.[9]

With his limited strength Bruce had little choice of tactics. Faced with such massively superior English garrisons and with the majority of Scottish nobles and their followers either continuing to support the Comyns or regarding Bruce as nothing better than a usurper following a lost cause, he had to remain in the rugged hill country and use the classic guerrilla methods of speed, surprise and elusiveness. Yet as Bruce's handful of followers continued to avoid capture, small numbers of men started to join him, including one sizeable party of forty men commanded by Bruce's former mistress, Christiana of Carrick. It was Christian who told Bruce about the fate of his womenfolk and the men who had been captured with them.

After despatching an escort to lead her back to her estate, legend has it that Bruce was so overcome by his misfortunes and the immensity of his self-appointed task to regain Scotland that he considered leaving the country for ever. When lying in a dark cave where he was accustomed to take his rest he noticed a small spider hanging from the roof by a thread. By agitated movements it attempted to swing on its thread until it could reach a wall and anchor itself before beginning a web. Six times he watched it swing and fall back before, on the seventh, it made itself fast. Bruce decided that if a little creature could so persevere the king of the Scots could do no less.

Whether or not inspired by the spider, from this time Bruce and his men conducted a series of breathtaking escapades against immeasurably stronger English forces commanded by Valence and his co-commander, Robert Clifford, who attempted to bring them into exposed positions where they could be destroyed. Bruce avoided their traps and through a combination of inspired tactics and notable physical energy even began to achieve a number of successes of his own.

Moving south into Galloway he established a base near Loch Trool within the deep glen of the same name. Warned of an impending attack by 1500 knights, Bruce and 300 spearmen successfully checked the horsemen before moving off into new fastnesses. The two English leaders directly involved, Sir Robert Clifford and Sir John Vaux, were so frustrated by Bruce's escape that they came to blows as they blamed each other for the rebuff. Bruce went north and on 10 May 1307 at Loudon Hill, a rocky upthrust near Kilmarnock, with a force of some 600 men, he deliberately chose to meet massively superior detachments of cavalry under Valence. Bruce selected a strong natural position where he could not be outflanked and he made the ground even more hazardous by cutting trenches to impede the English horses. As they galloped towards the Scottish lines the English cavalry came upon his hidden trenches and were thrown into confusion; more than 100 riders were unhorsed and the Scots thereupon went onto the attack. At this the 3000 English gave way and along with their commander retreated to the protection of Bothwell Castle. Loudon showed Bruce's evolving thought towards countering the offensive capability of English heavy cavalry. He selected a location where the opposing cavalry were funnelled onto a narrow front, and his man-made obstacles could both check their momentum and cause casualties at which his massed spearmen drawn up behind the three lines of trenches could themselves take up the initiative.

Just three days later Bruce and his men showed they had no undue fear of armoured horsemen for they met another large cavalry squadron, this time under Raoul de Monthermer, Earl of Gloucester and, despite superior English numbers, rebuffed them, forcing Gloucester to seek the protection of Ayr Castle. Such successes against those attempting to hunt Bruce down began to give new hope to others suffering from Edward I's savage repression. Men reasoned that if Bruce could go on winning it would be far preferable to join him than become declared outlaws threatened under English law by drawing and hanging. The Lanercost Chronicle reported bitterly about Bruce's gathering strength: 'Despite the fearful revenge inflicted upon the Scots who adhered to Bruce the number of those willing to strengthen him in his Kingship increased daily.'[10]

From now on Bruce's strategy became clear. He adopted the classic principles of guerrilla warfare devised by the Chinese General Sun Tzu eighteen centuries before by choosing engagements where the enemy appeared at a disadvantage, while at the same time attempting to give a sense of his own invulnerability. This approach was summed up later in the century by the following verse.

> In hidden spots keep every store
> And burn the plain lands them before
> So, when they find the land lie waste
> Needs must they pass away in haste
> Harried by cunning raids at night
> And threatening sounds from every height,
> Then as they leave, with great array
> Smite with the sword and chase away.
> This is the counsel and intent
> Of Good King Robert's Testament.[11]

Through such successes, limited as they were so far, Bruce aimed to convince those living in the vicinity of his operations that he was sure to overcome his enemies and they would do well to give him any information they had about the English and their allies. James Douglas had already shown the king by his despoiling and burning of Douglas Castle that, when the local inhabitants were hostile to the English, without the protection of such thick walls the invaders were put at a distinct disadvantage. Bruce realised that if he adopted the tactic of taking similar fortresses and then destroying them he would not only enjoy local successes but commence winning back the country.

On 7 July 1307 the Scottish insurgents received the news they must have been most eagerly awaiting. In his sixty-ninth year their fearsome adversary Edward I died at Burgh-on-Sands just south of the border as he was bringing another large army into Scotland. In the last nine months of his life he either lodged at Lanercost Priory near Carlisle or stayed in the city itself, and although becoming increasingly weak physically he despatched an unending stream of urgent instructions on how to deal with Bruce.[12] With the old king's death Bruce knew the slacker direction of his son Edward Caernarvon (now Edward II) would soon be likely to work to his advantage. In fact when the English army came under Caernarvon's command it only reached Cumnock in Ayrshire before returning to England. He was not to cross the border for another three years, thus giving Bruce the vital opportunity to challenge his most powerful Scottish enemies and extend his precarious fingerholds in the southwest to other regions of Scotland.

Edward II offered Bruce another bonus: on 13 September he replaced Valence, his father's tough and energetic, if not over-imaginative, Lieutenant of Scotland, with John of Brittany, Earl of Richmond. As a commander Brittany bore no comparison with Valence: he switched from actively hunting the insurgents down to a policy of containment, based on holding the line of Clydesdale. This eased the pressure on Bruce whose base at the time was still so small that his guerrilla fighters had to survive on whatever food they could take from others. He seized the increased opportunities for manoeuvre, and moved to attack the MacDoualls in Galloway who had captured his two brothers and delivered them up for execution. So successful was he and so thorough was his wasting of their lands that many of their tribesmen were compelled to leave their Scottish homes and drive their livestock into the forest of Inglewood in Cumberland.

From Galloway Bruce continued his offensive by marching north and breaking through the English defence line on the Clyde and moving into the Western Highlands, although he took pains to cover his back by leaving his keen young commander, James Douglas, in command of the southwest. The erstwhile guerrilla leader had now moved into the open as far as his Comyn opponents were concerned. And as Bruce proceeded up the west coast gathering strength all the while, he continued to enjoy the priceless support of Angus Og and his fleet of galleys. Command of the sea enabled him to make both rapid and surprise raids on his enemies. Whilst on his way to the far north, where he intended to break the Comyn power, he forced the MacDougalls of Argyll and Lorne to ask for a truce. John of Lorne tried to avoid the anger of the English king by excusing himself, saying, 'Robert Bruce approached these parts by land and sea with 10,000 men they say or 15,000. I have no more than 800 men.'[13] In fact, Bruce was unlikely to have that many more soldiers himself, but his string of successes against the English, together with his combined use of land and sea, alarmed less determined men and helped to disguise his relative weakness.

Protected by his truce with the MacDougalls Bruce moved northeast through the Great Glen, where he captured Inverlochy at its southern end before taking Urquhart and Inverness castles in the north. Emerging at Inverness he joined forces with the Bishop of Moray, his constant and long-standing supporter in that region. By October 1307 Bruce was in a position to threaten the Earl of Ross, whose estates stretched across a large swathe of the northeast coast. Ross had been responsible for the capture of Bruce's womenfolk but, putting aside any personal bitterness, Bruce offered him a truce until June 1308, which Ross accepted. Bruce's decision to start his campaign against Ross in the autumn was soundly based for the uncertain weather and rough seas made any English attempt to send military assistance extremely difficult if not impossible. Like John of Lorne, the cautious earl also wrote to Edward II with excuses, but Bruce believed that if he could gain further military successes the earl's allegiance was likely to change in his favour. With the Earl of Ross immobilised Bruce was now able to confront the Earl of Buchan, the greatest of the Comyn landowners, whose fertile estates stretched far along the northeast coast from the Moray Firth to Aberdeen. Bruce knew the proud Buchan was highly unlikely to offer terms and, as he drew near, Buchan duly came to meet him with his own army.

So far events had gone remarkably well for Bruce, whose forces were now joined by those of Sir William Wiseman and other knights of Moray. However, as he was about to make an assault on Inverurie, the capital of Buchan's estates in Garioch, he became desperately ill, most likely the result of the strain and ceaseless exertions of his eighteen months' campaigning. Encouraged by this, Buchan, supported by an English contingent and with others provided by David Strathbogie, Earl of Atholl and the Scottish baron John Moubray, threatened Bruce's forces who were compelled to retreat from the lowlands south of Banff to the more wooded uplands at Slioch near Huntly. It was winter and snow lay on the ground; Bruce's men were both cold and short of food while their leader, who lacked any medicine, remained very ill. However, Bruce's only surviving brother, Edward led the party by Huntly to the Garioch where they enjoyed some support but Buchan followed up and in late January his troops surprised Bruce's outposts and made ready for a full attack. At this Bruce, who had partially recovered, called for his horse and was lifted onto it. With a rider on each side to help him stay in the saddle he advanced and the king's appearance helped to put the attackers to flight.

Bruce took further time to recover fully but, on 23 May 1308, his forces met and defeated Buchan's close to Inverurie, following which he went on to destroy Inverurie Castle.[14] Edward Bruce was given the commission to ravage the Buchan estates and of smashing the main Comyn power base. So thoroughly did he go about his task by breaking down castles, killing, destroying homesteads, slaughtering, burning cattle and corn, that it was said men grieved over the herschip (harrying) of Buchan for fifty years or more.[15] Bruce was known for his comparative humanity and generosity but, like Edward I (and any successful medieval king), he showed he could also use terror effectively.

Bruce's barbarous treatment of the east coast served not only to crush a great Comyn, who fled to England where he died within a year, but also as a powerful incentive to persuade others to come to terms. In the meantime James Douglas was extending Bruce's control over Douglasdale, Upper Clydesdale and eastwards to Selkirk and Jedburgh. Douglas also captured Bruce's nephew Thomas Randolph and brought him to the king, with the result that Randolph eventually became another of his notable commanders. During the summer of 1308 Bruce continued his conquest of the north by capturing and destroying further Comyn fortresses such as Tarradale on the Black Isle, Slains and Dundarg to the east followed by English strongholds at Elgin, Fyvie and Aboyne, and with the surrender of Aberdeen in July he gained a major seaport through which he could resume the trade of Scottish products, particularly wool, with Scandinavia.

By mid-August 1308 Bruce was ready to take on the MacDougalls of Lorne, for which offensive he ordered James Douglas to join him. To reach the MacDougalls Bruce had to move through a narrow pass at Brander which was flanked on one side by the steep slope of Ben Cruachan (1124 metres) while on the other the ground fell away sharply into an arm of Loch Awe. The MacDougalls planned to ambush Bruce by rolling large rocks upon him and his men and then driving them into the loch but the king forestalled them by sending Highlanders under Douglas into positions above the attackers and by stringing out his forces. The tumbling rocks were successfully avoided and as Bruce's men charged uphill, the MacDoualls were assailed from above by Douglas' Highlanders. They were unable to resist the double attacks and Bruce pursued them to their headquarters at Dunstaffnage Castle near Dunbeg which quickly surrendered and was destroyed. In mid-August Bruce sent his brother to Galloway on another campaign of devastation and killing, in the process of which the MacDougalls were driven out of the region and some were forced to look for refuge in England.

Bruce's conquest over the Comyns and other Scottish nobles

who opposed him became virtually complete when the Earl of Ross submitted on 31 October 1308. Bruce's response was magnanimous. Ross was given back his lands together with the burgh of Dingwall and the lands of Creich in Sutherland. Such leniency gained its reward, for from now on Ross kept his promise to serve Bruce well and faithfully.

Within little more than a year Robert Bruce had transformed his military position. To the south he controlled a broad band of territory right across the country from Ayr to Roxburgh and Jedburgh. Galloway now paid him tribute and the MacDoualls there were scattered. Up the west coast in Argyll, he had defeated the chief branch of the MacDougall clan, while further north the Earl of Ross had become an adherent and, most importantly of all, the Earl of Buchan had fled to England. By conquest Bruce had forced many prominent members of the Scottish nobility to recognise him as king, but in private there were still a significant number, in addition to the Comyns, who doubted the legality of his claim to the throne.

While his achievements so far had been immense and gained against all the odds, the tasks still facing him were more difficult. A considerable number of castles remained in English hands, including those centres of power that stretched right across Lothian Scotland. Until the English garrisons were driven out of his land Bruce could never be recognised abroad as the legal monarch of an independent kingdom. Yet however difficult the task of clearing the castles might prove it was sure to bring him larger problems still. Despite the serious conflicts Edward II was experiencing with his nobles such action was bound before long to provoke the English king into sending overwhelming armies into Scotland both to relieve the castles, and to restore his military control there.

It had taken Bruce just eighteen months from spring 1307 until the autumn of 1308 to defeat his Scottish opponents (although some still opted to fight with the English), but he faced more than five years of further conflict before he would be brought to his ultimate test, the meeting of both countries' national armies in a full-scale engagement. Such a great battle was not directly of Bruce's seeking: his chosen policy so far was to continue

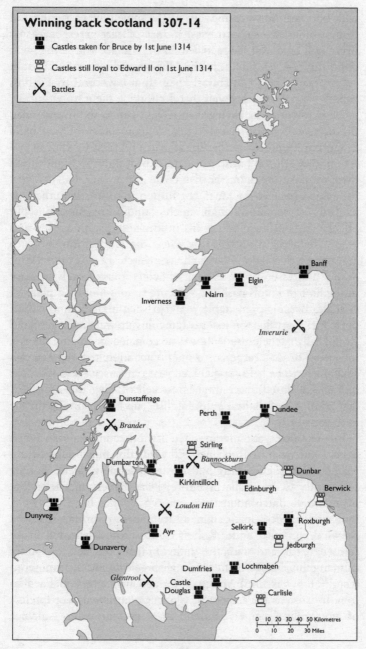

Winning back Scotland 1307-14

Castles taken for Bruce by 1st June 1314

Castles still loyal to Edward II on 1st June 1314

Battles

Banff

Elgin

Nairn

Inverness

Inverurie

Dunstaffnage

Brander

Perth

Dundee

Stirling

Dumbarton

Bannockburn

Kirkintilloch

Edinburgh

Dunbar

Berwick

Dunyveg

Loudon Hill

Ayr

Selkirk

Roxburgh

Jedburgh

Dunaverty

Dumfries

Lochmaben

Glentrool

Castle
Douglas

Carlisle

0 10 20 30 40 50 Kilometres

0   10   20   30 Miles

with his guerrilla warfare while at the same time capturing and demolishing English fortresses. In face of every invading army Bruce still favoured the tactics used by Wallace before the great opportunity given him at Stirling Bridge and his more reluctant acceptance of battle at Falkirk, namely using scorched earth to cut off his enemies' supplies thereby forcing them to withdraw, while in the process leaving themselves open to spoiling attacks. By such methods Bruce could take full advantage of Scotland's geography to persuade the English the conquest of the country was not worth the frustration and expense involved and bring them to make peace on Scottish terms.

Such a prospect lay far in the future: not only were the vast majority of Scotland's main castles still in English hands but Edward II continued to use his influence with the papacy and other European countries to prevent the recognition of Bruce as king of Scotland. Although by March 1309 Philip IV of France addressed Bruce as King of Scots, it was largely because of the French king's wish for Scotland to join him on a planned crusade. Bruce's predictable reply to such a request was that, once the English stopped ravaging his country, all Scotland would rally to the crusade. It was no coincidence that on the day following Bruce's response to the French king, the first Scottish parliament to be held for eighteen years endorsed its support for him and declared Bruce the nearest heir of King Alexander III, denigrating John Balliol as an English puppet put on the throne by Edward I.[16]

In the same year military activity took a new turn when Bruce was required to face Edward II's much-delayed invasion. The English king had come to terms with his barons sufficiently to bring his favourite, Piers Gaveston, back from exile and despatch major forces into Scotland. In fact Edward sent two armies north, one under the Earl of Hereford to Berwick, the other under Robert Clifford to Carlisle, but Bruce refused battle and with the unfavourable prospects of winter campaigning before them the English commanders proposed a truce. This was until March 1310 and was later extended to June because as the Lanercost Chronicle observed, 'the English do not willingly enter Scotland to wage war before summer chiefly because earlier in the year they find no food for their horses'.[17]

Meanwhile, Edward II's continuing problems with his nobles brought a surprising new twist, giving him a most powerful incentive to pursue the war with Scotland. The king faced fierce hostility from his nobles over his lavish gifts to Piers Gaveston, and from Philip of France who, furious at Edward's neglect of his daughter, Isabella (Edward's wife), had summoned him to Paris to justify himself. Edward II decided he could foil both challenges by gaining military successes in Scotland and accordingly a royal edict was issued for men to assemble at Berwick by 8 September for a new invasion attempt. (Piers Gaveston was, in fact, already in the north.) The army compared in size with any his father had led against Scotland although only three great barons, the earls of Cornwall, Gloucester and Surrey, answered the summons.

Characteristically, after devastating the country lying in the English army's path Bruce continued to avoid battle. When the English moved from Berwick to Biggar in central Scotland they found no corn nor cattle within an area that had not only been wasted but was suffering from widespread famine. To add to their difficulties James Douglas hovered nearby eager to kill or capture any stragglers. On 28 October Edward II was compelled to lead his army back to Berwick, harassed all the time by Bruce's raiders. The effectiveness of Bruce's tactics was fully acknowledged by a chronicler, the so-called English monk of Malmesbury who wrote:

> For Robert Bruce, knowing himself unequal to the strength of the King of England in strength or fortune, decided that it would be better to resist our King by secret warfare rather than dispute his right in open battle. Indeed I might be tempted to sound the praises of Sir Robert Bruce did not the guilt of homicide and the dark stain of treachery bid me keep silent.[18]

Edward (still accompanied by Piers Gaveston) continued to avoid the demands of his 'Lords Ordainers' by remaining at Berwick, although his army was now much reduced after many of the infantry had completed their forty days feudal service.

He stayed there for the next six months, during which time he attempted to refurbish his castles in Lothian by contracting with leading English commanders such as Robert Clifford (at Berwick), Henry Beaumont (at Perth) and Roger Mortimer (at Roxburgh), to occupy individual fortresses for a set period of time, usually not less than a year. However by midsummer 1311, despite such devices, he was so short of funds that he was forced to return to London having achieved very little militarily.

Once Edward II and his men had gone, Bruce assumed the offensive by making his first major raid across the border, moving into Northumberland where he burnt and looted crops before returning to Scotland fifteen days later. This opened Bruce's campaign of not only taking grain and livestock but extorting ransoms from the English northern counties, and so effective were his depredations in Northumberland that the county paid the enormous sum of £2000 as an immunity against any further raids until February 1312. One major advantage of these raids was that despite the valuable rewards such 'soft targets' brought virtually no risk to his soldiers.

Engrossed as never before in its civil war, England appeared to have no means of response. From mid-October 1311 until February 1312 Piers Gaveston was again banished and on his return Edward II sent him to York, whereupon the 'Lords Ordainers' decided to take military action. They assembled their individual armies and moved north against Gaveston, who surrendered to Valence, Earl of Pembroke, during May 1312. But as Gaveston was being moved into safe keeping he was captured by the Earl of Warwick and beheaded, at which the king – together with Valence who considered his honour had been compromised – took the field against the earls of Lancaster and Warwick. The king and Valence were successful and by October 1313 the majority of the estranged nobles indicated that they were anxious to make peace.

In the meantime, Bruce had both continued and extended his incursions. During July 1312 the parliament, meeting at Ayr, decided upon a large-scale invasion of England, and after crossing the border the Scottish forces sacked Lanercost Priory before moving on to Chester Le Street and Durham where they took immense booty. The leading men of Durham negotiated a truce to last for ten months until midsummer 1313 on the payment of £2000, with the additional humiliating condition that the Scots could retreat through Durham at their will. Fresh immunities were then granted to other counties but only upon the same heavy cash payments. Bruce's campaign, savage as it was, was a disciplined one. Those who paid were spared, those who did not had their estates ravaged and they themselves were taken back to Scotland. The aim was twofold: to restore Bruce's bankrupted kingdom and force the English to recognise Scotland; the former was so successful that within three years Bruce received more than £40,000 in tributes.[19]

Supported by such military successes Bruce continued with his political initiatives. On 29 October 1312, at Inchture near Perth, Bruce met with the envoys of King Hakon V of Norway and renewed the Treaty of Perth made in 1266 between the two countries, by which the Norwegians recognised the loss of the Hebrides in return for a perpetual annuity of 100 marks from the Scots. This restoration of links with Norway and that country's recognition of Robert Bruce as king marked another step towards the normalisation of relations between Scotland and the rest of Europe. By now regular trade was taking place with the Hanseatic League and other principalities of the Low Countries as well as unofficial – but significant – trade with some northern English sea ports and, of course, with Ulster.

Within the country, two thirds of which was under Bruce's control, the Scottish king won over David, Earl of Atholl, the son of John, Earl of Atholl, who had been hanged earlier by Edward I for supporting Bruce. Atholl's lands were restored to him and he was appointed Constable of Scotland. At the same time Bruce's nephew, Thomas Randolph, was created Earl of Moray with lands stretching between the earldoms of Ross and Atholl.

While Edward was embroiled with his barons, Bruce was able to continue with his dual strategy of making regular raids into northern England and continuing to take and destroy English castles in Scotland. Both elements yielded encouraging results. The raids were valuable because not only were they highly profitable but by terrorising the northern counties Bruce demonstrated the ineffectiveness of the English king. And by 1312 the number of castles under English control was being significantly reduced. North of the Tay, only Perth remained in English hands, with Stirling, Linlithgow and Bothwell occupying the line of the Firth of Forth and the Clyde; in the south-west Dalswinton, Dumfries, Buittle and Caerlaverock remained, while in Lothian, still mainly in English hands, the four strongest of all, Edinburgh, Roxburgh, Jedburgh and Berwick were unsubdued.

Taking and destroying such castles represented a mammoth task even for forces with heavy siege equipment. Without it, ingenuity and great daring were essential. In fact, it was the attempt to take one of these castles that led directly to the confrontation between the two countries at Bannockburn, although Bruce's threat in November 1313 that his Scottish enemies had but a year to make peace or suffer perpetual disinheritance also made another English attack on Scotland highly likely. Efforts to take these remaining castles met with mixed fortunes. On 6 December 1312 Bruce and Douglas attempted to seize the great castle of Berwick using hemp scaling ladders that could be lifted at spearpoint and placed over the walls for the attackers to ascend; on this occasion they did not succeed for the garrison was alerted by a dog barking. One month later on 7 January 1313 Bruce joined the troops who were unsuccessfully besieging Perth: feigning a move away (to understandable jeers from the garrison), they returned secretly eight days later when he personally led the attackers across a shallow point of the moat. Bruce himself placed a rope ladder on the wall and was the second to climb it. Next to fall was Dumfries, starved into surrender by 7 February 1313, followed quite quickly by Dalswinton, Buittle and Caerlaverock.

Outside Lothian only two castles held out, Stirling and Bothwell. Bothwell could be safely ignored as its governor remained inactive, waiting to give his allegiance to whoever gained the upper hand, but Stirling, which Edward Bruce was ordered to assault, was far different. Its massive fortifications could withstand any number of attacks, whether the assailants were equipped with siege engines or not. Edward Bruce had none; his only option was to starve the garrison into submission. For three months he camped round it and succeeded in sealing it off but, impatient and rash as he was, this was the very type of warfare for which he was not suited. The castle's governor was a Scot, Sir Philip Moubray, and he tempted Edward Bruce with the seemingly chivalrous proposal that 'if by midsummer a year hence (1314) he was not rescued by battle, he would yield the castle freely'. Robert Bruce was away seizing the Isle of Man, and Edward accepted Moubray's offer without bothering to consult the king.[20]

In mitigation, Edward Bruce might justly have thought the English king and his nobles would continue their warring and remain in no position to meet the challenge. But this was a rash assessment given that his agreement with Moubray was made for twelve months' time. The English could hardly have ignored Bruce's threat of perpetual disinheritance on his Scottish enemies but after things had been going so seriously against them, the agreement between Edward Bruce and Moubray gave a Godsent opportunity for relations to be patched up between the king and his nobles and for them to unite against the Scots apparently now ready to face them in open battle. On the Scottish side Bruce would have been understandably angry because of the challenge's unifying effect on the English, but much more importantly because he had been put on the spot by it. Barbour had him remarking, 'We are set in jeopardy to lose or win all at one throw.'[21] The pledge had been given by a brother who on the male side was nearest in succession to Robert Bruce's throne. Although Bruce had practised stealth and deception in his tactics against the English it was much more difficult for a man accused by many of being a usurper king not to honour his brother's word. Bruce was thus put under fierce pressure to meet the English in open battle, however much it went against his painstaking and hitherto successful strategy. At least he retained the advantage of choosing the terrain – for by the agreement the English had to come to Stirling. The agreement also still left him some choice about the nature of the conflict. Theoretically he could rebuff the invaders and then move off without pursuing things in a life or death struggle. Whether in the heat of battle such an option would be left open to him was, of course, incalculable.

Over the intervening months the Scottish king's chief task was to raise and train a force capable of meeting the English but he could also increase the invading army's logistical problems by capturing the other great castles of Lothian, a task which would keep his own forces occupied and alert. Edinburgh was of principal importance; it was closest to Stirling and presented a vital revictualling point, whereas Roxburgh and Berwick (which was also a seaport) were good starting off points for any invasion but still over fifty miles south of Edinburgh, with Jedburgh the most southerly of them all. Outside Lothian the closest castle to Stirling was Linlithgow, half-way between Stirling and Edinburgh.

The taking of Linlithgow Castle owed nothing to Bruce's eager commanders: it was achieved by a simple countryman named William Bunnock who conceived the idea of concealing eight men in a load of hay and jamming his cart under the portcullis. Bunnock himself killed the porter while those in the cart, along with others concealed near the gate, overcame the garrison. Roxburgh Castle fell to James Douglas during the night of Shrove Tuesday, 27 February 1314, who adopted the brilliant device of dressing his men in black cloaks and making them approach it on their hands and knees in the guise of the small black cattle of the time. The garrison was celebrating the last religious feast before Lent and Douglas and his sixty men were over the castle walls and among the roisterers in the great hall before they had time to react.

Not to be outdone, Thomas Randolph took Edinburgh Castle on 14 March. He and thirty men, all mountaineers, were led up the sheer crags by a certain William Francis, son of a watch-keeper in the castle. As a young man with a lover in the city he had regularly gone down one of the castle walls by rope ladder before descending the crags, and returned by the same route in the early hours of the morning. After one alarm when they thought they had been observed as they paused for breath on a ledge, Randolph and his men climbed over the castle wall as others created a diversion at the east port before the stronghold fell to his combined attacks.

Berwick Castle was not taken until 1318, and the English used it as a muster point for their cavalry before setting off to relieve Stirling Castle. Only two other castles remained uncaptured, Dunbar and Jedburgh. Dunbar was to play a vital part in the escape of Edward II after the battle but Jedburgh had no significant role.

With the fall of Edinburgh Castle in March 1314 the thirty-nine-year-old Robert Bruce had advanced his cause further than anyone could have imagined possible during the seven years since February 1307, when he and his small band of followers were fugitives in the Carrick hills. After a succession of victories all Scotland, except some pockets of Lothian, had come to acknowledge him as king, however many doubts might remain concerning the lawfulness of his claim to the throne, while his series of raids into northern England had not only confirmed his offensive powers but brought much-needed supplies and money to his impoverished country. Within Scotland at least three parliaments had approved the restoration of the country's fiscal and judicial system and the Church continued with its strong support, while trade and diplomatic relations had all but returned to normal with Europe.

However, Bruce had by no means secured Scotland. Edward Bruce's truce at Stirling Castle meant that the English had every motivation they needed to mount a major invasion. England still possessed the ability to assemble an army superior in both weaponry and numbers to any that Scotland could raise. It had, however, learned from its past mistakes, to use eastern sea ports such as Berwick and Dunbar, together with an accompanying wagon train, to keep the army adequately supplied during its northern campaigns. If Bruce could not find a way of defying such odds all his work could easily be reversed. If the English invasion was successful they could go on to rebuild their Scottish castles, restore their officials, reinstate the Comyns who accompanied them, purge the Scottish church of Bruce supporters and, if he were not killed, to arraign him like Wallace for his manifold crimes. With such an outcome Scotland's chance of becoming a fully independent country would be lost. No wonder Bruce had never opted for such a confrontation.

Section Two: *The Contenders*

CHAPTER FOUR

≈

THE TWO ARMIES

'They made ready weapons and armour, and all
that pertains to war.'

Barbour, *The Bruce*

IN THEIR PREPARATIONS FOR the expected confrontation
England and Scotland faced contrasting problems. Scotland's
primary difficulty was to raise sufficient numbers to match
those of the anticipated English invaders. Its population was
approximately 400,000, just a fifth of England's, and after
eighteen years of almost continuous fighting, including costly
civil warfare, the available manpower had been reduced still
further. If Bruce had attempted to use the decree of 'Servitum
Scoticanum' in 1313 to raise the country's traditional feudal host
of men aged between sixteen and sixty it is very doubtful if
he could have raised anything like the numbers that manned
Wallace's battle lines at Falkirk. There were also severe economic
constraints on both the equipment and food needed to support
a large army after years of fighting and enemy occupation
had seriously interrupted the country's legislative processes and
dislocated its economy. It was not until 1309, for instance, that
Robert Bruce was able to hold his first parliament, and his
request for burghers to attend the Inchture parliament of three
years later demonstrated the importance he came to place on
the burgh providing a vital source of state revenue, as well as
fighting men.

Although from 1310 onwards Bruce's financial problems
were helped by his raids on northern England, which brought
considerable sums in protection money together with cattle,
horses and corn, these were neither normal nor regular sources of

income. Compared with England, Scotland was a poor country and, until Bruce recaptured the Isle of Man (in 1313) English ships were able to threaten its shortest supply line from abroad through the southwestern approaches between Scotland and Ireland. In spite of the partial blockade, from 1310 at least the Scots had been receiving some foodstuffs from Ireland and, more importantly still, badly needed iron and steel weapons along with armour, in addition to the supplies of these coming from Scandanavia.[1] Military weapons were unlikely to have been made in Ireland and were probably re-exported after being obtained from the continent or from England.

Recruitment was not the major English dilemma. They normally had no need to order a full national levy for they could hardly have coped with the numbers that would have resulted, and so it became common practice to take men from specific regions. The reign of Edward I also saw a great extension in the system of paying troops and raising private contracts in addition to relying on the feudal or general duties of vassals. For the battle of Falkirk, for instance, the English infantry was levied from Wales, Chester and Lancashire, in all 29,400 foot, supplemented by mercenaries from Gascony.[2] Admittedly, prior to Bannockburn things were somewhat different, since the unsettled state of the country caused especial difficulties over raising men, and Edward II was obliged to extend his earlier calls to include thirteen midland and northern counties with specialist archers coming from the far south.[3] This brought further problems, particularly over the need to pay the militia once they served outside their county boundaries. Faced with the huge debt bequeathed by his father and dissatisfaction of his own making among the baronage Edward II attempted to raise additional foot soldiers by requiring one from each township, whose wages would be paid for by that community.[4]

Another of England's great strengths was in the qualitative superiority of its army. England's more numerous and wealthier aristocracy, together with the growing number of men who owned twenty librates of land or more, enabled it to raise far larger numbers of armoured cavalry, the battlefield-winning weapon of the day. Each English magnate was required to supply a fixed quota of knights, fully protected by chain mail, mounted on large and powerful shire horses which were themselves protected not only by heavy cloth trappings over their haunches but by metal chaffrons over their heads. chamFrons

By any standard it was undeniably expensive to equip a knight. When archers were paid two old pence a day, a heavy destrier horse cost between £40 and £80 and even cheaper horses cost between £10 and £20, quite apart from their other equipment. Each knight needed a minimum of two horses and most more still. Knights were customarily supported by at least two troopers on somewhat inferior horses that could be valued as low as £2 but on some expeditions even the English troopers were allowed three horses.[5] The shire horses needed to be powerful, for in addition to their riders' mail which could total more than 60lbs (27kg), their war saddles weighed from 21 to 33lbs (9.5 to 15kg).[6] Additionally, under their mail the knights wore heavy quilted garments to help absorb any blows and over it surcoats emblazoned with the knights' arms. By this time, as the contemporary inventory of Piers Gaveston revealed, many knights had come to enjoy the increased protection of iron plates over their chest and back which were often faced with silk or velvet.[7] When fully accoutred the knights topped off their layers of body protection with great metal helms covering their heads and faces which, despite admirable defensive qualities, brought attendant penalties, for even with slits or small windows for the eyes, their vision was much restricted.

For offensive action knights carried twelve-foot lances, together with swords and battle axes or maces for close quarter fighting. The heads of their lances were fitted with small pieces of cloth or silk, the forerunners of armoured pennons, which, when lances found their mark, prevented them from becoming embedded and enabled the weapons to be removed for further use.[8] Their swords were quite often highly decorated and most maces with their protruding 'knobs' were the work of skilled craftsmen. Some indication of the cost of armoured knights together with their weapons and horses can be gathered from Edward I's attempts to raise cavalry for an invasion of Scotland following the English defeat at Stirling Bridge. He subsidised several of his nobles by providing them with up to 500 horses at the amazing cost of £7691.16s.8d.[9]

Scotland could never match this outlay. Wallace was very weak in cavalry at both Stirling Bridge and Falkirk, while Bruce's cavalry contingent at the time of Bannockburn would not be much above a fifth of the English strength. Moreover his riders were mounted on small wiry ponies or 'hackneys', standing around 14 hands high, compared with a destrier of up to 17 hands with its much heavier build and more powerful shoulders and haunches. Although some of the Scottish riders wore mail, or were protected by stout coverings of boiled leather across their chests and backs, in the main their horses were incapable of carrying the equivalent of English knights equipped for battle. The Scottish cavalry were also incapable of withstanding charges from the English juggernauts, although they did have the advantage in manoeuvrability and adaptability: carrying such a weight of armour, English knights were most effective when charging in straight lines. Most seriously of all, if for some reason the English riders were unhorsed they became highly vulnerable to the weapons of ordinary foot soldiers. Daggers could be thrust within the eye slits of helms and axes swung against the unprotected backs of their legs. Notwithstanding, at this time armoured cavalry were still the unquestioned arbiters of the battlefield.

The English were also superior in bowmen. In England the shortbow was being replaced by the longbow with its much superior qualities, a fact well appreciated by Edward I at Falkirk. The longbow was strung with hemp whipped with light linen cord and its shafts of English yew were almost two metres long. These were equipped with different tips: some could pierce armour while others were designed for inflicting large flesh wounds. Although the longbow had a maximum range of 350 metres its armour-piercing qualities were best at the much shorter, if still considerable, distance of 100–150 metres. A good archer could fire as many as fifteen aimed arrows a minute and could be likened to a type of medieval machine gun. When the English used massed archers firing high in the air their shafts would make up a dense cloud of missiles, which descending with a destructive swishing noise could inflict heavy casualties on opposing infantry or cavalry. The English subsequently came to rate the longbow so highly as a weapon that six feathers from every goose killed were to be handed in for arrow fletching.[10] Like all weapons it was not without some limitations, the main one being the high draw power required – between 150–170 pounds. In battle longbowmen needed to take up their stations on firm ground standing side on with their feet planted well apart and even more than other infantrymen they were vulnerable to cavalry, if it could get amongst them. Good longbowmen needed strength and stamina and it took years rather than months for them to become fully effective. For protection the archers wore jerkins or chain-mail on their shoulders in addition to some form of head covering. As well as their bows they carried short swords or daggers.

The English army also had a considerable number of highly regarded crossbowmen. These had to crank their weapons for loading but once loaded they could be retained in that state without further effort. Some crossbows were carried by English-men and many by mercenary bowmen from regions such as Gascony. The weapon was equal or superior in range to the long-bow and very much superior to the shortbow. The penetrative power of its shafts were quite equal to those of the longbow as their leather or parchment flights made the shafts rotate thus increasing both their velocity and penetration. The crossbow's rate of fire, however, was slower with a maximum of six aimed bolts a minute. Nonetheless, it was at least as accurate and could be aimed precisely.

In comparison the Scottish shortbows had a far shorter range and poorer penetrative ability. They had, in fact, reached the limit of their development, although their skilled archers could fire even more quickly than the English longbowmen. Unlike the English the bulk of the Scottish bowmen tended to come from a particular location, in Bruce's time the forest of Ettrick.

In one arm only, that of infantry spearmen, were the Scots not outmatched qualitatively. Both sides were similarly equipped. For protection the English footsoldiers wore quilted coats, often topped by chain mail over their heads and shoulders, mail gloves and bassinets (iron hats), and each carried a shield. For armament they carried a twelve-foot spear together with a short sword or dagger. Their Scottish equivalents were also protected by quilted jackets. At the time of Bannockburn fewer had chainmail than the English but they also wore protective gloves and bassinets. Although contemporary evidence is lacking concerning their actual length, the Scottish spears were probably also between twelve and fourteen feet long.[11] In addition each Scottish soldier carried a dirk or an axe, as well as a circular wooden targe or shield. The latter was usually made by fastening layers of close-grained wood at right-angles to each other, making it very difficult for arrows to penetrate, although sometimes it was made out of string wickerwork. Even if their spears were no longer than twelve feet they were capable of keeping English cavalry at a distance, for the riders' twelve-foot lances were unlikely to stretch much more than six feet in front of their horses' heads. While their equipment was almost the same, the Scottish infantry had a distinct advantage in the calibre of the men who filled the ranks, as nobles, knights and yeomen farmers were accustomed to fight on foot together with their followers, whereas such men in the English army served with the cavalry.

The actual size of the two armies at Bannockburn has provoked much discussion. Apart from the contemporary chroniclers, two major studies have been made of the respective strengths. During 1913 both John Morris and William Mackay MacKenzie published books on the battle which included estimated totals for each side, although it has to be acknowledged that Mackay MacKenzie followed many of Morris' calculations.[12] Later writers, including the redoubtable Professor Barrow, have been generally content to follow Morris' and MacKenzies' figures, although Peter Traquair in his recent book *Freedom's Sword* has scaled down both armies still further.[13]

The total cavalry available in England at this time was about 7000 to 7500, but it is highly unlikely that such a number was mobilised.[14] Like his father Edward II used the feudal levy to raise the majority of his cavalry but for Bannockburn only three of the eight English earls answered his summons, the other five sending the minimum number of knights required. Fortunately for the English king many of his nobles below the rank of earl attended enthusiastically and were likely to have contributed more than the bare numbers of additional troopers required. Added to these were the Scottish knights still opposed to Bruce, as well as knights from Ireland and others from Europe. Between August and October 1313 Edward II took considerable pains to call on such men: he wrote eleven letters, for instance, to gain the release of a single – albeit outstanding – knight, Giles D'Argentan, to fight with him at Bannockburn.[15]

One contemporary English chronicler put the total English cavalry at Bannockburn at slightly more than 2000[16] although at the other extreme John Barbour set their cavalry strength at 3000 barded horses alone, i.e. those carrying fully armoured knights.[17] Following a careful calculation of the rolls John Morris came to the conclusion that the English cavalry at Bannockburn could not have been above 2400.[18] This, of course, would by no means be the total number of horses required. Apart from their front line mounts the English knights were likely to ride coursers or lighter horses on the approach march, saving their destriers for the anticipated battles. In fact, their battle chargers were normally led by the squire on the knight's right hand, for the name destrier comes directly from the Latin *dextra*, meaning right.

In contrast there is relative unanimity about the number of Scottish cavalry. Raised from among a much smaller force of knights and other magnates, quite apart from the fact that the feudal system of knight service did not operate countrywide, this was put at 500, all light horsemen since large-boned destrier horses were not available in Scotland and the English made sure they remained so. In January 1310 Edward II had banned exports of horses and arms to Scotland on pain of the highest penalties and under Edward III it was a felony to export horses there.[19] Taking the lowest estimated figures the English cavalry with their heavier horses still outnumbered their Scottish opponents by four to one.

Comparable discussion has taken place over the numbers of foot soldiers. Barbour, for instance, put the total strengths of the two armies (including cavalry) at 100,000 English and 30,000

Scots. In contrast, by painstaking analysis and working on the pattern of recruitment that operated during Edward I's Welsh wars, John Morris calculated that Edward II sent out writs for 21,640 men, including archers, and that he probably succeeded in assembling no more than 15,000, including 2400 cavalry. However these totals probably did not include the overseas and Irish contingents whom Barbour said were 'a great following'. W M MacKenzie comes to a somewhat higher total estimating the English cavalry and infantry combined at 20,000.

There is even less evidence to help calculate the size of the Scottish infantry. Working on Barbour's ratios between the two forces and using Morris' figures, the Scottish strength would total less than 7000. All authorities agree on the Scottish small folk (retainers and troops who came late to the battle) at some 3000.[20] These figures are not far from General Christison's, who in his study of the battle for the National Trust for Scotland calculated there were some 20,000 English foot faced by 5500 trained Scottish soldiers (together with the complement of small folk).[21] Only one English writer, Major A F Becke, whose conclusions are included within *The Complete Peerage*, and who lacks the distinction of authorities like Barrow, Morris or Christison, comes to the remarkable conclusion that the Scottish infantry was 'scarcely at all inferior in numbers to the English infantry'.[22]

These were the facts, along with the commentators' interpretations, that faced me and from which I needed to come to my own conclusions on the size of the opposing armies. Like all students of Bannockburn I found that although John Barbour's near contemporary account of the battle has proved remarkably accurate in so many respects (despite its Scottish bias), like other medieval chroniclers he tended to exaggerate the strengths of the respective armies. Such chroniclers' figures were not only highly inflated but wild differences occurred between them. Abbot Bernard of Arbroath, for instance, in his contemporary poem of the battle put the English foot at 40,000, with their cavalry at 3100.[23] This was remarkably at variance with Barbour's figure of 100,000 English infantry although not that far from Barbour's 3000 barded cavalry among a total of no fewer than 40,000 mounted troops! As far as many chroniclers were concerned the larger the figures the more dramatic would the clash appear. W M Mackenzie, however, comes to the more logical conclusion that Barbour's massive figures of footsoldiers probably arose from his guess that each of the English ten battles (or divisions) at Bannockburn were 10,000 strong.[24] Whatever inspired Barbour's figures for the English infantry it would have been impossible for Edward II to have marched this host from the Scottish border to Stirling in the time and manner described. However, Barbour's ratio of strength levels between the English and Scottish infantry of ten to three appears far more feasible where the account of the battle is concerned and neither I nor the majority of commentators find any good reason to discount it.

Of all the later writers John Morris made the most thorough investigation of the English methods of recruiting along with the proportions of men who were likely to have turned up during their Welsh and Scottish wars. Accordingly his estimated English strength at Bannockburn of 15,000 (including cavalry) plus Irish and overseas contingents has not been seriously disputed by the most distinguished later authorities, including Professor Barrow and General Christison.

Using Barbour's strength ratio the Scottish infantry would be expected to number no more than 6600. Morris' calculations of Scottish recruiting patterns also puts them at below 7000 with Professor Barrow inclining towards 6000 and General Christison going somewhat lower still. Although these levels seem very low in comparison with the English infantry it should be remembered that Bruce placed much more faith on personal qualities and skills than in mere numbers. After following the early descriptions of the battle and applying them to the ground I believe Bruce did in fact require something like 6000 men in order to form and hold his continuous spear walls against the English cavalry. I am therefore inclined to think Peter Traquair's estimate of 4500 spearmen rather too low, and for a whole number of reasons to discount the conclusions made in The Complete Peerage that the numbers of infantry were scarcely different on both sides.

On the question of the English heavy cavalry figures, at the higher end are the totals of 3100 and 3000 from Abbot Bernard and John Barbour with *Vita Edwardi Secundi* putting them two thirds lower at 2000. With regard to later commentators the meticulous John Morris reckons them at a maximum of 2400. It is impossible to be exact here although the English cavalry strength was highly unlikely to be less than the 2000 estimated by the English commentator in *Vita Edwardi*, who for patriotic reasons would be inclined to have reckoned them as low as possible. With less than 2000 the English would not have been able to mount such continuous attacks against the Scottish spearmen nor, after the bruising battle, to have supplied the two large bodies of English horsemen who left the field.

With regard to the Scottish light cavalry, John Barbour is quite definite in putting them at 500 strong, a figure supported by his account of the battle's final stages. Such a figure is fully in accordance with Scottish cavalry strengths both at Falkirk and somewhat later at Halidon Hill (1333) and it has not been contested by later commentators.

The most likely strength figures of the opposing armies at Bannockburn are therefore:

English

Cavalry of 2000–2400; infantry, including bowmen, 16,000–16,500.

Scottish

Light cavalry 500; trained infantry 5000–5750, together with 3000 'small folk' (including women).

By any standard, with or without their qualitative advantages, the English numerical superiority was overwhelming.

In addition to the numbers and armaments involved, the organisational arrangements for both armies are obviously important. As mentioned already Barbour has the English army split into ten battles for the march (the first of which was likely to be the vanguard), formations he suggested were retained in the conflict.[25] Most later authorities accept Barbour's 'battles', although Peter Traquair argues that ten battles would be unwieldy and points out the illogicality of great earls likely to be acting as joint commanders of cavalry battles when lesser nobles were in sole charge of some infantry ones. He suggests it is more likely the English would have adopted the traditional military formations of vanguard, main body and rearguard – which, of course, they could have done – as well as having ten battles. Despite Traquair's doubts, Barbour's account of the battle has proved remarkably accurate with the exception of his inflated force levels. In any case, the English aristocracy's love of cavalry is a long-standing tradition; at the beginning of the twenty-first century it is still safe to say that many British army officers would be willing to accept joint or lesser command roles with the cavalry than with the infantry.

In fact, the tenfold division of the battles could go far to explain many of the English difficulties during the battle. The army's strength was undoubtedly impressive, but gathered as it was from so many different sources, cohesion was particularly difficult. This was not all. An enquiry held during Edward II's reign discovered that local officials would sometimes choose good men at an assembly attended by the king's arrayers but substitute poor ones after the arrayers had departed.[26] The arrayer's task was to draw up the county muster rolls wherever the men could be grouped into vintenaries and centenaries strength (roughly equivalent to today's British army's platoons at somewhat under 30 men strong and companies of around 100 men). In any case whatever their quality, the army's 16,000 infantry were levied from counties across the face of central and northern England, with other detachments coming from much further south, together with 5000 from north and south Wales and perhaps a further 4000 from Ireland.

With the cavalry the pattern was similar, nobles answering the feudal summons came with their groups of knights and retainers from all over England and Ulster to join up with professional men at arms and cavalry paid for by the king's household. To add to such remarkable diversity additional soldiers, both infantry and cavalry, came from Europe to answer Edward II's general invitation for what he saw as a great military adventure.

Not only did they journey from widespread locations, they

had little or no time to practise together. Those infantry soldiers from south Wales or Lincolnshire who were gathered into their groups of 100 men (the centenaries) and put under an officer who was horsed, had to march 200 miles before they even joined the general muster on the border. It is likely the cavalry were first to arrive at Wark where they could have been formed into three of Barbour's battles, possibly the vanguard, then the force under Clifford's command and the third under the king (which would certainly have been the largest of the three). The other seven battles would have filled up as men arrived and no sooner had they assembled than they were required to set off on their move northwards into Scotland. During the march some sort of unit cohesion would be expected to develop but, even if they had thought it necessary, little or no tactical training could have been carried out.

As for the Scottish army all commentators (except Peter Traquair and the account in *The Complete Peerage*) accept they were formed into four battles. The probable reason for any disparity among the observers was because at Bannockburn Robert Bruce's battle followed behind the other three and it was therefore not immediately visible to the English. Barbour, however, gave specific details about the men in the king's battle. He 'had in his company all the men of Carrick and of Argyll, Kintyre and the Isles, among whom were Sir Angus of Islay and Bute and all his following. He had also a great host of armed men from the lowlands.'[27] Bruce relied here on the valuable leadership of Angus Og MacDonald, the Lord of Islay, who had been his firm supporter ever since Bruce made his bid for the Scottish throne. Professor Barrow reasonably concludes that those men in Bruce's battle, whom Barbour said came from the 'plainland', were from the Central Lowlands and perhaps Fife and Strathmore to the East.[28] With a larger formation than the other Scottish commanders such a wide area of recruitment was likely to have been required.

Working on the premise that each of Bruce's senior commanders would be expected to follow the king's lead and command men who owed them prior allegiance, Ronald McNair Scott makes valid assumptions about the composition of the three other battles. Edward Bruce, he concluded, drew on men from the southeast, from Buchan, Mar, Angus, the Mearns, Menteith, Strathearn and Lennox, including some from Galloway. Those in James Douglas' and Walter Stewart's battle would come from Lanark, Renfrew and the border region, while Thomas Randolph, Earl of Moray's battle was made up with men from Moray's earldom, from Ross and other parts of the far north, including burghers from Inverness, Elgin, Nairn and Forres.[29] This was not all. Men coming from certain localities were likely to be kept together under their own sub-commanders and appointed to particular stations in the spear lines. There they would occupy all three or four ranks of the segment. If Bruce came to inspect a schiltron he would know that a particular flank would be the responsibility of the MacDonalds while further on he would come upon his own men of Carrick. By such methods loyalty and responsibility were encouraged within the small Scottish army.

On paper English superiority was such that Bannockburn should have been no contest. As in past battles, however, neither favourable strength levels nor superior equipment can guarantee victory. Qualities of leadership, training and force cohesion are all important too. The armies' commanders are described in the next two chapters but Bruce had not only selected his well before the coming battle but under his tutelage he made sure they had progressed. With the dangers facing him he could not afford to retain commanders of moderate ability. Many of the soldiers in the Scottish battles had also been together long enough to develop a firm trust in their leaders and many were justly proud of what they had already achieved under their direction.

Edward II enjoyed no such relationship having clashed with all the senior English commanders over his favourite, Piers Gaveston. Mutual trust was not only lacking between the king and his nobles but amongst the nobles themselves depending on how far they had opposed their monarch. As for the Scottish commanders serving in Edward II's ranks, they were Comyn supporters primarily motivated by the wish for revenge against

Robert Bruce and for the restitution of their possessions in Scotland rather than any devotion for the English king.

In his role as defender Bruce had another advantage, the opportunity of selecting the likely site of the battle and preparing his men for the anticipated shape of the encounter. The English were coming to relieve the garrison at Stirling Castle and just before the castle their ways of approach were limited. He could therefore determine the pattern of the likely confrontation. In fact, after Edward Bruce and Sir Philip Moubray made their compact, both sides had the best part of a year to prepare, a period which they used in rather different ways. Bruce kept his forces sharp by setting them to capture the remaining English castles in Lothian (in the full awareness that any successes could only make things more difficult for an invading army), but as the time for Stirling Castle's relief drew closer he concentrated on training his men in the tactics he believed could best match the English invaders. Bruce was very likely to have talked to some of the survivors from Falkirk, and he had already used massed spearmen, if still in relatively small formations, at Loudon Hill and Glen Trool against English heavy cavalry. Unlike Wallace's spearmen at Falkirk Bruce had made them advance but only when their flanks were secured by steeply sloping ground. After their success at Loudon Bruce, like Wallace, determined to make his spearmen the nucleus of the army that he was preparing to meet the English. They would constitute the human anvil of impenetrable pikes against which the English cavalry would shatter their lances and, hopefully, break their hearts.

As with the Greek phalanxes, drill masters were needed to train his men to change their formation, notably from straight files three to six ranks deep, often facing both ways, to a circular formation offering all-round defence. When in motion the schiltrons would have to move with measured steps in order to preserve their order and formation. When in circular formation with the front rank grounding their pikes and pointing them outwards, the rear ones would need to practise leaning their pikes forward upon the shoulders of the first rank. Endless drill was also required to strengthen arms and shoulder muscles the better to handle the clumsy, head-heavy spears and hold them straight forward for relatively long periods. Above all the spearmen had to be trained to act in unison, thus preserving cohesion, the essential strength of such a formation.

Even if Edward had wanted to undertake a training programme with his army, which was extremely doubtful, he had first to settle matters between himself and his nobles following Gaveston's execution. Only after much diplomatic persuasion by Valence and Louis, brother of Philip IV of France, did the nobles apologise for their crimes and it was not until October 1313, after the king granted them a general pardon, that he could start his detailed preparations to assemble an invasion force. It was December before he sent out writs to eight earls and eighty-seven barons, ordering them to bring themselves and their contingents to Berwick by 10 June 1314. During February Edward repeated his intention of leading an army against Bruce but surprised his followers by letting them know he intended a mainly infantry campaign.[30] This was not a popular announcement: his barons wanted a cavalry enterprise. It was not until March 1314, after restoring Valence to his post as Viceroy of Scotland, that the king was able to issue a succession of detailed orders to raise both men and supplies.

In any event Edward II faced a most formidable logistical undertaking and it was problems of movement and supply rather than training that occupied the English command. More than sixty ships were required to support the expedition, quite apart from the organisation required to bring the levies together, and in May an embargo was put on the export of food from England. At about the same time more than two hundred wagons, together with the animals needed to draw them, were commissioned to help transport the army north. In fact, the scale of the victualling required exceeded anything achieved by Edward I. Funds for the campaign came through arrangements made with the Italian banker, Antonio Pessagno. In the months leading up to the campaign he lent at least £21,000 to the English exchequer together with funds for three quarters of the wheat and oats stockpiled at Berwick.[31]

In early June 1314 Edward moved to Berwick and awaited the

concentration of his invasion force. At nearby Wark, where they gathered, no monarch could have failed to be moved or to feel anything but optimism as the great assembly of heavy cavalry and the endless infantry detachments came marching in, however raw some of them might be. He could be sure he had sufficient resources of infantry, including highly regarded Welsh bowmen, to complement his unparalleled force of heavy cavalry against which the Scots apparently had no counter. In a show of confidence he distributed the estates of the opposing Scottish commanders to his supporters. Some of his proud knights so shared his certainty of victory that they brought tapestries, plate and furniture to deck the houses they would possess.[32]

On the other hand, in Scotland as Bruce drilled and redrilled his men he knew that if he met the English he would be fighting for his own and his country's very existence. He had still not resolved the question of where best to meet them on their way to Stirling, and it was still theoretically possible he would avoid a full scale encounter.

In spite of their overwhelming superiority it was one thing for the English to assemble an army, quite another to move it into the battle area in good heart and then bring its full strength to play against a smaller but battle-hardened adversary.

≈

CHAPTER FIVE

THE SCOTTISH COMMANDERS

> 'It greatly pleased his [Bruce's] heart, and he was
> persuaded that men of such mind, if they set
> their strength to it, must be indeed right hard to
> vanquish.'
>
> John Barbour, *The Bruce*

MUCH HAS ALREADY BEEN said about the achievements,
both militarily and politically, of Robert Bruce before
the expected battle, actions which had enabled him and his
group of followers, originally hemmed in by enemies on all
sides, to become the masters of Scotland with the exception
of isolated English strongholds. His military successes owed
much to his natural vigour but also to his growing mastery
of tactical and strategic factors which reinforced his undoubted
skill at arms. In their turn his chosen commanders had Bruce
as both model and tutor; two of them, his brother Edward
and James Douglas, had shared the dangers and reverses of
his early days and when the tide began to turn they were
given major responsibilities. In 1307–8 for instance, Douglas,
who as yet had few men and still needed the protection offered
by the wide forests of Ettrick, Selkirk and Jedburgh was given
the massive task of winning back the border regions. No past
achievements by Bruce or his leaders, however, could compare
with the task of having to meet a massive English army under
its king.

From the perilous days following his coronation the mantle
of the leader sat well on Bruce's shoulders and his determination and cool nerve (notably illustrated during 1306 when,

surrounded by large numbers of enemy, he openly read a light-hearted French romance while waiting for his few supporters to rejoin him) were coupled with undoubted acumen and graciousness.

Bruce's antecedents were of obvious importance in his development as a leader, although the adversity of his early days as a fugitive king probably never allowed him to forget the common fate he shared with those who kept faith with him. Both Bruce's parents were accustomed to exercise power and responsibility. As Countess of Carrick, Bruce's mother was directly descended from Fergus, Lord of Galloway, the proud prince who had ruled a virtually independent Celtic kingdom in southwest Scotland and it is possible that in the Gaelic fashion during his early boyhood Robert Bruce had the egalitarian experience of being fostered in another household. On his mother's union with the Bruces she brought the vast estates of Carrick, close by their principal Scottish possessions at Annandale, which themselves totalled some 200,000 acres. The Bruces, on the other hand, were of Anglo-Norman stock who came over to England with William the Conqueror and for their role in overcoming the native resistance they were granted much land in the north of England as well as in Scotland.

So powerful, in fact, were the Bruces in Scotland that by 1238 when the ageing Scottish king, Alexander II, had no heir, his Great Council decreed that unless he had further issue, Robert Bruce, Lord of Annandale (Robert Bruce's grandfather, known later as the Competitor) a self confident, vibrant man who was descended from Henry of Northumberland, son and heir of the Scottish king, David I, should be the true and legitimate heir to the kingdom.[1] In fact, Alexander II remarried and the son born to him relatively late in life became King Alexander III. Yet on Alexander III's death, despite the presence of his royal grand-daughter, the 'Maid of Norway', Robert Bruce claimed he was, in fact, the proper heir, not only by right of succession but by virtue of the nomination made during the reign of Alexander II.

Whatever criteria came to be used by Edward I in 1292 in deciding the succession to the vacant Scottish throne and however much he took care to demonstrate that John Balliol was the strongest claimant to it (which by the law of primogeniture he undoubtedly was) the Competitor still argued that as the son of a younger child of King David he should take precedence over Balliol's right through the daughter of an older child. The Bruces always regarded Edward I's decision unjust and themselves as the rightful heirs. Apart from his powerful legal claims, Robert Bruce the Competitor could justly feel he had personal qualities that marked him as a worthy bearer of the Crown. The *Lanercost Chronicle* described him as a gifted speaker, of handsome appearance, remarkable for his influence and, of equal importance, 'most devoted to God and the Clergy'.[2] He was amazingly hospitable and, like his grandson, renowned for abundant energy. At the age of sixty, after resigning all his offices, he took his son on an extended crusade to the Holy Land at a time when such campaigning was extremely hazardous and carried high risks from disease. On his return in 1272, discovering Edward I had ascended the English throne, he decided to settle on his Scottish lands and in the following year strengthened his Scottish connections by marrying again, taking as his wife a widow, Christiana of Ireby, from an adjoining estate.

In 1286 on the death of Alexander III the seventy-six-year-old Competitor still had the energy and belief to emerge from retirement and press his claims for the throne as he would do even later on the Maid of Norway's death when, at eighty years of age, he moved with a strong body of armed men to Perth, where the Scottish council was in session, to 'safeguard' his royal title. Once his claims had been rebuffed by the decision of King Edward's adjudicators, Bruce returned to his estates but roundly refused to pay homage to Balliol.

Robert Bruce, the future Robert I of Scotland, was born in 1274 (the same year as William Wallace) at Turnberry Castle in Carrick, about sixty miles from his grandfather's seat at Lochmaben. As a boy he saw a considerable amount of the indomitable Competitor and would have been left in no doubt about his grandfather's opinions regarding the rightful position of the Bruces with respect to the Scottish crown.

McNair Scott is sure, for instance, that as a sixteen-year-old squire he accompanied the force raised by the Competitor and his father which went to Perth to further the Bruces' case there.[3] In his turn the old man would be sure to have recognised the future promise of his grandson, compared with his calculating, if spineless son.

In November 1292 the Competitor formally invested the Bruce claims to the Scottish throne upon his son (Bruce's father) Lord of Annandale and Earl of Carrick, and his heirs after him. In his turn, two days later, Bruce's father resigned the earldom of Carrick to the future Robert I. Bruce's father also took considerable pains to avoid doing homage to John Balliol as king of Scotland, since it would have jeopardised the family's claim to the throne, and he went on a protracted visit to Norway with his daughter Isabel to give her in marriage to King Eric of Norway.[4] This left young Robert Bruce as the virtual head of the large family. When Bruce's father returned to England on the Competitor's death in 1295 he still refused to pay homage to John Balliol and Edward I appointed him governor of Carlisle Castle, probably to make certain of his loyalty.

Edward's decision seemed soundly based for during 1297, the year following the Scottish defeat at Dunbar and the submission of John Balliol to the English king, the Earl of Annandale felt compelled to remind Edward I of the Bruce claims to the Scottish throne. This was met with Edward's scornful and negative reply, 'Have we nothing else to do but win kingdoms for you?' When the future Robert I came out against Edward I at Irvine during 1297 the English king relieved his father of his governor's post at Carlisle following which he put himself out of contention, retiring permanently to his English estates, and remaining there until he died in 1304.

From 1297 the Bruces' hopes of gaining the kingship would rely on the Competitor's grandson. The mainsprings of Robert Bruce's actions thereafter were his determination to right the injustice done to his family together with his own fierce ambition for the throne of Scotland. Unlike his father and for all his loyalty to a family with strong connections in both England and Scotland, Robert Bruce identified himself strongly with

Scotland. This is less surprising than some observers might believe when one realises that he was in fact the first born of a union between a mother whose Celtic ancestry stretched back to antiquity and a father who was one of Scotland's premier earls whose family while originally Norman (from Norse descent) had direct connections with Scotland, including its Royal House, for over six generations. Robert Bruce's connection with Scotland had been strengthened by his marriage to Isabel, daughter of the Earl of Mar, who was a great friend of the old Competitor. Although a daughter, Marjorie, resulted from the union, Isabel died tragically early, probably in 1297.

As we have seen already, from 1297 until 1301 Robert Bruce supported his country's national cause against successive invasions by Edward I, but it was Comyn attempts to sideline him from the senior decision-making processes in his own country, as well as the possible return of John Balliol to Scotland, that led him to join an English king who at least professed to acknowledge his claim to the Scottish throne. The decision was also likely to have been influenced by his desire for a male heir and with it his interest in marrying for a second time to Elizabeth, daughter of the powerful Richard de Burgh, Earl of Ulster, a strong supporter of Edward I. Whatever the outcome of Edward's attempts to subjugate Scotland the match promised to bring benefits to the twenty-eight-year-old Bruce. It would serve to revive the Carrick alliance with the Earl of Ulster and, 'as Bruce's future wife was James Stewart's niece by marriage, it would confirm the long-standing Bruce/Stewart friendship too'.[5] The prominence of the Stewart family within Scotland at this time was seen by the fact that James Stewart had been appointed as one of the joint guardians following the death of King Alexander III.

Bruce's behaviour during his five years at the English court before being forced to flee to Scotland can also be seen both in terms of attempting to balance his regard for Scotland while preserving his own regal prospects. No doubt his Comyn rivals in Scotland, struggling against Edward I's invasions, would have observed that compared with their continuing armed struggle his ambition for the throne seemed equal or greater than any feelings of patriotism. On the other hand anyone who believed in the justice of his royal claims as strongly as Robert Bruce was not likely to give his support – even conditionally – to an English king who had annexed Scotland and had dealt unfairly with the Competitor and his own father without strong reasons. The astute English king would know this well enough and he favoured both Bruce and other members of his family – Edward took Edward Bruce into the household of the Prince of Wales while another brother, Alexander, was made Dean of Glasgow. Despite their differences it is also quite possible that some degree of genuine respect existed between Bruce and Edward I. Bruce would be likely to acknowledge the ability and determination along with the harsh cruelty of a great medieval king while Edward was sure to see in Bruce not only courage and great skill at arms but a longsightedness quite absent in his own son. No recognition of the other's qualities, however, stopped either Bruce or Edward I from pursuing his chosen aims, in Edward's case the subjection of Scotland, with Bruce his country's throne. As Edward's siege engines pummelled the garrison of Stirling Castle, Bruce made a secret compact with Bishop Lamberton over a future bid for the throne. Two years later while still in Edward's peace he concluded a further contract with John Comyn (the Red), his most powerful rival in Scotland, with the same purpose.

In an age when men still felt free to change their allegiance if they considered their oaths of fealty had been given under duress or when promises made for such oaths had not been kept – like Edward's promise to Bruce over the Scottish throne – Bruce's commanders could better appreciate his marked opportunism during 1297–1306 than some later commentators.[6] What none of them could fail to appreciate was his long-felt determination to be king and once king his commitment to Scotland. Under the most adverse conditions this one-time duplicitous courtier went on to display qualities of resolution and perseverance that brought them notable military successes. While Randolph might not, at first, understand Bruce's tactics of guerrilla warfare he would soon do so. Moreover once men gave their allegiance to such a spirited and attractive leader they quickly tended to give him their devotion as well.

To a greater degree than Edward I with his habitually superior forces and in a way unknown to Edward II with his limited experience on campaigns, Bruce had shared the hazards of his commanders, usually against adverse odds. By the nature of society at the time they would normally be selected from a relatively small group of privileged men but, because, with the exception of Edward Bruce, all the king's brothers, along with his other senior leaders, had been executed, he needed to spread his net further than normal to look for senior military commanders. As a result Bruce discovered the outstanding James Douglas, a minor noble and unlikely candidate, as well as the justiciar and administrator Sir Robert Keith, who so ably took the field at Bannockburn when Bruce needed his regular cavalry commanders to command the schiltrons.

Traditionally the most successful commanders have taken pains to appoint subordinates whom they can be sure are willing to carry out their directives whether in a single battle or throughout a protracted campaign. When, for instance, during the early nineteenth century, the Duke of Wellington was fighting the French in the Iberian peninsula he chose as subordinate commanders men such as Roland Hill and Thomas Picton, steady soldiers who gave him the unquestioning concurrence his method of leadership required. Under his direction they proved immensely difficult soldiers to beat. At Bannockburn under Bruce, his commanders needed to exercise equal steadiness against superior English numbers. Sometimes commanders have had to value the unquestioned loyalty of their subordinates more than their ability, as for instance Hannibal, the outstanding Carthaginian commander of ancient times, who not only had to face the Romans but also many enemies from within his own homeland. As a result he used his two brothers, Hasdrubal and Hamilcar, as supporting army commanders but, although he undoubtedly had their loyalty, they failed to match either his military skills or those of his Roman enemies. At Bannockburn Bruce was more fortunate because his commanders not only had the opportunity to show their loyalty but their skills had been developed in earlier engagements. During the battle his luck held because all his important leaders survived and were able fully to justify his faith in them.

Thomas Randolph, 1st Earl of Moray (d 1332)

The first schiltron at Bannockburn was given to Thomas Randolph, first Earl of Moray, Bruce's nephew. Randolph was accustomed since childhood to being involved in important affairs of state, and as a minor he accompanied his father to Norham during December 1292, where he witnessed John Balliol swearing fealty to Edward I for the crown of Scotland. However, despite his father's support for John Balliol, after his marriage into the Bruce family, Randolph was expected to assist Robert Bruce. After Bruce's murder of the Red Comyn and his rout at Methven in June 1306, Randolph was taken prisoner along with other close family members. While those like Neil Bruce and Simon Fraser were drawn, hanged and beheaded, Randolph was the only major figure to be spared execution, very probably as a result of his family's friendship with Aymer de Valence, the English commander.

Despite this Randolph could not expect to escape Edward I's wrath completely and on 24 July the English king ordered him to be kept under close guard in the castle of Inverkip until he should be arraigned at either Carlisle or Perth.[7] It was probably to save his life that Randolph swore fealty to the English king and agreed to take up arms against Bruce, yet once he had given his pledge he served Edward I faithfully. His knowledge of Bruce's bases and likely movements proved invaluable to the English. Valence, using Randolph as a guide, together with help from one of Bruce's pet blood hounds, narrowly failed to capture the Scottish king and Randolph got close enough to seize his banner.

In the following year the tables were turned when Bruce's own commander, James Douglas, surprised and captured Randolph at the waters of Lyne near Peebles. Randolph remained defiant when brought before Bruce, even reproaching the king for cowardice because of his reluctance to meet the English in open warfare. According to Barbour, Bruce replied with heavy irony, 'Mayhap it shall come ere very long to such endeavour. But since thou speakest so royally, there is much reason to reprove thy proud words, till thou knowest what is right and bowest to it as thou oughtest'.[8] In fact, Bruce appreciated such honesty and boldness, even against himself. He ordered Randolph 'to be kept in firm keeping', but Randolph was soon his loyal follower and in the years to come, next to Douglas, he became his most famous general. Bruce's own trust was demonstrated in 1312 when he made him earl over the warlike men of Moray, who had already served the cause of Scottish independence so well, and partly as compensation to Randolph for his estates in England that were forfeited and subsequently transferred to Hugh Despenser.[9]

The approving Barbour described Randolph as being 'of medium height' with a 'broad visage, pleasant and fair, courteous at all points' and a man 'full of all nobleness and made of all virtues' who 'esteemed honour and liberality and ever upheld righteousness'.[10] Barbour's eulogy aside, Randolph went on to prove himself a brave and popular commander. Most importantly he showed himself capable of learning the more subtle arts of warfare from the sharper minds of the king and James Douglas. It was Douglas' seizure of Roxburgh Castle that led Randolph to explore unorthodox ways of capturing Edinburgh Castle, which seemed so secure on its daunting volcanic crag. His brilliant success there on 14 March 1314 made it certain he would be given command of a main Scottish division at Bannockburn.

Edward Bruce (d 1318)

Bruce's second schiltron commander was an obvious choice. Edward Bruce, the king's brother and overall commander in the king's absence, was just a year younger than Robert and the only one of Bruce's four brothers to escape Edward I's executioners. He was undoubtedly an ambitious and arrogant man – qualities that may have been fed to some degree by the removal of his three brothers – although as the next in line to Robert he would, in any case, have enjoyed superior rights of succession over them. His closeness to the crown was shown by a tailzie or entail published by Bruce's Ayr parliament of 1315, stating 'with the consent of Marjorie Bruce, the king's daughter, that if the king died without a male heir the crown should go to Edward: as a man of great prowess in warlike actions for the defence of the rights and liberties of the Scottish realm'.[11] Barbour hinted at a strong rivalry between Edward and the king when he wrote that Edward 'thought Scotland too small for his brother and himself'.[12] If Edward had regal ambitions himself, he was also autocratic and rash by nature, and after Bannockburn the man who so coveted a crown was given his brother's permission and support to invade Ireland and take to himself the title King of Ireland. It was always an optimistic venture and eminent Scottish historian Geoffrey Barrow was in no doubt 'the notion that he could lead a successful national revolt in Ireland and rule there as king on the same footing as his brother ruled in Scotland was preposterous and foredoomed to extinction'.[13] However, it can also be argued he was taking no greater risks than those of his elder brother in 1306–7, but support from the Irish proved variable and at Dundalk in 1318 he was defeated and killed.

The manner of his death was entirely in character. At the head of a thousand Scots, together with a number of Irish, Edward set out to attack Dundalk. Their route was barred by Richard Clare, Lord Lieutenant of Ireland, with a force of knights many times greater than that of the Scots. Edward Bruce had, according to custom, divided his forces into a vanguard, main body and rearguard, but his initial briefing had been sketchy and they failed to keep contact with each other. The first two bodies of men were separately destroyed and when Edward's three veteran commanders, Sir John Soules, Sir Philip Moubray and Sir John Stewart, advised him to turn back as reinforcements were not far away he refused to listen, flew into a rage and swore 'that no man, while he lived should ever say that an enemy had made him give way'.[14] The Irish among his forces refused to fight such a superior force but his small body of Scottish knights stayed and were killed taking part in the headstrong attack.

Such irresponsibility made Edward Bruce totally unsuitable for the highest level of command, but under Robert Bruce's close direction he played an important role prior to and during the battle of Bannockburn. He was never happier than when in sight of the enemy. Ronald McNair Scott was sure that, like the hero of the Chanson de Geste, Edward Bruce would have declared, 'If I had one foot in Paradise I would withdraw it to go and fight'.[15] There was no shortage of hard fighting during Robert Bruce's early days and acting as his brother's mailed fist Edward gained more responsibility as the king's successes accumulated. After Robert Bruce had defeated the Earl of Buchan at Inverurie on 23 May 1308 he used Edward, the heedless and hard thrusting cavalry commander, to ravage the Buchan province from end to end. Bruce then appointed him to range over the rugged province of Galloway, 'killing rebellious nobles and making all subject to the king'. Well aware of his brother's love of titles, meaningful or not, Bruce followed this by naming him Lord of Galloway.

Edward Bruce also took part with James Douglas in lightning and destructive raids into northern England, before going on to attack the English-held castles which, with his troop of engineers, he dismantled. It was, of course, Edward's dislike of sieges that led him to be trapped by Sir Philip Moubray, Stirling Castle's wily commander, into the agreement to fight that brought strong pressure on Robert Bruce to depart from the careful strategy he had so far successfully pursued. And it was typical of Edward Bruce that he made no attempt to consult the king beforehand.

The same lack of judgement was seen in his personal life: he seduced the Earl of Atholl's sister Isabel, made her pregnant and then deserted her in favour of the Earl of Ross' daughter. As with his decision at Stirling, this was to have wider repercussions for, partly as a result, during the first night of the battle at Bannockburn, the Earl of Atholl, who was apparently coming to join Bruce, surprised Sir William Airth and killed him along with many others who were guarding the Scottish base camp. While not without emotion Edward was not a commander particularly sensitive to his men's needs: he was said to have wept twice in his life, once when at Bannockburn he heard about the death of his friend and paramour's brother, Sir Walter Ross, and two years later at Carrickfergus in Ireland when Neil Fleming and a group of knights sold their lives to give him the necessary time to recover from a surprise attack.

In many ways Edward Bruce was a loose cannon. When left to his own devices he could be almost as dangerous to his own side as the enemy, but for all that he was a doughty soldier, practised and hardened in war who, under Robert Bruce's guidance, was a fearsome and irrepressible opponent.

James Douglas (the 'Black' or 'Good' Douglas d 1330)

Bruce's third division of spearmen in the great battle, though nominally under the command of Walter Stewart, High Steward of Scotland, was led by Stewart's cousin James Douglas, Bruce's finest soldier. Tradition precluded the subordination of the Stewart to a commander of lesser social rank and for Bruce's sake Douglas accepted the title of joint commander for a force that was, in fact, largely peopled by his own followers and under his control. John Barbour's *Bruce* made Douglas its co-hero and he had, in fact, been with Bruce since his crowning, distinguishing himself in countless actions before Bannockburn. While a veteran in terms of combats Douglas was only twenty-seven years of age at the time of the battle and his still unscarred face bore testimony to his amazing skill at arms.

Douglas came from a military family. William, his father, also fought against the English and in 1296 commanded Berwick Castle during its siege by Edward I. After Edward put Berwick to the sword William Douglas surrendered the castle and was sent into captivity from which he either escaped or was released since he joined William Wallace at the commencement of Wallace's rebellion. He left Wallace to join Bruce and the Stewart, and was among other Scottish leaders who surrendered to the English at Irvine. Most were allowed to go free providing they produced hostages to guarantee their future good behaviour but William Douglas refused to surrender his son, James, who would certainly have been acceptable. He was therefore sent in chains to Berwick Castle where his captors dubbed him 'savage and abusive'. Such an obstinate prisoner was bound to have been dealt with severely and in 1299 after his transfer to the dreaded

Tower of London, William Douglas died, still a declared enemy of the English. John Barbour for one was sure he had been murdered there.[16]

James Douglas was sent away to complete his education in Paris, not for the quality of the instruction but to remove him from English eyes. Alone in a foreign city, among people of all classes, he enjoyed no favours and it was while in Paris that Douglas learned of his father's death and the forfeiture of the Douglas estates which Edward I gave to his own commander, Sir Robert Clifford. From then on James' whole purpose in life was to fight the English and regain all that was rightfully his. Fortunately for Douglas he met Bishop Lamberton in Paris, who took the destitute young man into his household. By the time Douglas returned to Scotland, Lamberton (together with the vast majority of the Scottish nobility) had made his peace with the English king. In 1305 when Edward I was mounting his showpiece siege against Stirling Castle – the last stronghold still in Scottish hands – Lamberton brought his ward before Edward hoping the clemency he had shown to other rebels would be extended to a young man whose only offence was being his father's son. But the eighteen-year-old's petition for a return of his lands was brusquely refused and Douglas was quickly removed from Edward's sight.

In March of the following year Douglas was with Bishop Lamberton at Berwick when they received the momentous news that Robert Bruce had proclaimed himself King of Scots. Although Bruce, obeying Edward's orders, had in 1297 ravished Douglasdale and earlier abducted Douglas' mother and her other children, the situation had much changed. Bruce was now Edward's declared enemy and at odds with the Comyns too. Under the circumstances Douglas had reason to hope an embattled Bruce would welcome his pledge of support. The prudent Lamberton gave Douglas permission to seek Bruce out (and also some money to help him on his way) providing he did not go as the bishop's official representative. John Barbour has Douglas leaving Berwick on the bishop's own palfrey, Ferrand, to meet with Bruce as he made his way to his crowning at Scone:[17]

And when Douglas saw him coming he rode forward in haste and greeted him and made obeisance very courteously and told him all his conditions and who he was and how Clifford held his inheritance. Also that he came to do homage to him as his rightful king and was ready in everything to share his fortune. And when Bruce had heard his desire he received him with much pleasure and gave him men and arms. He felt assured he should be worthy, for his fathers all were doughty men. Thus they made their acquaintance that never afterwards by any chance of any kind was broken while they lived.[18]

The young slim figure with his pale complexion and black hair who sought Bruce out was soon to be known for a personality that captured men's loyalty and for a pronounced and unorthodox military ability. In normal circumstances he was said to be gentle and courteous, speaking quietly with a slight lisp, but in battle he became a different man – bold, swift in thought and act, 'always bent on plots' to deceive his enemy. For the time being he was one of Robert Bruce's least impressive followers, bringing neither money nor followers, not even the basic military equipage of a gentleman.

Whatever his initial disadvantages James Douglas quickly distinguished himself during Bruce's disastrous campaigns of 1306. Physical hardships did not deter him and he soon established a close bond with the king. After Bruce's rout at Methven and with enemies all around them, the king and his companions arrived at the west shore of Loch Lomond. To avoid a long detour they were desperate to cross the loch and, after tirelessly scouring its banks, James Douglas discovered a little sunken boat in which they laboriously crossed two at a time, the first two being Bruce and Douglas. Bruce then split his forces and, as a mark of the confidence he already felt, entrusted the twenty-year-old Douglas with the second group.

In the following year Bruce's forces were reduced to a few score men seeking refuge in the hills near Turnberry; their capture or death seemed only a matter of time for most of their supporters were cowed by the terror campaign waged by the English king. Even at this time Douglas continued to think aggressively and he asked Bruce for permission to try to redeem his property at Douglasdale, only some fifty miles away. With just two companions he reached his estates and identified himself to Thomas Dickson, one of his most loyal tenants, who succeeded in gathering a few extra supporters. With this added strength Douglas decided to ambush the garrison of Douglas Castle as they attended church on Palm Sunday three days later. Although the ambush was revealed prematurely, it eventually succeeded and Douglas either killed or took prisoner all the soldiers in church. With characteristic nerve he led his followers back to the castle where they sat down to the dinner prepared for the garrison on its expected return. After ransacking the castle's stores and poisoning its water supply they piled any equipment surplus to their requirements in the cellar, brought in the prisoners and beheaded them before setting fire to the castle.

The grim affair became known as 'the Douglas larder' but Douglas' act, like William Wallace's assassinations of English officials ten years before, posted a warning of Scottish intent and raised the spirits of Bruce's beleaguered party. At first sight his killing of the prisoners appears barbaric, but it should be remembered the English king had already instituted the policy of executing any of Bruce's supporters without trial, for the most part hanging, drawing and quartering them, and Douglas could not risk the prisoners giving information liable to jeopardise the families of those retainers who had recently joined him. In Douglas' case, as in Wallace's, it was total war against an enemy who not only made him destitute but was committed to destroying his master Bruce and all his supporters.

The same intensity accounted for Douglas' treatment of English archers. Every one caught by him or his men suffered the loss of either his right hand or right eye. No longer able to take more Scottish lives they were then released. The side-effect of such action was to terrorise any bowmen acting against him and there were instances of them being filled with wine before agreeing to fight him.[19]

Over the months following 'the Douglas larder' he played a leading role in harassing Bruce's opponents, always placing the greatest emphasis on reconnaissance and good intelligence.

After Edward I's death, when Bruce was able to display more aggression, Douglas' speed and skill at deception made him the ideal commander for tactics that depended on swiftness and surprise.

By 1310 Bruce had succeeded in bringing the greater part of Scotland under his control and had turned to harrying northern England, at the same time attempting to capture the Scottish castles that were still in English hands, and for both activities James Douglas was ideally suited. He showed himself a master at lightning raids where much spoil and many prisoners were taken before the defenders had time to retaliate, while his audacity and resourcefulness were invaluable when it came to capturing castles. He devised a collapsible scaling ladder with rope sides and wooden steps that was subsequently used by other commanders. Its topmost rung was of iron equipped with a socket into which a spear point could be placed to raise the ladder up and hook it over a castle wall.

On 27 February 1314 (Shrove Tuesday) Douglas' ingenuity came into full play when he captured Roxburgh Castle. At nightfall Douglas and his men at arms wore black surcoats over their armour, approaching the castle like a herd of the small black cattle common at the time. Some of them carried collapsible ladders suspended beneath their bodies and when all arrived below the castle walls and the ladders were raised on the tips of their spears, they climbed rapidly over the ramparts and overcame the garrison. As the cattle-like raiders approached they had been observed by two sentries who remarked to each other that their farmer-owner must have been feasting to let them escape and become possible prey for the marauding Black Douglas.

This was the calibre of the man who commanded Bruce's third infantry division at Bannockburn, but his responsibilities during the battle by no means ended there . He played a premier role in the pursuit and had he been granted more cavalry for this purpose the outcome would have been far worse for the English and the war might even have been ended.

Robert Keith, Marischal of Scotland (d 1346)

Apart from his long-time and much-valued ally Angus Og MacDonald, Lord of the Isles, who fought directly under Bruce's command with the fourth and reserve schiltron, Bruce's other eminent commander at Bannockburn was Sir Robert Keith, leader of his light cavalry. Older than Bruce's infantry commanders, Keith had held posts of high responsibility for both the Scots and the English until he became convinced of Bruce's importance to Scotland's future independence. As early as 1294 Keith acted as Great Marischal of Scotland under John Balliol. In 1300 he was captured by the English and imprisoned in Carlisle Castle. Reported to Edward I as 'one of his worst enemies' and 'of bad repute', Keith was then removed further into England. On his release he became active on behalf of the Scots until their general submission to the English king in 1304. Following this Keith acted as one of two English justices whose jurisdiction stretched between the Forth and the Mounth, for which he was variously rewarded for his loyal and efficient service.[20] As an abiding patriot he might well have reasoned that in such a capacity he could at least ensure that impartiality was given to his countrymen as well as the English.

In 1308 Keith became the first Lothian lord to join Bruce, and in the following year he united with other Scottish nobles in sending a letter to France requesting that country's recognition and support for Scottish independence. Bruce reinstated him in his post as Marischal of Scotland, an office held by the Keith family for more than a century, and also made him Justiciar of Scotland from the Forth to Orkney.[21] At the same time the king brought Keith closer to him by granting him extensive land in the northeast of Scotland far away from the family's former main interests in Lothian. In Keith, Bruce felt he had yet another commander in whom he could place his full trust. The decision to make Keith commander of the cavalry at Bannockburn was shrewd because he was not merely an able man but one of high rank, an important factor as the cavalry was certain to contain a greater proportion of nobles than the divisions of spearmen. Such men expected a commander of equal status and, although Keith was not nearly as experienced in cavalry tactics as either Edward Bruce or James Douglas, Bruce knew that, unlike William Wallace's horsemen at Falkirk, Keith's cavalry at Bannockburn could be relied upon to carry out his orders, however demanding.

CHAPTER SIX

≈

THE ENGLISH COMMANDERS

'Right brave were they, and believed if they came
to battle no strength could withstand them.'

John Barbour, *The Bruce*

IN THE SAME WAY as the character of Robert Bruce would
set the tone and unite the purpose of the Scottish forces,
the character of the English king, Edward II, formerly Edward
Caernarvon, first Prince of Wales, was of equal importance to
the English army. In their ruler the Scots were well-served; the
English were not. In fact his biographer, Michael Prestwich, concluded that Edward II 'was one of the most unsuccessful kings
ever to rule England'.[1] However, by 1314 the reign was only
a third of the way through and, despite the grievous divisions
that had occurred between Edward II and his nobles, the king's
much-hated favourite, Piers Gaveston, was dead and an uneasy
peace existed between them. A major battle with Scotland presented a classic occasion for the leading English nobles to close
ranks round their king. However, divisions were so deep that
only three of the English earls agreed to serve personally under
him, although the others sent the retinues required by their feudal
obligations and many of the younger nobility gave him their
personal support. This support was not always offered for purely
patriotic reasons and certainly not out of love for this particular
king but because success on the battlefield was the goal of any
feudal knight: for the ambitious it offered unique opportunities
to be granted land, the basis of all wealth at this time, and for
advancement into the more senior ranks of the peerage.

*   *   *

Edward Caernarvon was ten years younger than Robert Bruce, the fourth son of Edward I and his queen, Eleanor of Castile. By the time he was four months old the last of his older brothers had died leaving him heir apparent to one of England's most formidable kings. One penalty of Edward I's success was that for much of the prince's boyhood his father was away fighting and up to her death when he was just seven parental guidance came largely from his mother. As a result, the robust young prince spent much time in the hands of his general tutor, Sir Guy Ferre, who apparently kept his royal charge on a very loose rein. The prince did not distinguish himself educationally although he undoubtedly developed a wide range of interests, including a love for 'gambling on dice' that was shared by many of his subjects. In an age when everyone could ride he was soon considered an excellent horseman, albeit favouring the more self-indulgent activities of hunting and horse racing rather than the jousts that trained men for war and allowed a future king the chance to assess their potential worth on the battlefield. In addition the prince enjoyed boating and swimming and, more controversially, rustic crafts such as thatching and ditching, wrought iron work, even shoeing horses.[2] He was musical and, when king, Genoese instrumentalists were commissioned to entertain him, while he himself played the crwth or Celtic violin.

An orthodox rather than fervent believer, he was far less inclined to pay public tribute to his God than either his father or, for that matter, his future opponent at Bannockburn. In fact, the English chronicler from Lanercost strongly criticised him for not commending himself to the saints when campaigning. On Edward's journey to Bannockburn the same chronicler went on to say he marched with great pomp and elaborate state purloining goods from the monasteries as he went; it was also reported that he did and said things to the prejudice and injury of the saints.[3] The pleasure-loving Edward could also be amazingly generous: he once gave £50 to a surgeon who cured one of his stable boys who was bitten by a stallion from the royal stable and, more controversially, in March 1312, the same amount to Geoffrey de Sellinges, one of Piers Gaveston's retainers, when he learned that Gaveston had decided to remain in England.[4]

He was less celebrated for his emotional stability, for losing his temper over relatively minor issues and, more importantly, being hesitant or mistaken over major ones. Denholm Young's withering introduction to *Vita Edwardi Secundi* attributed many of the king's shortcomings to a lack of good preparation for his role, calling him an aimless man without poise or sense of values.

In spite of any deficiencies in Edward II's training for kingship whether serious or not, it would be wrong to say that Edward I lacked paternal regard for he took considerable pains to help his son gain command experience in Scotland, but by 1300 the old king was struggling with many serious problems, and after the loss of his first wife he became noticeably more impatient and harsh. In that year the prince accompanied his father on a major campaign against Scotland where he undoubtedly cut a fine figure and about whom it was said:

> He was of a well-proportioned handsome person,
> Of a courteous disposition, and well bred
> And desirous of finding an occasion
> To make proof of his strength.[5]

In the event the expedition, like so many others against that inhospitable and determined country, proved disappointing. Confronted by such a strong English army the Scots were understandably unwilling to risk a major engagement and the prince's active role was limited to a single skirmish. Nonetheless his father was not displeased with his demeanour, appointing him Prince of Wales and Earl of Chester.

In 1301 he joined his father on another invasion of Scotland and this time the king entrusted him with command of a separate force due to enter the country from the southwest, with the intention that 'the chief honour of taming the pride of the Scots should fall to his son'.[6] Unfortunately, the Scots proved too strong and far too elusive for the Prince of Wales to gain the glory for which his father had hoped. He reached no further than Whithorn and Loch Ryan along the coast of Galloway before he was compelled to rejoin his father who had moved into quarters at Linlithgow. Two years later Edward I assembled another major army and completed his occupation of Scotland (except for Stirling Castle) but since he met with only nominal resistance his son gained little further experience in battlefield command.

Apart from such difficulties, Edward I's tutelage of his son as future king and military commander was punctuated by violent disputes between them. One incident occurred in 1305 when the nominal cause was the prince's poaching deer from the estate of Walter Langton, the king's favourite minister. In reality it resulted from the prince's continuing obsession with Piers Gaveston, the handsome and witty son of one of Edward I's household knights. Gaveston was required to leave the country and the prince was humiliated by being banned from court and required to follow its progress at a distance of some ten leagues.

In 1306, following Bruce's revolt, Edward I's health began to fail and he realised that his son would soon have to lead the English forces against Scotland. In fact, a writ dated 25 April 1306 described the projected movement north in that year as an 'expedition by Edward, Prince of Wales, to be joined afterwards by the King'.[7] The king mended relations between them and, to seal the prince's more influential role, held a magnificent ceremony to knight him before he set off for Scotland, a ceremony that brought together the largest grouping of knights ever seen at Westminster. Unfortunately the solemnity of the occasion was marred when the preceding night of fasting and prayer turned into one of drunkenness and turmoil with the prince taking a leading part. Edward knighted the prince in the palace chapel, assisted by the earls of Lincoln and Hereford who fastened on his spurs, and the prince himself then knighted a further 267 young men, including Piers Gaveston. A banquet followed at which all present pledged themselves to defeat the Scots and subsequently go on crusade; the prince, for instance, swore he would never sleep twice in the one place until he had reached Scotland and revenged Robert Bruce's murder of John Comyn. However, in the resultant campaign, it was Aymer de Valence, Earl of Pembroke, who gained the initial battlefield successes against Bruce, while the Prince of Wales followed up behind. At this time he became known more for his harsh treatment of the ordinary people in southwest Scotland than for his prowess in battle, a tactic however that succeeded in driving underground any support remaining there for Robert Bruce.[8] Although the prince undoubtedly shared his father's determination to subdue Scotland, it soon became apparent that, compared with Edward I's fierce dedication, his own pleasures would take an equally high priority.

During the winter of 1306–7 when Edward I was staying with his son at Lanercost Priory near Carlisle in preparation for a renewed campaign against Scotland, fresh trouble flared up between them. The cause was again Piers Gaveston who, with twenty-two other young knights, had angered Edward by deserting the war in Scotland (which with Bruce's second defeat at the hands of John MacDougall seemed virtually over) and moving across to the continent to attend a tournament there. All their lands were seized but at the intervention of his young queen, Marguerite, Edward I pardoned them with the exception of Piers Gaveston. Despite his father's strong displeasure at their relationship and Gaveston's recent behaviour, the prince rashly attempted to use the king's treasurer, Walter Langton, to help gain his father's permission to bestow one of the prince's own titles, Count of Ponthieu, on his beloved. His father's response left the prince in no doubt about the king's feelings or about his estimate of his son's achievements so far: 'You baseborn whoreson! Do you want to give lands away now, you who never gained any? As the Lord lives, if it were not for fear of breaking up the Kingdom you should never enjoy your inheritance!' In his rage Edward seized the prince by the hair and tore out as much as he could before throwing him out of his presence. The Prince of Wales delayed carrying out the king's order to banish Piers Gaveston for as long as he dared before accompanying his favourite to Dover, where he showered him with gifts of tapestries and rich tunics.[9] He had, in fact, not yet rejoined his father for the projected campaign northwards when Edward I died at Burgh-upon-Sands near the border.

With Edward I's death the new king moved back into England and did not return to Scotland for three years, a decision that gave Bruce the priceless opportunity to extend his power. Characteristically, Edward II's first act was a selfish one that antagonised his nobles; he brought Gaveston back and created him Earl of Cornwall, a title customarily given to a member of the royal family. In spite of such ill-judgement Edward II's reign appeared to start promisingly with his marriage in France to Isabella, daughter of the French king, although on his return to court, the king's kisses and repeated embraces for his favourite, whom he had appointed Keeper of the Realm while he was in France, allied to his obvious preference for Gaveston's company to that of his queen, infuriated both her and other senior nobles. As if this were not enough, at Edward II's coronation on 25 February 1308 while other nobles were content to wear cloth of gold, Gaveston, in his vanity, wore regal purple trimmed with pearls. The barons – assisted by the queen – banded together and demanded Gaveston's banishment by 25 June at the latest. In the face of such opposition Edward II was forced to concur, but even then he continued to make grants of land to his favourite and softened the sentence of exile by appointing him as his Lieutenant in Ireland in place of the powerful Richard de Burgh, Earl of Ulster.

One of Edward II's most serious shortcomings as king was his carelessness at alienating some of the men he needed most. However, with Gaveston no longer on the scene Edward II showed that when he was minded he could use royal patronage as well as other kings. By a shrewd use of bribes he succeeded in dividing the baronial opposition and persuading them to allow his favourite's return, but in his delight at their reunion he no longer bothered to treat his senior barons with the degree of tact they warranted, while Gaveston too soon showed how little he had learned by becoming even more abusive, calling Ralph de Monthermer, Earl of Gloucester, 'a whoreson' and the venerable Earl of Lincoln, who headed the opposition to him, 'old burst belly'. As a result the earls understandably refused to attend Parliament if Gaveston was present and instead held a Royal Council of Assembly which they attended in armour and where they forced the king to agree to a commission of reform comprising twenty-one of their number called the 'Lords

Ordainers'. Their main grievance was against Gaveston, but many of their complaints were about the state's finances and the expenses involved in military expeditions.

While they were considering their findings Edward embarked on a long overdue campaign against Scotland, as much from personal motives as objectives of state, for whilst on campaign he would be excused from being in London to face the report of the Ordainers' committee and avoid having to explain the treatment of his queen to her father, Philip of France. Only two earls, Gloucester and Warwick, agreed to take part in the projected campaign and in the event its modest objectives of strengthening and reprovisioning the garrisons still in English hands were not fully achieved.

With the defection of the other earls, Gaveston had an opportunity to demonstrate his military ability but, although he marched north to Perth while Gloucester concentrated his forces in the great forest of Selkirk, the Scottish forces stayed out of reach, denying him any chance of battlefield success. If Gaveston had proved a notable military leader it would have strengthened the king's case against his critics and possibly reversed English misfortunes in Scotland; but he did not and by November the king was back in the border fortress of Berwick where he remained until June 1311. Although Edward II intended to lead another expedition that summer, a crippling shortage of money forced him to return to Westminster and hear the Ordainers' verdict. Their main demands included the renewed exile of Piers Gaveston and a re-ordering of royal finances, which they considered had been squandered on the king's favourite rather than used in pursuit of the Scottish war, but after another short exile the king allowed Gaveston to return and by January 1312 all his lands had been restored to him.

At this, even those barons who had remained sympathetic towards the king united in arms against Gaveston. After his capture and subsequent execution the king was so enraged that he began to gather armed forces against his nobles. In such a situation any warlike operations against the Scots were necessarily suspended – there was no question even of countering the Scottish raids against northern England – and as the Scottish chronicler Fordun wrote, exultantly, 'The fruitless English nation, which had unrighteously attacked many a man, was now, by God's righteous judgement made to undergo awful scourges.'[10]

In April 1312 the Scots took further advantage of English inaction by recapturing Berwick, but the power vacuum in London could only be temporary and gradually the balance began to swing back in the king's favour. A certain revulsion developed against the earls who had executed Gaveston and in November 1312 the king's cause was further aided by the birth of an heir to his queen, Isabella. The more moderate among the nobles began actively seeking a reconciliation. Two papal emissaries, together with the King of France's brother, Louis of Evreaux, toiled for several months to bring about a settlement between the king and his nobles and, after long and bitter exchanges, not least over the custody of the valuable jewels which the king had given his favourite, a final settlement was reached on 14 October 1313. By this the earls admitted their fault and offered a humble apology to the king who, in turn, granted a general pardon to them and their followers.

No amount of agreement, however, could alter the fact that for more than six years after his accession Edward II had outrageously misused his royal patronage in favour of one man. Nor could the settlement bring immediate concord; the king's hatred for Lancaster, for instance, was far too marked for that. Serious differences remained, not only between the nobles and the king but also amongst themselves. The full price of Edward's infatuation with Piers Gaveston to the exclusion of all else was only too likely to be paid in the coming battle with Scotland.[11] As a leader largely inexperienced in war, Edward II would command a group of nobles lacking some of their most powerful representatives, while those who remained, however sincere their loyalty, had long been accustomed to such rancour and discord between monarch and others of his nobles that the actions of the king no longer bore the full stamp of authority. In such circumstances it needed a stronger king possessing better judgement than Edward II to obtain the best from his subordinate commanders who in any case had yet to witness his demeanour and powers of decision-making in the heat of battle. Their own fixation on attacking the enemy, whatever the situation, would probably cause them serious difficulties, as at Falkirk when they had needed the restraining influence of Edward I.

The three earls who answered Edward II's call and could be expected to take senior positions of command during the coming battle were Aymer de Valence, Earl of Pembroke, Gilbert de Clare, Earl of Gloucester and Humphrey de Bohun, Earl of Hereford.

Aymer de Valence, Earl of Pembroke (d 1324)

Valence's biographer, J R S Phillips, was critical of all the English nobles who served under Edward II at this time but, although not judging his subject an Alexander in war, he 'came to rate him the best of a moderate group and a man essentially faithful to the monarch'.[12] Valence was the son of William de Valence, one of Edward I's marcher lords. With extensive possessions both in Wales and Montignac in Europe, and twice married to French women of distinction, Valence could be expected to take a wider view of affairs than some others of his peers, whose interests were confined to England and Scotland. With such immaculate French connections he was uniquely qualified to conduct relations between England and France and his high level of performance on such missions led Professor Barrow to rate him as the one English noble during the early years of the fourteenth century who displayed qualities of statesmanship. While it is Valence's military qualities that are of prime concern, his diplomatic talents were not irrelevant to his role as a commander nor, in such troubled times, was the fact that he loyally supported both Edwards until his death in 1324. It needed exceptional stupidity on the part of Edward II to drive Valence into opposition but, although he allied himself with his fellow Ordainers between 1310–12, it is more than likely that at heart he remained loyal to the concept of kingship as opposed to any alignments of rival nobles.

Valence's military career began in 1296 with Edward I in Flanders and he fought at the battle of Falkirk. From then on, with the exception of besieging Piers Gaveston in Scarborough Castle, he was exclusively concerned with the Scottish wars. Although Valence was the Red Comyn's brother-in-law and therefore not likely to feel any warmth for Robert Bruce, his appointment by Edward I as his Lieutenant in Scotland at the time of Bruce's revolt also demonstrated confidence in his military ability. Valence's success over Bruce at Methven has already been discussed, though his conduct on that occasion was heavily influenced by the Scot, Sir Ingram Umfraville, who also hated Bruce and who advised Valence to ignore accepted practice by moving against Bruce during the night.[13]

At Edward II's accession Valence was deprived of his Scottish lieutenancy, apparently on the advice of Piers Gaveston who in an age of universal hatred for Jews also insulted him (and amused Edward II) by nicknaming him 'Joseph the Jew' because of his height and pallid complexion. When in 1310 Edward II marched to Scotland with Gaveston, Valence, along with most of his fellow nobles, understandably refused to accompany the king, although he sent his feudal quota of knights, about ten in number.[14] As a supporter of the Ordainers he removed Gaveston from Scarborough Castle and imprisoned him in Deddington but it was seemingly without his knowledge that Warwick had the king's favourite removed and executed. In apparent disgust Valence returned to the court party, although he was certainly no firm supporter of the king's policy regarding Gaveston.[15] In spite of their serious differences over the royal favourite Valence continued to enjoy close personal relations with Edward II who, for instance, even went so far as to give him a number of falcons that had previously belonged to Gaveston, while the king also used Valence's diplomatic skills to conduct peace negotiations with his nobles and with the French king.[16]

In 1314 Valence supplanted the feeble John of Brittany as Lieutenant of Scotland and was given correspondingly wide responsibilities. He went on to play an energetic and creditable role at Bannockburn, although, unfortunately, there is no evidence as to the nature of his participation in the English councils of war there. Militarily, particularly in terms of personal energy, Valence appears to stand comparison with Bruce's much younger commander Thomas Randolph, Earl of Moray. However, under Edward II Valence was not given the same opportunities as Moray to develop his skills on the battlefield and the critical J R S Phillips came to conclude that neither his average military virtues nor his leadership qualities in the field of politics were equal to the demands placed upon him by the serious crises of Edward II's reign.[17]

Gilbert de Clare, Earl of Gloucester (d 1314)

The Clares were another marcher family that served with Edward I in Wales. Despite Phillips' sombre judgement of all English barons at this time the young Earl of Gloucester, a grandson of Edward I and nephew of Edward II, was considered one of the outstanding nobles of his generation and 'both intellectually and morally the noblest representative of his great house'.[18] His mother was Edward I's third daughter, Joan of Acre and his father Gilbert de Clare. A boy prodigy, at fifteen years of age he was made a companion to Edward II and served him in Scotland during 1306. Despite his tender years Gloucester not only attended a muster of the English forces at Carlisle but was selected to negotiate a truce there with Robert Bruce.[19] Rapid advancement followed: on 3 December 1308 he was appointed commander of the English forces sent to relieve Rutherglen Castle and in the following year – when still only 18 – he became commander of the English forces on both sides of the Forth.[20]

In spite of such swift promotion for one so young, Gloucester lacked practical battlefield experience. His advancement was very probably due to his seeming incorruptibility and to the fact that he was a consistent supporter of Edward II when so many others were against him. While Gloucester, like Valence, supported some of the reforms proposed by the Earl of Lancaster's Ordainers – in particular those designed to check the king's undue generosity towards Gaveston – he opposed the use of extreme measures in obtaining them. In 1308 he distanced himself from those who called for Gaveston's banishment, although he appeared to have no personal sympathy for the favourite. As a mark of Edward II's trust in him, in 1313, while the king was absent in France, he was appointed regent of England.[21]

Gloucester brought a large retinue to Bannockburn, although it was certainly smaller than the 500 men attributed to him by Barbour. In his eagerness to be first to meet the Scots in battle Gloucester disputed with Hereford over who should lead the vanguard but, this apart, he was widely known for his level-headedness: after the disappointments of the first encounters he was one of those who advised the king to delay until the full strength of the English army could be mobilised. His death at the outset of the main battle deprived the king of someone capable of understanding the dangers in which the English army had placed itself and the need to take fundamental, if unpopular, decisions to improve the situation.

Humphrey de Bohun, Earl of Hereford (d 1322)

Humphrey de Bohun's father had served Edward I in Wales and Humphrey himself had accompanied him during his invasion of Scotland in 1300. At the time of Bannockburn the twenty-eight-year-old baron was Constable of England and was married to Elizabeth, seventh daughter of Edward I and widow of Count John of Hainault. A man of vast wealth, De Bohun was a noble of considerable importance with a fortune sufficient for him to leave the amazing sums of £2000 to each of his four younger sons and 1000 marks to his son-in-law, Hugh de Courtenay.[22] Although he lacked the campaigning experience of men like the veteran Henry de Lacey, Earl of Lincoln (who died in 1311),

De Bohun enjoyed the strong confidence of his peers and was chosen, with Valence, as a negotiator in the quarrels between the king and his nobles both over Piers Gaveston and then, following Bannockburn, with the Despensers. While De Bohun shared his peers' alarm and anger concerning Edward II's favourite he was, like Valence and Gloucester, a moderate opponent. Skilled in personal combat, De Bohun listed (unsuccessfully) against Gaveston in the great tournaments held at Fulham in 1305 and 1307 but like his brother earls, his experience of military leadership was strictly limited. Apart from joining Edward I's disappointing Scottish campaign of 1300 he accompanied the Earl of Gloucester against Robert Bruce in 1308 without having any chance to distinguish himself, and was afterwards present at the bloodless siege of Piers Gaveston in Scarborough Castle.

Having returned to the king's peace after Gaveston's death, Hereford enthusiastically answered Edward II's call in 1314 but although he fought bravely enough at Bannockburn, his distinction arose not from his ability as a commander there but as the Scots' most notable prisoner. Despite his eminent position and the large retinue he brought onto the field, he had little practical experience of command in war and none of large-scale engagements. His battlefield philosophy was to reach the enemy as soon as possible, and he was unlikely to have contributed anything original to the councils of war held the night before the main encounter. During the battle itself he was behind the forward elements of his vanguard when they clashed with Bruce on day one, and during the main action he became too quickly involved in hand to hand fighting to exercise an overall influence.

The two other English commanders with an opportunity to influence events at Bannockburn, particularly in its early stages, were the joint leaders of the English army's second cavalry division, Sir Robert Clifford and Sir Henry Beaumont.

Sir Robert Clifford (d 1314)

Clifford came from Northumbria, and his father had been a friend and companion to Edward I from their crusading days together. Clifford himself was involved in several of the clashes that took place between England and Scotland from the 1290s into the early years of the new century. His military career began promisingly when, together with Henry Percy, he made a brilliant raid into Scotland which was rewarded by the surrender of the Scottish forces at Irvine in June 1297. During April of the previous year, when just twenty-three years of age, he had been present at the English victory at Dunbar[23] and over a period of almost twenty years the spirited and determined cavalry commander accompanied a succession of English invasions northwards until his death in battle. On Edward I's expedition in 1300 Clifford was responsible for the campaign's one notable success, the capture of Caerlaverock Castle near Dumfries in July and as a reward Edward made him its guardian.

In the light of such long experience of the Anglo-Scottish clashes Clifford would have been familiar with the ground on which Bannockburn was fought. A trusted supporter of the old king, Clifford was present at his deathbed where he was given instructions relating to the banishment of Piers Gaveston of whom, with the majority of his peers, Clifford was a strong opponent. Notwithstanding this Edward II also had a high opinion of Clifford both with regard to his military ability and for his honesty and directness. In 1308, for instance, he appointed Clifford, along with the Earl of Angus, as Captain Guardian of Scotland on either side of the Firths. As late as March 1310 Clifford showed he had not yet fully aligned himself with the fiercest baronial opposition to Edward II by stating that any concessions made by the king to them should not be seen as a precedent.[24] However, in 1312 on rumours of Gaveston's return from exile, Clifford guarded the northern counties against any possible collusion between the favourite and England's enemy, Robert Bruce. Clifford despised Gaveston and on 4 May 1312, he joined with the Earl of Lancaster, the king's bitterest enemy, to besiege him in Scarborough Castle.

Yet Gaveston apart, Clifford was as loyal to his sovereign, Edward II, as to his father, willingly answering his call to muster at Berwick for the relief of Stirling Castle. He was already at Berwick in April 1314, for he was excused attendance at the April parliament for that reason. A measure of the regard both monarchs felt for Clifford's military and administrative abilities could be seen in their generous awards which made him one of the largest English landowners. He was, for instance, granted Robert Bruce's forfeited manor of Hert and Hertlepool, Christopher Seton's estate at Skelton in Cumberland and William Douglas' Douglasdale (this on payment of 500 crowns a year).

At Bannockburn Edward II's own trust in this vigorous soldier and long-time opponent of the Scots was shown by appointing him (along with Sir Henry Beaumont) as commander of the English army's second cavalry division. His death at Bannockburn during the opening moves of the main battle undoubtedly robbed the English king of a capable and highly respected commander whom the chronicler Rishanger referred to as a 'miles illustris'. In the light of Clifford's unhappy experience against spearmen the day before it is virtually certain he would have tried to bring up bowmen as soon as possible in support of the English cavalry during the main battle.

Sir Henry Beaumont (d 1340)

Although Clifford was undoubtedly the more experienced soldier, Edward II unwisely attempted to spread his bounty by appointing Sir Henry Beaumont as co-commander of the second cavalry division. Originally from Beaumont in France, Sir Henry was Edward II's cousin and a knight of the royal household who had served with Edward I and then with the Prince of Wales in their Scottish wars. At Edward II's accession Beaumont stood high in the new king's favour and received extensive lands in

Lincolnshire and, more contentiously, the Isle of Man – to the fury of other English nobles. In 1310 Beaumont married Alice Comyn, niece of John Comyn, third Earl of Buchan, and this gave him even more reason to fight against Robert Bruce. Certainly no more capable than Robert Clifford, during his and Clifford's first exchange with the Scots Beaumont had one idea only, how best to attack. When a more cautious approach was suggested by a fellow commander, Thomas Grey, he utterly rejected it and continued in the energetic but ultimately fruitless assaults against the Scots. Despite suffering such unexpected failure, on the second day he continued with the English vanguard, but again without success since insufficient bowmen were brought up in its support. Beaumont was demonstrably not an outstanding tactician, preferring to bludgeon in all-out attack with little respect for his opponents.

There appear to be no grounds whatever for querying Beaumont's loyalty to Edward II during the battle, either during the preliminary clashes, or when among the large contingent of cavalry that fought with and gave the king protection as he left the field. Later he became involved in conspiracies at court against his king and showed himself as an adventurer. He turned his coat, paying allegiance to Queen Isabella in her attempt to depose Edward II, and later along with Edward Balliol he became chief of the disinherited nobles pledged to regain their Scottish estates.

It is not known whom Edward II selected to command the English forces at Bannockburn in the event of his becoming a casualty. One is left to wonder whether the relatively inexperienced but arrogant monarch, for instance, ever felt the need to appoint a deputy. If so it is likely to have been Valence, but in the light of Edward's idiosyncratic decision-making this is by no means certain. There is also no record of who commanded the large numbers of English infantry and bowmen, but whoever they were, they were allowed little opportunity to swing the battle in favour of the English. A strong and self-willed leader such as Edward I permitted little deviation from his orders, and this gave poor training for the senior English commanders under him, while the seven years under Edward II prior to Bannock-burn were highly undistinguished in the military sense.

Phillips could well have been right in rating the ability of Edward II's subordinate commanders as moderate, even if they were undoubtedly vigorous and brave; after tricking Bruce at Methven Valence allowed himself to be consistently outfoxed and outfought by the Scots; Gloucester remained startlingly inexperienced and his death prevented him showing any out-standing qualities at Bannockburn; and despite his greater age De Bohun had been as much engaged in conflicts with Edward II as he had with the Scots. Beaumont proved himself as a good middle piece commander, but no more. Clifford was the possible exception but he was killed before he could distinguish himself further. Among other experienced soldiers there was Sir Maurice Berkeley, who appeared to have acted as a senior retainer to Valence rather than as a commander in his own right, and Sir Pain Tiptoft (also killed in the main battle's early stages) who had acted as companion to Edward II from his early years without acquiring significant command experience. One of the most charismatic figures among the English at Bannockburn was Giles D'Argentan, a magnificent fighting soldier said by John Barbour to rate as the third best knight in Christendom for his skill at arms (the first two were Emperor Henry and King Robert Bruce in that order).[25] D'Argentan enjoyed no similar rating for his powers of command. Edward II went to great pains to bring the paladin back from his crusading to support him at Bannockburn but, while brave to a fault, D'Argentan made no impression as a commander there.

Together with Valence the most senior of Edward II's advisers was Ingram Umfraville, cousin of the Earl of Angus, related to John Balliol, and long-time opponent of the Bruces. Umfraville had held a number of significant civil and military posts in Scotland and in 1302 he acted as a senior envoy during the negotiations held in Paris to agree a peace treaty between France and Scotland. During 1300 he replaced Bruce as joint guardian of Scotland along with Bishop Lamberton and John Comyn (the Red). He had been active militarily since 1299 when, with other Scottish nobles he conducted a large-scale raid south of the Forth with both barded horse and infantry. In 1301, he and John Soules conducted spoiling attacks against the English forces commanded by both Edward I and the Prince of Wales, including a bold assault on Lochmaben Castle. With Scotland's general submission to Edward I in 1304 Umfraville's estates were forfeited, the conditions set for their redemption being the payment of up to a maximum of five years' income. It was a mark of Umfraville's importance in the rebellion along with his late submission that his redemption terms were the harshest of all the Scottish nobles, i.e. for the full five years value.[26]

By 1308 Umfraville was fighting on behalf of the English against Edward Bruce in Galloway but it would therefore have been amazing if, as a Scot, even one who had changed allegiance, his advice had been given precedence over that of Edward II's English councillors. In any event, experienced soldier or not, by Bannockburn his judgement seemed to be clouded by hate. His advice to King Edward at the outset of the main battle (as will be seen) was fanciful in the extreme and although positioned near the king in order to inform him about the Scottish method of fighting, it is unlikely that he would have been trusted with the main direction of the army.

Sadly for the English, in the coming battle their high command would be headed by an unpopular king largely untried in war and supported by a considerable body of nobles, all of whom had previously opposed him for favouring another over themselves or like the Scot, Umfraville, joined Edward II because of his hate for Robert Bruce. Like the Earl of Gloucester they had grown up in a climate of feuding and did not seem prepared to subordinate their own interests to the general advantage on the field of battle. While many had considerable experience of warfare both in Britain and elsewhere they had been given relatively little opportunity for independent command, and during the battle's early stages some of the most promising became fatalities. In any case, so confident were they in their superior numbers and armament bringing success that the English leaders felt no need to dwell on the tactical problems facing them or to consider overmuch ways of best combining their fighting strength. Apart from the battle at Stirling Bridge against William Wallace in 1297, when the main English army was led by Warenne, Earl of Surrey, rather than their king, and where it had been prevented from using even half its strength, the English simply did not lose to the Scots. Their opponents might elude them and they might even have to turn back for want of food and provisions, but defeat in open battle was unthinkable.

Section Three: *Bruce's Masterstroke*

≈

CHAPTER SEVEN

ADVANCE TO BATTLE

'We are so few against so many.'

Barbour, *The Bruce*

WHETHER IT WAS DUE to a measure of overconfidence, or, more likely, because some important units had still to reach the concentration area, Edward II did not give the order for his army to cross the border before 17 June 1314, a week later than planned. To fulfil the challenge, Stirling had to be relieved by the 24th for which he had allowed himself no leeway for unexpected delays or enemy action along the arduous ninety-mile journey. Whatever his commanders thought about such a restricted timetable they must have been pleasantly surprised by the weather: instead of rain, which had accompanied so many other English armies into Scotland, it was hot and dry. This, however, brought problems of its own: the potholes on the uneven roads were iron hard, causing carts to jolt and buck, while the unyielding surface led to sore feet for animals and men alike.

Most of the heavy transport would probably have gone on from Wark to Berwick, where it would cross the Tweed before taking the Roman road over the Lammermuir hills. Other detachments probably crossed the river at the village of Coldstream. Evidence that the English did, in fact, use the Roman road came from a royal despatch made at Soutra (probably from the ancient hospital there) on 18 June which was sent to the king's council and the Archbishop of Canterbury.[1] From the heights of Soutra where the road climbed to over 1000 feet the invaders had their first clear sight of Edinburgh and, depending on the amount of heat haze, possibly glimpses of Stirling too, lying further north beyond the western shoulder of the Pentland hills. They had done well to reach Soutra, almost forty miles from Coldstream by the end of day two but Edward's strong pace was far faster than the Monk of Malmesbury liked. 'He hastened day by day to the appointed place, not as if he were leading an army to battle but as if he was on a pilgrimage to St James of Compostella. Brief were the halts for sleep, briefer still for food, hence horses, horsemen and infantry were worn out with toil and hunger.'[2] The chronicler's observations were surely justified when one realises that with such extended columns of marching men interspersed with heavily burdened carts, progress could not be reckoned to exceed two miles per hour. At times the men would be marching somewhat faster than this but in accordance with normal military practice they were likely to have paused fairly frequently, possibly for ten minutes each hour, to deal with blisters and to patch up their crude footwear.

To reach Soutra within two days the marching columns would have been on the road for at least twelve hours each day. (From Soutra they had another sixteen-mile journey before entering Edinburgh.)

Despite his criticism of the king the same chronicler observed with pride that he led 'a very fine and large army' with 'more than 2000 armoured horse and a very large number of infantry' and added proudly that all 'who were present agreed that never in our times has such an army gone forth from England' with 'enough waggons to have stretched for twenty miles if they had lined up end to end'. Another contemporary source was quite specific about their numbers: '106 waggons drawn by four horses each, and 110 waggons each drawn by eight oxen, making a total of 424 horses and 880 oxen.'[3] These numbers applied to the draught animals alone, and the cavalry horses, whose feet needed careful maintenance, were numbered in thousands rather than hundreds. For Edward I's earlier invasion of Scotland in 1300, 3000 horseshoes and 50,000 nails were required to be carried in seven three-horse carts.[4] Far more shoes were required in 1314 when just 200lbs was the normal load for horse-drawn carts.[5] Even more important than horseshoes were the war supplies, including bows, together with their shafts, lances and other spare personal weapons. Along with such military equipment they carried food, including grain, bacon, mutton, fish and wine. Whatever grass was available on the way, some hay would also have been needed for the vast number of horses.

With so many waggons the army's movement was bound to be tedious and it needs no imagination to realise the difficulties experienced when it came to steep gradients at the base of which were streams that needed fording or other places where the road had been partially washed away. If the vehicles had carried food and war materials only the logistical problems would have been difficult enough, but with the pleasure-loving Edward this was far from the case. Where the king led his nobles were virtually bound to follow, carrying with them not only their personal tentage but other material comforts such as silver eating vessels and a wide choice of wines. In the expectation of certain victory some, like the younger Hugh Despenser, whose rights to his lands and tenements in Scotland had been restored to him by the king's charter, carried domestic equipment to assist in their re-occupation.[6]

Whatever the mandatory halts, straggling was inevitable and the army's line of march became so extended that Barbour described it as covering 'hills and valleys'. Local people who had removed themselves from its path to watch from the safety of adjacent hill tops had no difficulty whatever in tracking it. The vanguard's progress, for instance, was distinguishable by a moving cloud of dust through which the sun's rays caught fire upon burnished breastplates, lance points and the brass bosses of harnesses. Accompanying these came the sounds of massed horses, not only destriers but second line animals and remounts; the jingling of tackle and the clatter of hooves on the boulder-strewn road would have easily marked out the horsemen from the more regular crunching noises of the accompanying carts.

This evidence was as nothing compared to the sounds of the main body with its endless line of cumbersome waggons, over half of which were drawn by teams of slow phlegmatic oxen, heads swaying at each stride. The banshee-like squeals made by the wooden axles might well have taken their toll

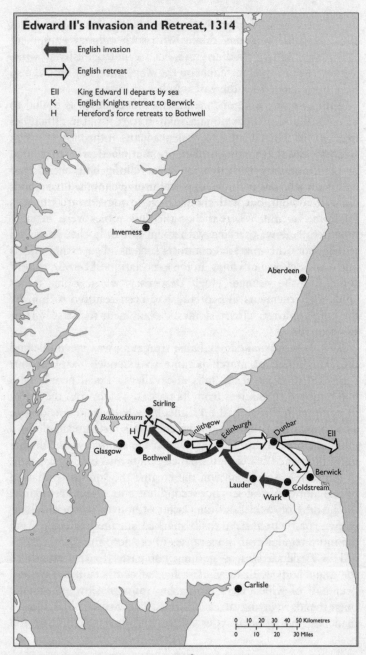

Edward II's Invasion and Retreat, 1314

English invasion

English retreat

EII   King Edward II departs by sea
K   English Knights retreat to Berwick
H   Hereford's force retreats to Bothwell

Inverness

Aberdeen

Stirling

Bannockburn

H

Linlithgow

Edinburgh

Dunbar

EII

Glasgow

Bothwell

K

Berwick

Lauder

Wark

Coldstream

Carlisle

0 10 20 30 40 50 Kilometres

0   10   20   30 Miles

on the accompanying troops, as they did almost five centuries later when they almost drove Sir John Moore's soldiers to distraction during their epic retreat across northern Spain to the seaport of Corunna. With such repetitious and nerve-fraying screeching came the rhythm of marching feet, thousands of them, interspersed with sporadic shouts of command and snatches of song. As the Monk of Malmesbury had already observed, for the majority of those involved, particularly the footsoldiers, it was undoubtedly a demanding experience. Burdened by thick jerkins, or mail, and carrying unwieldy spears along with their other equipment they were forced to plod through choking dust clouds amid the droppings and the ammoniac pools of the horses, unable to see much further than the rank immediately to their front, while from time to time selected detachments would be ordered to break ranks in order to manhandle carts stuck fast in potholes. During the overnight halts the need to take their turn at standing guard further deprived the soldiers of much-needed rest.

Such a march was certain to tell on both men and animals. Some of the men who sustained gashed or raw feet might be allowed to ride in the waggons but others with strained muscles or broken bones would have been left under escort in one of the villages on the way. As the army advanced ever further into a country stripped of food and shelter, initial optimism was also liable to have given way to some feelings of vulnerability. The Scots' reputation for raiding had been well-earned and, as part of a seemingly endless column, men must have thought they presented a near perfect target for attacks by marauders on fast horses. The English were not to know that Bruce had no plans to attack them until much later, but they dared not ignore the possibility.

Although the daylight hours were long at that time of year, many soldiers had additional responsibilities to perform by the light of their camp fires. Men not allocated for guard duties, for instance, still faced the enormous task of feeding and watering the animals before they could rest their own leg muscles and aching shoulders and begin preparing food. No wonder some of them remained hungry for most of the journey and were 'out on their feet' by the end of it.

The king had badly underestimated the time needed to move such a massive army but failure to meet the date agreed by Edward Bruce and Sir Philip Moubray would mean handing the castle over to the Scots. After so much time allowed for mobilisation it would represent a massive blow to English prestige apart from the even more important military considerations. Foremost among these would be Robert Bruce's release from the compact made with Sir Philip Moubray. He could therefore place a strong garrison in the castle and keep his main army hidden in the surrounding woods, ready to harass any assault made on it by the English whose army in any case was designed for open combat rather than for siege operations. By keeping his forces in being, and not hazarding them in battle, Bruce could wait until the English experienced inevitable logistical problems, whether or not they came from mounting a major siege. In the event of an English withdrawal the advantage would pass to Bruce and he could resume his guerrilla tactics. The army was, therefore, driven on rigorously. The English reached Edinburgh on 19 June but more time was lost when two days were spent taking on and distributing stores from the ships waiting at Leith docks. This was a very necessary procedure as not only was it the army's first opportunity for replenishment since setting out over the hills[7] but it was of particular importance to those who had joined the army following a long approach march, and whose footwear and clothing was probably already in tatters. It was not until 22 June, with just two days before the castle was due to be relieved, that the host set off again. Completing a punishing march in the hot, dry weather they covered the twenty-two miles to Falkirk in a single day – but even then ten miles separated them from their goal, which by the agreement was a point three miles or less from Stirling Castle.

Under such an insensitive commander the English army undoubtedly became more leg weary than it needed to be and infantry soldiers and their commanders were likely to have reacted angrily. Yet with the cavalry it would have been different. Rapid movement was everything to them and they would have found the great army's progress painfully slow. For both infantry and cavalry, however, the problems set by the march were bound to prevent any consideration about their detailed dispositions or the degree of necessary co-operation between them when they finally brought the Scots to battle.

The Scottish forces faced quite different problems. Being relatively close to the anticipated battle area, no debilitating approach march was needed although nothing could change the fact that they were heavily outnumbered and had a less well-balanced force. To help offset this Bruce continued with his plans to bring his army up to the highest standards of training. Constant drilling with heavy lances helped his infantrymen's level of fitness and after inevitable difficulties in the early stages the smooth movements by which his individual schiltrons were able to change formation from massed lozenge to circular patterns must have done wonders for their confidence. At the end of May, before the English had even come to muster, his initial training had gone so well that he was able to move his schiltrons from inside the Torwood to the more open – and likely battle – area of New Park where they could practise against dummy attacks mounted by Scottish cavalry units. New Park had been King Alexander III's hunting demesne, close to Stirling Castle and immediately south of the King's Park, the royal hunting ground of earlier centuries.

From New Park's higher ground the Scottish forces would be able to watch the English army approaching along the Roman road before it descended into the valley containing the Bannock Burn. If the English kept to the road they would soon come into view again as they ascended the valley's nearside and entered the park on their route towards the castle. As a defensive position it was a good one; the park's forward hills were perfect for observing the English while its crests and rear slopes had enough wooded areas to give Bruce the opportunity to withdraw and make his army safe from any possible attacks from English cavalry. When, on the morning of Saturday, 22 June, Bruce's scouts galloped up to tell him the English had at last set out from Edinburgh with less than two days before the midsummer deadline, he must have reasoned they had little choice but to keep to the direct route of the Roman road to Stirling which ran east to west roughly in line with the old Antonine wall. After the English forces reached the point where the Bannock Burn crossed the road they would be entering the zone where he could bring his defensive preparations into play.

Before considering the attributes of his position it is necessary to become familiar with the terrain involved. Of particular interest is the rectangular piece of land bounded on its west side by the forward hills of New Park and the Roman road where it crossed the Bannock Burn, and on its eastern side by the crossing places close to the tiny settlement of Skeoch and the point where the Pelstream and the Bannock Burn meet (see map). To the west of the rectangle the road to Stirling is bounded by Gillies Hill and the King's Park while to its east the Bannock Burn eventually disgorges into the River Forth. The rectangle itself splits conveniently into two, with the Pelstream Burn as its dividing line.

On the upper section and to the west of the rectangle is the relatively dry land of the King's Park where horsemen could gallop along its wooded rides, while to the east of the Roman road cultivated land stretches for a quarter of a mile until a steep bank (sheer in places) descends at the 30 metre contour on to flat, wet meadows (carse) stretching to the River Forth. During the fourteenth century the area close below the castle was still used for gathering peats for fuel and it was wet and uneven, but in any case the whole carse of Stirling south of the castle was dangerous ground intersected by sluggish streams called 'pols' from the Celtic, or 'pows' in later Scots.[8] Professor Barrow described these as tending to run through 'deep peaty pools with crumbling, overhanging banks'.[9] The largest pow was the Bannock Burn itself but the entire area of the carse was known in the fourteenth century as Les Polles, the area of sluggish streams.[10]

The lower section of the rectangle below the Pelstream was, in fact, where the main battlefield action would take place. Here, looking again from west to east, there are the rolling (and wooded) hills of New Park with thickets of trees bordering the side of the Roman road. Beyond the road is the small plain of

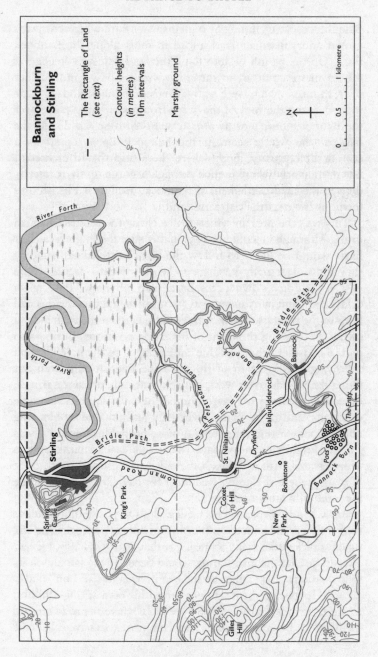

Bannockburn and Stirling

- - - The Rectangle of Land (see text)

Contour heights (in metres) 10m intervals

Marshy ground

N

0   0.5   1 kilometre

River Forth

River Forth

Stirling

Stirling Castle

Bridle Path

Roman Road

King's Park

Coxet Hill

St. Ninians

Dryfield

Balquhidderock

Borestone

New Park

Gilles Hill

Pelstream Burn

Bannock Burn

Bannock

Bridle Path

The Entry

Pots

Bannock Burn

Balquhiderock, including St Ninians township, where corn was grown and subsequently threshed in mills along the Bannock Burn. On the plain's eastern flank the land descends steeply, at the 30 metre contour, to the carse with its pows and patches of fresh moss which were as treacherous as quicksand. A track follows along the foot of the scarp from its crossing place over the Bannock Burn northwards towards Stirling Castle. At the base of the whole segment the Bannock Burn represents a considerable barrier, both where the Roman road crossed it but particularly where it runs through a gorge up to 10 metres deep at the small settlement of Bannock, until its banks become lower as it enters the flat carse land.

This was the area in which Bruce chose to meet the English army. Although he could be reasonably sure the English in their haste would be likely to follow the line of the Roman road (if they did not actually keep to it) he still had to decide where best to position his own forces. Bruce no doubt hoped the English army, confident in its superiority, would attempt the obvious and keep to the road itself, which he could then straddle with hidden obstacles covering the front of his troop positions. But he also had to consider other possible choices open to them. While still following the direction of the road the English could fan out along the woods to its west, but this was unlikely since armies, especially those with a large number of cavalry, are vulnerable in woods, and Bruce made it virtually unthinkable by blocking all the tracks within the forest. A more probable alternative was for the English to move onto the road's eastern flank and to keep parallel with it through the cultivated ground south of St Ninians, where the going was ideal for cavalry. This would be far more difficult to counter.

Bruce had to display all his tactical skills to position his soldiers so that they could both cover the obvious lines of approach and still retain sufficient flexibility to meet any that were less likely. He had already decided his main army would depend very largely on its four divisions of spearmen in schiltron formation and on Sunday 23 June he posted them. He positioned his own strong schiltron to meet the most likely English approach, where the road crossed the Bannock Burn, at the place later commentators have called 'the entry'. The other three schiltrons were committed to blocking the relatively good ground to the east of the road should the English decide to fan out there. This was much the more difficult option to counter; as vanguard he placed Moray's schiltron at St Ninian's kirk to the north end of New Park with the two schiltrons of Douglas and Edward Bruce lying some way between him and Moray, Douglas being nearer to Moray (see map). In the event of the English declining to use 'the entry' and approaching along the cornfields, the plan was for Moray to block their advance, at which point Bruce and the other two schiltrons could fall on the exposed English flanks and rear.

In addition to the schiltrons the Scots had their 500 light cavalry which their king was unwilling to commit too soon. Much would depend on how the English decided to use their archers. If they were unwise enough to move them onto open ground without protection from cavalry or spearmen his small body of horsemen might yet play a decisive part. Finally there was the question of what role he might give to his camp followers and servants who were collectively termed 'small folk', along with others who arrived late for muster and who were either too ill-armed or not sufficiently trained to enter the ranks of the schiltrons. In the event Bruce decided to place them to the rear in the valley between Gillies and Coxet hills, from where they could be brought up into the action if the situation became critical.

Having decided on his dispositions the king assembled his commanders and formally revealed his plans. Bruce's own style of leadership and the intrinsic merit and confidence of his leaders would almost certainly have led to questions and some discussion. In a confident tone he confirmed what most had already come to believe, that the English were likely to pass through New Park, 'unless they marched beneath (us) and go over the morass. Thus shall we have them at advantage . . . If we fight on foot we shall always have the advantage for in the Park among the trees the horsemen must always be encumbered and the ditches below must also throw them into confusion'.[11] To reinforce his advantage Bruce also adopted a device which he had used earlier at Loudon Hill, where he canalised his opponents along a narrow track. At 'the entry' he honeycombed the ground on each side of the Roman road with small pits, or pots, the depth of a man's knee (and about a foot across), so close that Barbour likened them to the wax comb of a hive.[12] Bruce and his men toiled all Saturday night, digging them and then covering the relatively small snares with sticks and grass. This 'medieval minefield' would be quite enough to break horses' legs and Barbour for one was satisfied with the effectiveness of such devices. However, a single contemporary authority, Friar Baston, who accompanied the English, says that Bruce made them more deadly still by placing iron spikes in the holes. Two later commentators, Christison and Traquair, have gone further and speak of calthrops (three-pronged iron spikes) standing in the pots to maim the horses.[13] Bruce's intention was to force the English into a position where they could not use their greater numbers, particularly of horsemen, to advantage. With 'minefields' of pots on both flanks they would be forced onto a narrow front where he would meet them with massed spearmen. In any case with horses trapped in the pots the whole momentum of the charge would slacken.

On the morning of Sunday 23 June, the eve of the feast of St John the Baptist, the Scots heard mass and ate a frugal breakfast. After mass Bruce inspected the pots and then assembled his forces. A commander's address was often transmitted (section by section) by appointed heralds to the whole army but Bruce's force was so small and close-packed that he went down the lines talking and looking into the faces of his men. Even then, after so many engagements together, he offered them a choice, namely 'whatsoever man found his heart not assured to stand and win all, and to maintain that mighty struggle or die with honour, should betimes leave the field, and that none should remain but those who would stand by him to the end, and take the fortune God sent'.[14] As the king fully expected, all answered with a great shout that they would not fail him for fear of death until the battle was won. At this point the servants and 'small folk' were sent to the base of Gillies Hill for their protection.

Meanwhile the English army had begun the final leg of its

journey. Two men had particular reasons for wanting to learn more about the English line of advance and the tactics they were likely to adopt. They were, of course, Moubray, the Scot who governed Stirling Castle for the English and had watched with growing unease the careful and thorough Scottish preparations for defence, and Bruce himself. Bruce decided to send out James Douglas together with Keith, his cavalry commander, to report on the English army's progress. What they in fact saw has been graphically described by Barbour who would certainly not want to under-emphasise the task Bruce faced, '. . . so many braided banners, standards, and spear pennons, and so many mounted knights all flaming in gay attire, and so many broad battles taking such vast space as they rode, as might, by their number and battle array, have dismayed the greatest and boldest and best host in Christendom'.[15]

The observers, of course, could not know how tired the English felt although they could have suspected that under Edward II's direction the army was probably not as well trained as it might be. There would, of course, be opportunities to test their opponent's cohesion and their discipline later but, meanwhile, Bruce ordered his observers to say that the enemy were in 'ill-array' to help raise the spirits of his men.

Sir Philip Moubray came upon the English army just after midday when it was still about three miles from the castle. To reach them he had ridden round the Scots' flank by way of Gillies Hill and it appears he might have been given safe conduct to do so by Bruce.[16] Bruce's purpose here is not altogether clear but Moubray asked to see the king and told him the Scots had blocked 'the entry' and that any attack upon them in that region could therefore prove difficult. In any case – and this could have been Bruce's reason for the safe conduct – he reminded Edward that by coming within three miles of the castle the army had technically relieved it.[17] In practice the large numbers of Scots close by still controlled the area.

What happened then will never be completely clear. While Moubray was meeting Edward, the English advance party continued to make its way towards the castle along the Roman road. We do not know whether the king took Moubray's warnings seriously or not, nor whether he felt he was unable – or unwilling – to stop the advance party's approach. However, both the Lanercost chronicler and Thomas Grey in his *Scalcronica*, are agreed that for some reason or other the advance party did not stop but that – in the highly unlikely case of it suffering some check – the English decided to send forward an additional force of 300 horsemen under Sir Robert Clifford and Sir Henry Beaumont (Barbour had their numbers as high as 800) along open ground to the east of the road either to help relieve the castle or to surround the woods at its base to prevent the Scots getting away.[18]

Whether the English main body halted before Clifford and Beaumont's powerful detachment was despatched is not altogether clear. It is more than possible that it did. However, the direction Clifford and Beaumont chose for their own sweep is indisputable. To reach the castle unawares their obvious approach was by Moubray's route, fording the Bannock Burn at a point west of the Roman road and making their way round the back of Gillies Hill. In fact, they opted for a much shorter route, crossing the burn where the gorge levelled out and following the bridle path that ran below the sharp descent onto the carse. They must have thought it a good decision for they could see Stirling Castle directly ahead of them outlined in the bright sun. To their immediate front the plain appeared to be clear of enemy troops and, after they had forded the fast-flowing Pelstream and spurred their horses up its further bank, it seemed as if nothing could prevent them from reaching their goal.

Meanwhile, the English vanguard continued its progression up the Roman road directly towards the Scottish positions. If Moubray had come upon the English column at a point behind the vanguard he would not have been able to tell them about the Scots' dispositions and, even if the king had taken Moubray's warnings seriously and despatched a herald forward, he would not have reached the vanguard before they met the Scottish opposition. Barbour, for one is quite clear the vanguard were told nothing of Moubray's warnings for he describes the army halting and taking council whether they should pitch camp that night or join battle at once. But, says Barbour, 'the vanguard knew nothing of this halt and delay and rode with good array, without stopping, straight to the Park'.[19] For this to happen one must question whether the English king was fully in control of events and, if not, whether he had appointed one of his veteran commanders, such as Valence, to co-ordinate matters on his behalf. For whatever reasons, two separate groups were now rapidly approaching the Scottish positions, the cavalry battle under Clifford and Beaumont moving by way of a bridle path below the scarp, seeking a route to Stirling Castle in order to relieve it, and the vanguard, the corps d'élite of the English army, moving towards the castle by way of the Roman road. Neither seemed aware of the other. The English command system was already starting to unravel.

Equally serious, the English problems of command were not only felt at the highest level, but further down the hierarchy as well, for the king had allowed both detachments to be under joint command, a disastrous situation during a battle. The Romans had operated the unwieldy command system of consuls taking control on alternate days, but on each day no one could doubt who was in charge. Barbour suggests that Clifford had the chief command of his and Beaumont's forces, although this is by no means certain. More serious still, there was no acknowledged commander of the vanguard where the young, spirited Gilbert de Clare, Earl of Gloucester, the king's nephew, shared command with the imperious Humphrey de Bohun, Earl of Hereford, hereditary constable of England, and a bitter rival of the Clares.

Both advancing formations moved with a lack of caution suggesting they were still far from convinced the Scots would dare to take on heavy cavalry in open battle. A clash between the English and Scottish forces was now certain: on what scale and with what results would soon become evident.

CHAPTER EIGHT

≈

ENCOUNTERS – DAY ONE

'Hast thou found me, O mine enemy?'

1 Kings 21:20

THE ENGLISH VANGUARD PRESSED on through the Torwood. After being restricted earlier to the pace of the main body it must have been exhilarating swinging along the road towards the castle. They could hardly believe they would be allowed to reach it unopposed, but after the long march the previous day they had been slow to set off from Falkirk and as it was now late afternoon Hereford was conscious there was little time to strike at the Scots that day. A detachment of young knights and esquires along with some of Hereford's Welsh soldiers, all well-mounted, rode ahead of their seniors. Coming out of Torwood at Snabhead they caught sight of their goal, the great castle standing on its lofty grey crags, seemingly close enough to touch, with trails of smoke from its kitchen fires drifting lazily above. Before them they saw the road descend into a valley and, after making their way down its steep incline, they came upon a considerable stream (the Bannock Burn) that crossed it.

They splashed through it and after climbing the road on the other side shouted to each other in delight when they sighted a number of Scottish footsoldiers apparently withdrawing into the woods of the New Park.[1] In reality they were being marshalled into formation. Bruce's scouts would certainly have kept him posted about the progress of the English main body but he might well have been surprised by the speedy progress of the vanguard. It never seemed to have crossed the minds of the young men that the defenders, who so far had not contested their invasion, would dare to withstand armoured horsemen in broad daylight and in open country. Most of the riders had one thought, to catch the Scots before they entered the protection of the woods. Spurring their horses forward the leading horsemen rode pell-mell for the enemy. As they were seemingly not affected by Robert Bruce's 'pots' positioned on both sides of the road it is likely they rode straight down it and continued to follow its course up the hill towards the enemy's position.

To the rear of the group was Hereford's nephew, Sir Henry de Bohun, who, rather more thoughtful than his bellicose companions, noticed that although the Scots had undoubtedly seen them they were not in fact running for the protection of the woods. He paused and shrewdly signalled his men to pull back a little towards the burn to await further reinforcements. De Bohun then caught sight of a figure who rode out some 30 metres in front of the Scottish soldiers, dressed in mail, riding a sturdy grey hack with a light hand axe hanging from its saddle. On his head he wore a conical steel head piece and above it a cap of hardened leather surmounted by a crown. In spite of his earlier cautiousness this was something de Bohun could not resist: he realised he had been given a unique chance not only to end what seemed an interminable war but to gain personal fame, for did men not say that the Scottish king was the second most renowned knight in Christendom? De Bohun himself was mounted on a barded horse and was fully armed and protected. He did not hesitate. From some 200 metres away he lowered his helm, pointed his lance straight forward and picking up his horse cantered across the rough grass towards his opponent before accelerating into a full charge over the final 50 metres. With such an uneven contest, Bruce had good reason to seek the protection of his spearmen before re-emerging when he was properly equipped. But whatever prudence might have dictated, the Scottish king was standing in front of soldiers prepared to hazard their lives for him. In any case, as he caught sight of the De Bohun arms on the young knight's surcoat, it would have been hard for him to forget that it was the De Bohuns who had received his Annandale and Carrick estates after they had been seized by Edward I. Bruce coolly held his ground and let the young knight thunder close until, a moment before the galloping rider could impale him, he pulled away from De Bohun's line of strike, remaining close enough to raise himself in his stirrups and swing his axe down upon the knight's helmet. His stroke was to such good effect that the axe 'clove skull and brain' before its shaft broke.

Bruce's first blow of the campaign had a predictable effect on his followers. With a triumphant shout they made a concerted forward movement with their spears extended to meet the rest of the English vanguard that had followed De Bohun but as the vanguard attempted to form up into battle order it experienced serious difficulties with Bruce's 'pots'. In the subsequent meleé De Bohun's squire, who gallantly rushed forward to stand over his fallen master, was killed, while Gloucester the English co-commander was unhorsed. The clash developed into a considerable engagement in which Bruce's full schiltron took part. It ended when, after suffering a number of casualties and being unsure how far the 'pots' extended on both sides of the road, the English withdrew down the line of the road to the south of the Bannock Burn. The Scots commenced to pursue but they were recalled by Bruce lest they lost cohesion and let themselves become vulnerable to the horsemen. When they came back the soldiers gathered round their king in delight, although their commanders, conscious of his unique importance to their cause, reproached him for his rash action. Bruce made no attempt to justify himself and seemed quite content to let his deeds speak for themselves, except for making the wry comment that he was sorry to have broken his good axe.[2]

While this engagement was taking place, the second English cavalry force had also been advancing; after crossing the Pelstream they were almost level with St Ninians. The route they had taken along the carse had not been anticipated by Bruce, although Moray's scouts should have picked them up below St Ninian's kirk. In the stress of action Scottish leadership was also showing some deficiencies, although, if the English acted predictably, there was still a fair chance to retrieve the situation. Inevitably it was Bruce who spotted Clifford and Beaumont riding northwards in their attempt to circle New Park from the east. Moray

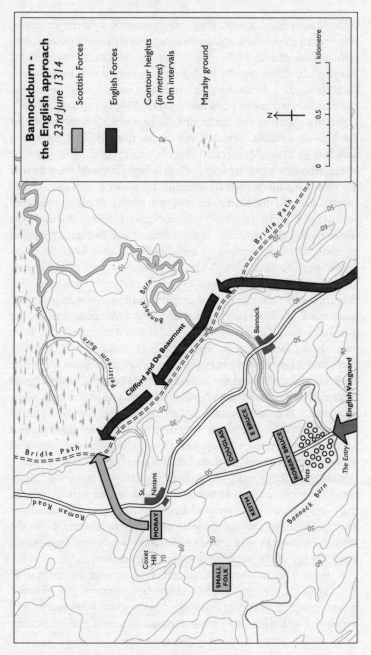

**Bannockburn –
the English approach**
23rd June 1314

Scottish Forces

English Forces

Contour heights
(in metres)
10m intervals

Marshy ground

N

0   0.5   1 kilometre

Bridle Path

Bannock Burn

Pelstream Burn

Clifford and De Beaumont

Bannock

English Vanguard

Bridle Path

E BRUCE

DOUGLAS

ROBERT BRUCE

Pots

The Entry

Bannock Burn

St. Ninians

Roman Road

KEITH

MORAY

Coxet Hill

SMALL FOLK

himself who was with the king rather than his own schiltron was quite unaware of the English movement and Bruce turned on him with a flash of anger telling him that, 'a rose had fallen from his chaplet'. In other words, he had let his king down by allowing English cavalry to move past him, thus heavily compromising the Scottish defensive position. At this, Moray turned and rode hurriedly back to his men, just in time to lead them out of the woods near St Ninians and make towards the armoured knights.

Beaumont was in the lead and although he could have swung his riders round the spearmen and, by making straight for the castle, cut off the Scots' retreat, no Englishman at this time seemed willing to avoid a battle. Beaumont's first reaction was the need to make space in order to surround the spearmen and he shouted at those close to him, 'Let us wait a little; let them come on; give them room'.[3] Beside him the veteran Sir Thomas Grey was less sanguine about seeking battle in this way and with the prospects of unsupported cavalry against massed spearmen. He turned to Beaumont and said: 'My lord, give them what you like now; I'm afraid that in a short while they will have everything.' What Grey's sombre words meant is not clear but there was likely to have been bad ground to one or more of their flanks which prevented the English from taking full advantage of their mobility. With the exception of Grey and, no doubt, some few others, the vast majority of English knights seemed haunted by the possibility of showing any trace of fear against their Scottish opponents and incapable of considering more measured actions against them. Beaumont's hot and utterly inappropriate rejoinder to Grey was, 'Flee then. Flee if you're afraid.' Grey shouted back, 'Fear will not make me flee, my Lord,' and, in mindless gallantry, he spurred his horse on between Beaumont and Sir William Deyncourt who were heading straight for the spears. Deyncourt was killed immediately while the Scots pulled Grey off his dying horse and took him prisoner.

A fierce and prolonged engagement followed as the rest of the cavalry came up. Under Moray's command the Scottish infantry took up circular formation as they had been taught and presented a double line of spear points towards the horsemen.

They, lacking archers, had no choice but to move around them, then charge forward at any possible gap appearing in the ranks. The spearmen set their points straight forward, directly at the horses, probing for vulnerable areas. If the mounts could be brought down their armoured riders were likely to be pinned under them, or if the horses reared up in face of the blood-stained tips, some riders would suffer heavy falls and find themselves lying helpless on the ground amid threshing hooves.

It was the same story as Falkirk until Edward I brought up his archers. As the members of the schiltron stood shoulder to shoulder offering an impenetrable wall of spears it appeared invincible. The English mounted attack after attack without success and, in their rage and frustration at not breaking through the shield wall their knights hurled spears, darts and maces – even swords – into the heart of the formation in vain attempts to maim its occupants, until a pile of such weapons built up inside it. Whereas the English were without bowmen, there were possibly some men within the schiltrons carrying shortbows who brought down both men and horses, although Evan Barron, for one, was sure the Lanercost chronicler was more likely to be describing individual footsoldiers who, dashing out from the spear walls, stabbed and cut down their fallen assailants at close quarters or, as happened with Thomas Grey, dragged them inside the spear walls to be held prisoner.

The noise and movement created by the horsemen surrounding the beleaguered schiltron was unceasing. Yet although the English cavalry, like a pack of hunting dogs around a boar, had trapped the spearmen they were quite unable to get beneath their spear tusks to reach the formation's soft underbelly. All thoughts about the cavalry's tactical objective of joining up with the castle's garrison were forgotten as, in their pride and rage at being thwarted by footsoldiers, they mounted sally after sally against their obdurate opponents. The plunging horses raised choking clouds of dust around the schiltron while a cloud of steam rose above it from the close-packed spearmen clad in thick tunics and clumsy bassinets, as they strained to keep the heads of their long, unwieldy spears facing forward.

James Douglas, who commanded the schiltron nearest to

Moray's, and was never happier than when he was fighting, approached the king with offers of help. At first Bruce refused. He was confident of the schiltron in such conditions, and sure that he detected some wavering amongst the attackers. Moray should be allowed to take his rightful credit. However, when after a further period of din and dust matters still remained unresolved Bruce eventually agreed to Douglas joining in. As Douglas brought his spearmen closer to Moray he saw the king was right: the English attacks were plainly losing momentum as their knights became baffled and frustrated at being kept at spears' length by the Scottish formation. Chivalrously he stopped his own schiltron to allow Moray a well-earned victory, but the very sight of his approach confused the English cavalry and some attempted to wheel about to meet the fresh enemy.

At this Moray saw his opportunity and assumed the offensive, charging right through their ranks. One part of the broken English squadron galloped towards the castle, while the larger one made for the main army. Both were seen to be in great disorder after suffering serious casualties and following such a surprising turn of events. Amazingly, during the whole engagement Moray's schiltron lost just one yeoman, although many of his men were bound to have sustained cuts and bruises. Worn out and soaked in sweat, at Moray's command his men slumped down on the ground, took off their helmets and began to relish their triumph. They had seen off the enemy – for a time at least. After a scout reported their victory to the king, together with the amazingly low casualty figures, the rest of the army moved over to congratulate them and salute the earl.[4]

In the exhilaration of the moment such men – or their opponents for that matter – would scarcely have been aware that their success marked a new development in warfare. The signs had been there at Falkirk before Edward I intervened with his archers, but now spearmen had not only defended themselves successfully against armoured cavalry, they had then moved onto the offensive and driven them off the field. While in 1302, at Courtrai, Flemish peasant infantry protected by a stream had defeated French nobility on their horses, Moray's men, unlike the Flemings, challenged cavalry in the open and on good ground.

By the time Clifford returned to the main English army he was compelled to admit he had failed to open up a route for them to relieve Stirling. In any case, it was now so late that no further offensive action could be contemplated before the following day.

Although the English losses during that afternoon had not been heavy and they still retained their great numerical superiority, the effect of the two clashes on the morale of both armies was tremendous. As the English chronicler of Lanercost said: 'From that moment began a panic among the English and the Scots grew bolder.'[5] Napoleon, a great commander by any standard, considered good morale crucial for success, going as far as to say that this was to the material as three is to one. If that were really so, the events at Bannockburn on day one were worth a minimum of 5000 extra men to Robert Bruce and his army. Whatever the effects, with a break in hostilities commanders on both sides had the opportunity to digest the lessons of the early encounters and decide on their actions for the next day.

CHAPTER NINE

WEIGHING THE ODDS

'He either fears his fate too much,
Or his desserts are small
That puts it not unto the touch
To win or lose it all.'

James Graham, 1st Marquis of Montrose

BOTH SIDES NOW HAD to consider their next moves. Among the English there was some confusion and a mood of new caution,[1] replacing the earlier blind presumption of victory and contempt for their enemy. As yet, however, apart from the cavalry detachments, no one in the English army had even seen the enemy, much less contacted them. Most of the soldiers were not only unaware of what was going on but were unable to break ranks to find out. In the circumstances, the cavalry would have been reluctant to proclaim their misfortunes, and hard news would be substituted by rumours, the scourge of any military organisation. However, the sight of once proud knights returning, weaponless, some with their surcoats ripped or missing, others bloodstained and leading injured horses, needed no embellishing. Rumours said they had run from infantry spearmen and some of the footsoldiers would have been less than human if they had not been pleased to see the cavalry 'peacocks' so humbled. At the same time these men were bound to feel that if Scottish spearmen could beat English cavalry what chance would they, ordinary English levies so despised by their own horsemen, have against them? Standing immobile along the roadside the English had ample time to wonder whether their latest invasion would prove as easy as they had been led to believe. Barbour had the traditionally superstitious soldiers whispering together 'in five hundred places or more' saying, 'Our Lords will always use their might against the right and when they wage war unrighteously God is offended and brings misfortune and so it may happen now'.[2]

Many must have suspected that something had already gone seriously wrong for a king whom everyone knew was no equal to his father when it came to either fighting or praying. The rank and file quite expected him to share their own barons' scorn for footsoldiers but to their alarm he was also generally thought to have little regard for archers either.[3] As they waited amid the lengthening shadows their draught animals would have grown fractious in their need for water and grazing. After the physical demands of the journey both men and animals were tired and the longer the army stood immobile the greater the soldiers' conviction – and for many their relief – that there would be no further fighting that day. Not all the levies swept into the ranks by the sheriffs' summons were the most enthusiastic or fittest of soldiers, nor were they enamoured by the long hot hours spent plodding along dusty roads in a country stripped of people and livestock. Such men would not hesitate to admit their weariness and start enquiring when and where they would be making camp.

In such circumstances good leadership was of the greatest importance, but instead of showing himself to his army the king sent heralds down the seemingly endless column to explain and justify the recent setbacks. The message they carried was reasonable enough. So far, they told the soldiers, there had been only skirmishing but 'in the great battle they could by no means fail, and that when the Scots fled full amends should indeed be made'.[4] No hint of plunder, however, could change what these men already knew. Their so-called invincible knights had already been given bloody noses. In all fairness one has to wonder what else could have been done, although the same message delivered with an air of authority by the king or his senior representative would surely have been far more effective. But it is unlikely Edward appointed a deputy; it probably suited him better to keep his nobles in perpetual rivalry of each other.

Yet a decision was required urgently; it was getting late and the Scots still held the entry route to the castle. An army stretched along miles of road had to be gathered into a suitable assembly area before it could resume offensive action the next day. The English commanders knew it was imperative they made camp and brought their scattered units together but given Bruce's renowned aggressiveness – and recent successes – the chosen location had to be suitable for defence against any surprise hit and run attacks during the night. The nature of the ground before the castle and the very size of the force made selection difficult. The army could, of course, have been drawn back into Torwood but retracing their steps in such a way would not have been good for morale and the forest would give the enemy good opportunities to approach unobserved. Equally important in such a location, water was likely to be short and their animals, including the precious horses, were becoming dehydrated.

After the army had learned about the unexpected rebuffs to its cavalry any decision was bound to be something of a compromise, especially as there seems to have been no prior consideration about suitable laagering areas before the castle. It had never been thought they would be needed. In the event the English commanders decided to send their cavalry, and the greater part of their infantry onto the carse land two miles eastwards away from the Scots' positions both at the entry and in the region of St Ninians. Most of the heavy transport would, however, have to laager nearer the road. Another seeming advantage of the site was that it allowed the cavalry and infantry to move beyond the deep gorge containing the Bannock Burn to a point where the land levelled out and they would be able to ford the burn relatively easily. Although many of their accompanying wagons would still be unable to cross over, the carse promised plenty of water and it was open enough to prevent any surprise attacks from the Scots. Such thinking was legitimate enough; but what the English did not fully anticipate was the scale of the problems involved in making camp on such wet and treacherous terrain, nor those posed by its confining water courses.

Both Barbour and Grey described the chosen locality. Barbour is quite matter-of-fact: 'The host therefore quartered that night in the carse and made all ready, and got their gear in order against the battle. Because of the pools in the carse they broke down house and thatch and carried them to make bridges that they might pass over . . . so that before day they had bridged the pools, and the host had all passed over, and with their horses occupied the firm ground, and, arrayed in their gear, stood ready to give battle.'[5] Barbour probably thought he hardly needed to emphasise they had struggled all night to get so organised, especially as any colourful description of English exhaustion would tend to detract from the performance of his Scottish champions the following day. The Englishman Grey gives an altogether darker picture. 'The king's host which having already left the road through the wood had debauched upon a plain near the water of the River Forth, beyond Bannockburn, an evil, deep, wet marsh where the said English army unharnessed and remained all night, having sadly lost confidence and being too much disaffected by the events of the day.'[6] The *Life of Edward II* confirmed the English had moved over the Bannock Burn to the carse, as did the *Lanercost Chronicle*, describing the obstacle as 'a great ditch into which the tide comes from the sea, called the Bannockburn'.[7]

The massive English forces, unsettled by conflicting rumours about the reverses suffered by their heavy cavalry, were about to spend an exhausting and sleepless night on the carse with their high command still far from unanimous about the king's wish to fight the next day.

The Scots were in a very different position although at this stage they had not decided on their own course of action. By now Bruce knew any coming battle would not take place on his chosen site where the Bannock Burn crossed the Roman road to Stirling. He could not expect to trap the English in his minefield a second time. In any case having moved onto the carse the English were most unlikely to return to the entry point before resuming their progress to the castle. Bruce's knowledge of the ground and the decision taken by the English commanders to camp on the carse led him to think the invaders would now choose to advance over the open ground between the New Park and the carse, where defenders could not use woodland for protection and which was too wide for 'pots' to be dug to hamper them. It also represented relatively good terrain for cavalry. Bruce, too, had an important decision to make. Having inflicted two humiliating reverses on his opponents he could either be satisfied with that and withdraw westwards to wild country where the English could not pursue him, or opt for the much more hazardous choice of taking on the great English host. While the first was by much the safer course of action it would allow the English to claim they had in fact succeeded in their campaign objective, namely the relief of Stirling Castle. There are two versions of how he arrived at his decision.

The first account by Barbour referred to the period before the English had made camp when Moray's victorious schiltron rejoined the Scots' main army and was surrounded by happy and excited men. Barbour has Bruce taking the opportunity of sounding out many of the soldiers standing together by putting the most crucial of questions to them, speaking as follows:

'I am full well assured that many an (English) heart shall waver that seemed erstwhile of mighty valour. And if the heart be dismayed, the body is not worth a mite. I trow, therefore, that a good ending shall follow this beginning. Nevertheless, I say not this to you in order that ye shall follow my desire to fight; for with you will rest the whole matter. If you think it expedient that we fight, we shall fight; and if ye will that we depart, your desire will be fulfilled. I shall consent to do in either fashion right as ye shall decide. Therefore speak plainly your desire.'

Barbour has them responding in a heroic vein:

'Good King, without more delay, tomorrow, as soon as ye see light, ordain you wholly for the battle. We shall not fail you for fear of death, nor shall any effort be wanting till we have made our country free.'[8]

It sounds almost too good to be true, although the Scots' initial success against the English cavalry would have done wonders for morale and a portion of these men would have already accompanied Bruce during some of his earlier engagements against English forces. After his successes they were quite likely to be happy to go on following him. The Englishman Grey gave another version. He said the Scots being well satisfied with their day's work after calling a conference of their senior commanders, had decided to break off hostilities and were on the point 'of decamping in order to march during the night to the Lennox' when Sir Alexander Seton, a Scots knight in the English service, repelled by the lack of leadership and sense of defeatism in their camp, made his way to Bruce and told the king, 'My Lord King, this is the time if ever you intend to undertake to reconquer Scotland. The English have lost heart and are discouraged, and expect nothing but a sudden, open attack.' He described their unhappy condition and pledged his head on pain of being hanged and drawn, that if he (Bruce) would attack them on the morrow he would defeat them easily without (much) loss.[9]

Seton was unlikely to have been fully trusted in spite of his offering to stake his life on the accuracy of his report. The news he brought, though, gave Bruce further evidence for his growing conviction that the English actions so far had been far from impressive. He realised well enough that as yet he had repulsed only two relatively small English divisions, albeit from the cream of the English cavalry and it would inevitably be very different when his soldiers had to face the full English army, with its unrivalled complement of cavalry who this time would be supported by archers and overwhelming numbers of infantry. Conversely after blundering into his prepared positions the English had compounded their difficulties by deciding to make camp on a stretch of wet and broken carseland. For such reasons, whether or not Bruce and his commanders had actually decided to move away, they now decided to take on the massive English army.

Understandably, neither side enjoyed much sleep. The English cavalry spent virtually the whole night in utilising planks and beams stripped from nearby houses to help move their horses and stores onto firm ground and, once there they kept a proportion of their excitable chargers bitted and tacked up to meet any surprise Scottish attacks. As for the English infantry allotted the wettest part of the carse, with no tents for shelter, they dulled their discomfort from sodden garments and clouds of voracious

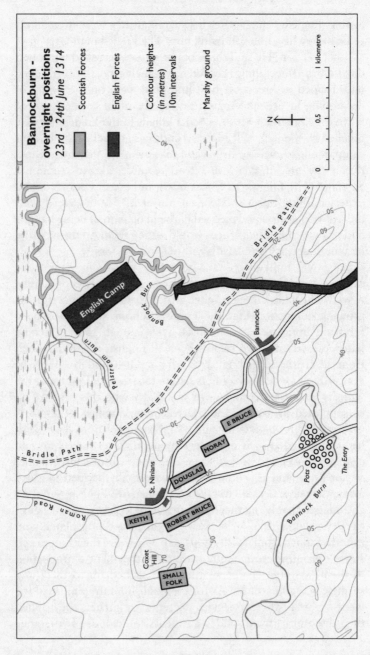

Bannockburn –
overnight positions
23rd – 24th June 1314

Scottish Forces

English Forces

Contour heights
(in metres)
10m intervals

Marshy ground

insects with strong drink, keeping up their courage with endless shouts of 'Wassail' and 'Drinkhail'.[10] The few who did not join in would have found it difficult if not impossible to sleep through the noise. Such revelling, which must have been countenanced by their leaders, was not good for discipline nor for the cool heads needed on the coming day. As Friar Baston subsequently wrote bitingly about their revels, 'They kill thee Scotland with vain words upbraiding'.[11] In any case, at this time of year the night was remarkably short; at Stirling it was down to three hours of dusk rather than full darkness, and as early as 3.45 a.m. on the 24 June the lightening of dawn began to be apparent.

By then the Scottish king in a repeat of Edward I's actions before the battle of Falkirk, when he had sent his army to hear mass, made his confession to Maurice, Abbot of Inchaffray and commanded him and other priests to offer mass for his soldiers which they did on a small feature at the edge of a wood.[12] Abbot Maurice had brought the relics of St Fillan to whom Bruce was devoted, and Abbot Bernard of Arbroath carried the casket containing the remains of St Columba (the Monymusk reliquary) with which to bless the army. By such means Bruce had his troops commit their bodies and souls into the safekeeping of their Maker and as a further pledge of their faith on this important feast day of St John the Baptist they ate plain bread and water. After their frugal meal they began to assemble in their respective schiltrons carrying distinguishing banners as the king had commanded them. When the ranks were drawn up they watched Bruce carrying out the traditional ceremony of knighting selected individuals, including the young Walter Stewart and he created James Douglas a knight Banneret (a senior cavalry commander), an award conferred only on the battlefield. They would have seen the king slashing off the forks of Douglas' knight's pennon with his sword and replacing it with the banneret's square standard.

Such religions and civil ceremonies both helped to remind Bruce's men what was required of them and also served to emphasise the worth of their leaders. Shortly afterwards Bruce addressed the assembled army with words that sounded the same themes. His speech was recorded by Bernard, Abbot of Arbroath, Bruce's chancellor who, some six years later, was almost certainly responsible for the declaration sent from Arbroath to the Pope in support of Scotland's independence. Bruce's address was notable not only for its powerful moral and patriotic tone but also for its egalitarianism:

> My lords, my people, accustomed to enjoy that full freedom for which in times gone by the Kings of Scotland have fought many a battle. For eight years or more I have struggled with much labour for my right to the Kingdom and for honourable liberty. I have lost brothers, friends and kinsmen. Your own kinsmen have been made captive, and bishops and priests are locked in prison. Our country's nobility has poured forth its blood in war. These barons you can see before you, clad in mail, are bent upon destroying me and obliterating my kingdom, nay, our whole nation. They do not believe we can survive. They glory in their warhorses and equipment. For us, the name of the Lord must be our hope of victory in battle . . . if you heartily repent of your sins you will be victorious, under God's command.

Finally Bruce offered material benefits to those among his men who like many other soldiers down the ages, would have joined him to escape from the law, probably for misdemeanours committed in their native townships or localities 'As for offences committed against the Crown, I proclaim a pardon, by virtue of my royal power, to all those who fight manfully for the kingdom of our fathers'.[13]

For the men of substance Bruce promised the remission of feudal dues for the heirs of any killed in battle. Bruce's order to commence hostilities followed immediately. Not only had he decided to fight but he devised a calculating and highly daring plan, one that depended on his army being able to confine the English within the area of their chosen camp. With the two armies so close together he was unable to conceal his preparations and as it became fully light English scouts reported that the Scots seemed fully prepared for battle.

In contrast, on the English side there was no such urgency,

virtually their whole concern over the last few hours had been making camp in what had turned out to be most difficult circumstances. They assumed they would be able to move their army's different units into battle formation before proceeding towards the castle, whether or not they were to meet opposing forces on the way. The news of the Scots' preparedness therefore caught the English leaders off guard. The night before Edward's veteran commanders, together with the Earl of Gloucester, had recommended postponing any advance on Stirling Castle for twenty-four hours. Both moral and practical arguments were voiced against advancing the next day, namely that it was a saints day – a fact not rated that highly by the king – but more importantly because much reordering of their formations was needed before they could meet an assembled enemy, and in any case, after its hard march, the army was close to exhaustion. None of these considerations seemed to carry much weight with the king nor with the hot-bloods among his councillors to whom any further delay was anathema.

Notwithstanding such different points of view within the English camp, even those who counselled caution and time to balance the army did not propose taking up a position of all-round defence involving mixed units of cavalry, bowmen and infantry. None of the English commanders considered the possibility of an attack by the Scottish main army. This was particularly so with the king. While he may have felt some slight reservations after the outcome of the previous day, he declared himself fully confident in his far superior force and it seems that detailed tactics were apparently not discussed at any time. In fairness, standing there on broken ground enclosed by two tidal streams with a major river at his back, any commander would know that major changes in formation would best be left until the army moved out onto the plain, where it could expect to meet the Scots if they tried to block its progress to the castle. In any event, there seemed no undue haste for, although the Scots were apparently ready to meet them, and they had put cavalry to flight on the previous day, they would never dare leave the shelter of their prepared positions to attack the entire English army.

Before recounting the dramatic events of the battle it is worth being as clear as possible about its location and it is hoped the reader will find the map at p123 helpful here. Although we are fortunate to have contemporary descriptions of the battle, recounted as they are in considerable detail, there are still conflicting theories about exactly where the main Scottish and English armies met. The initial problem arises because in their descriptions, neither John Barbour nor Thomas Grey gave the battle a clear name (which would surely have helped to pinpoint it). In fact, two names were used in letters written about it from 1314–19: Englishmen called it the battle of Stirling and early Scottish writers (from the early fourteenth until the fifteenth century) referred to it as the battle of Bannock,[14] both versions giving way to the general title, the battle of Bannockburn.

It would be far simpler if the different interpretations had been restricted to these place names but over the years historians on the battle have come up with four different sites with a variation of up to two miles. It seems hardly credible that despite the highly acidic nature of the soil, there should be no evidence of the mass graves dug after the battle which would materially help define its location. However, a detailed analysis of the soil in the most likely areas has yet to be carried out and unfortunately much recent building has made any such study considerably more difficult, if not impossible. With no clear scientific proof one can only continue, like earlier historians, to make deductions from the contemporary accounts, combined with a detailed examination of the ground.

The first, or traditional, site was at the borestone to the west of the map's lower segment which adjoins the present National Trust heritage centre and Robert Bruce's great equestrian statue. This can be rapidly eliminated. While Bruce conceivably used the area of the borestone to watch the English army approach the Bannock Burn and placed his reserve in its general vicinity, it is virtually certain that the main battle on 24 June was not fought there. Admittedly in 1913, the same year as William Mackay MacKenzie published his pioneering account of the battle, another commentator was still of the belief that the site of the borestone was not open to doubt, but following MacKenzie's powerful arguments against this location no serious authority has subsequently supported it.[15] Contemporary accounts of the battle describe enclosed flanks and the difficulties experienced by the English in getting their infantry forward – but while the borestone site to the north of the Bannock Burn offers some protection for the Scottish east flank by a steep slope, on the opposite flank open ground gives ample opportunity for cavalry, together with supporting infantry, to circle and thus compromise the whole Scottish position.

MacKenzie argued that the true site was on the carse of Stirling, near Muirtown, some two miles northeast of the borestone and almost the same distance from the village of Bannock. On this site the opposing forces would be confined within the water courses of the Forth and the Bannock Burn. Yet MacKenzie's site was only half the story. Unlike earlier commentators, who placed the Scottish army north of the Bannock Burn and the English to its south, MacKenzie turned the opposing forces round almost ninety degrees to have the Scots facing east and the English confronting them from a westerly direction within an area bounded by the Bannock Burn and an enclosing bend of the river Forth. Along with his relentless and careful reasoning MacKenzie cited in confirmation an illustration from an early manuscript of the *Scotichronicon* which shows the Scots at Bannockburn with Stirling Castle to their left and the Bannock Burn on their right.[16]

Although subsequent commentators have accepted MacKenzie's east/west alignment they have disputed his proposed location. Professor Barrow, for instance, has pointed out that MacKenzie mistakenly interpreted the Celtic word 'pol' as pool, whereas pols were, in fact, sluggish streams. Barrow concluded that MacKenzie's confusion about the pols led him to place his site in the buckle of the Forth further to the east of Bannockburn village than the descriptions indicated. According to Barrow the name of the battle also contradicted MacKenzie's 'far eastern' site. If the battle had been fought that far east it would have continued to be named after Stirling rather than Bannock, a long-established settlement quoted, for instance, in the *Chronicle of Melsa* during the early fifteenth century.[17] If, following MacKenzie's detailed arguments, the borestone site to the extreme west is rejected and, following Barrow, MacKenzie's Muirtown site to the extreme east is also rejected, one is left with a location within an area stretching from the Dryfield (where corn was planted) eastwards to the carse of Balquhiderock.

Although this rules out the sites at the two extremities the problem remains of where the two sides clashed within the carse of Balquhiderock. The Rev Thomas Miller writing with Brigadier General Carruthers in 1931,[18] favoured the area of the Dryfield to the west of the carse (also supported by Professor Barrow) but in the late 1950s General Christison argued powerfully for a site somewhat further east, at the mouth of a triangle formed by the Bannock Burn, its tributary the Pelstream Burn, and the steep slope descending from the Dryfield at the base of which runs the bridle path from Bannock to Stirling.[19] Christison cites the Pelstream Burn as playing a vital part in confining the English army. This site is currently supported by the National Trust for Scotland, although later writers remain divided on the question. Ronald McNair Scott[20] supports Christison's version, while Peter Traquair[21] in 1998 reverted to the Miller/Carruthers interpretation, reasoning that with his relatively small forces Bruce needed to fight on a narrower front than that of Christison's site. To support his interpretation Traquair endeavoured to point out instances of deep gullies on the Dryfield that he believes could have protected Bruce's flanks.

After walking the ground and considering the different proposals against a series of early maps uncluttered by the wide-ranging modern buildings and before the land was so extensively drained, the author comes to virtually the same conclusions as Christison. Christison's main contributions have been to consider the role of the Pelstream Burn in confining the English right flank – for the Scots to think they could win they must have been confident about some obstacle here in addition to the Bannock Burn on the English left flank – and to reject the possibility of heavy cavalry climbing the steep escarpment bordering the Dryfield in order to approach the Scots position. In fact, the old general was very fierce with Mr Hugo Millar, secretary of the Glasgow Archaeological Society – and other civilian analysts – who were quite prepared to accept that the English climbed onto the escarpment. As an experienced soldier he told Millar that 'a critical study of the military factors of time and space, physical obstacles, fatigue, morale, training, discipline, armament, leadership and tactics is absolutely vital in appraising any battle, however old'. Christison asked him whether he (could) really see Edward II moving up it at night or even less probably, sending his heavy cavalry charging up such a steep escarpment against the Scots entrenched in a well-prepared position.[22] After checking the scarp, it is indeed hard to envisage heavy destriers being set up it, especially as there are no references in the contemporary descriptions to the monumental difficulties that would have been experienced during such an undertaking or to the Scots moving back to enable the English to occupy it. If the English did not climb the scarp, then General Christison's picture of the English being trapped within a narrow pocket of carse east of the scarp, bounded by the Pelstream and Bannock burns, with the Forth to their rear, carries the most conviction.

Another problem is raised with Peter Traquair's assertion that the neck of land between the two burns was over one and a half miles wide. In this case, one must agree with him that the small Scottish army could not block the mouth of the pocket effectively. However, further work on the maps reveals that the actual dimensions of the land between the two burns is not 1.5 miles but somewhat less than 0.7 of a mile wide, a distance which the Scottish forces could certainly have occupied with their spearmen. This was confirmed by re-walking the ground and checking the course of the two burns on either side of the choke point. The Bannock Burn gave no trouble since it is well defined throughout, although it has been robbed of much water by hydro schemes and is no longer the torrent it was in the fourteenth century when its level was raised further by tidal waters from the River Forth. With the extensive drainage of the surrounding area its banks are no longer so slippery although the depth of the gorge on both sides of the present township of Bannockburn is still daunting. The Pelstream Burn is very much diminished due to major changes in the surrounding water table together with drainage and 'smoothing' of the once broken carseland for agricultural use. However, despite everything its course is still clearly definable and the burn continues to be fast flowing. Although today it is difficult to imagine such a narrow stream acting as a genuine obstacle against both cavalry and infantry it must be remembered that in the fourteenth century it, too, was tidal where it flanked the area of the battlefield. In addition within living memory the belt of land stretching from its further bank continued to be exceedingly treacherous and local people have cited instances of horses being drowned there as late as the 1950s. After checking the dimensions between the two burns and considering the nature of the two water courses during the fourteenth century, Christison's arguments for the battle taking place eastwards of the Dryfield within the carse of Balquihiderock seem overwhelming.

Working on such premises, I have indicated on map 3 where I believe the English were camped, together with the positions of their Scottish adversaries during the night of 23/24 June 1314, and where the clash between the two armies took place.

CHAPTER TEN

BATTLE JOINED

'Let us do or die!'

Robert Burns, *Bruce's March to Bannockburn*

HAVING CONCLUDED THE RELIGIOUS and knightly ceremonies and delivered his powerful, if traditional, address before battle, Bruce gave the momentous order to advance across the open carse against the mighty English army, treble the strength of his front line units and equipped with far superior weapons, lying in its encampment between the Bannock and Pelstream burns.

This was the second definitive moment for Scotland in the Wars of Independence, the first being William Wallace's blast on his horn at Stirling Bridge that signalled the charge of his troops down the slopes of Abbey Craig onto the English formations confined in the bend of the river below. Given the enormous risks, Bruce's directive was only possible because of the innovative way he had trained his schiltrons to move forward in echelon formation. Despite the clashes of the previous day, and the forward dash made by Moray's schiltron against Clifford's opposing cavalry, Bruce hoped the English would still view his schiltrons as essentially defensive formations, like William Wallace's, and fail to appreciate fully how vital their mobility was for his plans.

Leaving the protection of the woods the first three schiltrons picked their way down the steep incline of the Dryfield and formed up at its base before starting their move eastwards up the gently rising ground of the carse. Compared with the English the Scottish army travelled light. Their many recent engagements had compelled them to jettison unnecessary stores and their fighting men were remarkably self-sufficient, which was fortunate since there was no question of waggons being used in support. Spearmen had to rely on their personal weapons and the equipment they carried, including spare spears. Bruce had ordered each schiltron to carry banners bearing their leader's arms, such as the three white stars on a blue background of Sir James Douglas or the proud emblem of the black galley against a yellow backcloth for Angus Og MacDonald, Lord of the Isles.

From the base of the scarp they had something over half a mile to travel before reaching the enemy. As they ascended the gentle slope they could see flashes of colour – reds and blues, bright greens and gold, from among the many domed tents in the cavalry lines. Sounds carried across on the clear morning air, swords being sharpened on whet stones, horses whinnying, the burble of talk together with the clanking of cooking pots being stowed away as the English appeared to be breaking camp. The Scottish spearmen knew that if the English brought even a fraction of their archers forward, their deadly firepower would make the task of crossing the grassy plain fronting the English position beyond them. Bruce gambled on the element of surprise and the fact that, although the English were unquestionably far stronger, they were as yet disorganised and above all lacked a planned response.

The Lanercost chronicler had the schiltrons preceded by Scottish archers acting in the role of skirmishers, an excellent way of using the limited number of Scottish shortbowmen. Apart from sacrificing his small cavalry force in a preliminary attack, it was Bruce's one means of giving his spearmen some degree of protection. Some English bowmen, probably those attached to the cavalry units, immediately moved forward to counter this and, although their numbers were only a fraction of those serving with the main body of English infantry, the battlefield observer from Lanercost reported that they scattered their Scottish opponents. However, this clash of archers inevitably diverted fire from the schiltrons as they pressed on to reduce the gap between the two armies and Traquair has the English archers unable to follow up their early successes because of the English vanguard charging out across their line of fire.

Edward Bruce's schiltron took the lead with the appointed task of anchoring its right flank against the Bannock Burn. Coming after him and immediately to his left was Moray, followed by Douglas. Moving up in this order the spearmen began to usher the opposing archers against the English right flank by the Pelstream Burn. The Lanercost chronicler referred to just three Scottish schiltrons and these were all the English could have seen at this stage, although the fourth and largest formation of spearmen directly under the king's command followed some distance behind them.[1] Bruce's concern for his men was, of course, by no means confined to the dangers from English archers, deadly as these might prove. The main threat would come from their cavalry, and his audacity in giving the order to advance over ground favourable for horsemen is all the more remarkable. It should not be forgotten, however, as other Scottish commanders did at Flodden two centuries later, that a schiltron's strength lay in keeping its formation and for this it too needed good ground. Pre-eminently, Bruce knew that in order to reduce the odds he had first to seize and then retain the initiative and it was imperative to meet the enemy head on to give his plan any chance of success. Only then could he succeed in imprisoning the English within their treacherous grassy rectangle, encompassed on three sides by the barriers of the River Forth, the Bannock Burn and the Pelstream Burn, all swollen by the morning's tidal floodwaters. At high tide the waters of the Forth (and its tributaries) were only one or two feet below the general level of the carse and in places they spilled over into adjoining pools.

Given the packed nature of the English forces within the rivers, Bruce's tactics were an even more effective version of those used by William Wallace under the lea of Stirling Castle seventeen years before. If Bruce could first trap and then, equally importantly, start compressing the English, they were bound to experience grave difficulties in bringing more than a small proportion of their forces into action against his lines of spearmen that had proved so effective the previous day. Speed and surprise were vital for, if the English emerged from their camp area and moved onto the plain of Balquhiderock, their numbers would be able to envelop the Scottish infantry and subject it to deadly volleys of arrows before crushing it with combined assaults from cavalry and infantry. Whether or not the English high command at Bannockburn was actually capable of rapidly mounting and then co-ordinating their attacks in such a way was something Bruce could not risk. He had to push his advance forward with all speed.

Whatever their shortcomings in leadership and despite their king's aversion to bowmen, if the English had suspected for a moment that the Scots would emerge from the woods and attack as they did, the more experienced of Edward's commanders would doubtless have already brought forward numbers of foot archers to provide direct support for the cavalry. From their experiences of the day before, Beaumont and Gloucester especially would have been aware of the problems experienced by cavalry against Scottish spearmen and it was, therefore, somewhat surprising that no one pressed for some detachments of foot archers to be placed in the forward lines, however unlikely the event of a Scottish attack. No Englishman could have doubted Bruce's previous successes against adverse odds, nor his ability as a commander, marks of which he had demonstrated only the day before. However, in that particular army, with Edward II as its commander, the English cavalry were unlikely to yield their positions on the carse or jeopardise their opportunity of being the first to engage the enemy for such an improbable situation.

The English archers were sure to have been much in the thoughts of Bruce's spearmen as they moved across open ground in close formations. Veterans from Falkirk would have told their companions how arrows could tear into them in a hissing, death-dealing cloud. As experienced soldiers they would know that in spite of carrying their proud armorial banners, the schiltrons could rapidly have holes rent in them by the lethal shafts. Even if they did arrive within arm's length of the enemy positions they were still likely to meet archers able to fire point blank into their ranks. As seasoned soldiers they would try to blank out such dangers and concentrate on the immediate problems in hand, striving to obey their sergeants' instructions to keep good lines, to point their spears straight ahead and, with the hummocks in the ground, to take especial care over their footing. As they continued to advance, though, they must have felt the urge to tilt their helmeted heads forward and hunch their backs the better to meet the expected arrow cloud. In such a religious age, and conscious of their vulnerability, they would also have welcomed the signal from the Abbot of Inchaffray, who was preceding them bearing a crucifix, for them to kneel briefly and join him in reciting the Paternoster.

But once on the open carse there was no turning back. Bruce's most experienced soldiers customarily held the flank positions but in any case, walking shoulder to shoulder with friends from their own clans and from their own localities – like those members of Pals battalions in an infinitely more costly war 600 years later – such men were better able to subdue their fears and even grow in confidence as they approached ever closer to the enemy. Had they not done well the previous day under the same commanders? In any case, all shared the heady feeling of being committed to a long-awaited battle and, above all, of going onto the attack.

On the English side arrangements were, of course, at a much earlier stage. Whichever cavalry commander had despatched the archers forward as skirmishers probably sent word for the king to join him with all speed. Once among the front detachments, Edward could only watch in amazement as the Scottish spearmen, in virtual silence, moved steadily across the carse towards his position. By now they were less than two bowshots away and the forward phalanx continued its relentless advance with the other schiltrons following close behind. In their tight formations the king must have thought them remarkably few compared with his own great army spread over the carse behind him, especially as he had not seen how the same spearmen performed on the previous day. Most importantly, they showed no signs of slowing.

'What?' he shouted to those beside him. 'Will those Scots fight?' Barbour's account of the battle places the veteran Scotsman, Sir Ingram Umfraville, past guardian of his country, long-standing Balliol supporter and enemy of the Bruces, beside the king to advise him. Initially Umfraville's reply seemed to reflect admiration for his countrymen, as well as the certainty they were coming to their death. 'Of truth, sir, now I see the most marvellous sight by far that ever I beheld – Scotsmen undertaking to fight against the might of England and to give battle in the hard open field.' This Scot who so hated the Scottish king must then have had second thoughts about the result, for he proposed a strategem for the English to fall back beyond their baggage thereby tempting the Scots into plundering it, when they could easily be attacked and destroyed. Umfraville plainly did not appreciate the iron discipline exerted by Bruce nor could he have properly anticipated the difficulties of such an undertaking within the cramped English position. The king rightly rejected the absurd suggestion out of hand, largely because he had no intention of giving way in front of 'such rabble', but also due to the fact that he still could not bring himself to believe the Scots had actually come to fight him. As the schiltrons stopped and knelt in prayer he grasped at the possibility that they might be asking for mercy. This time Umfraville knew his fellow Scots well enough to answer him, 'You are right; they ask for mercy, but not from you. They cry to God for forgiveness. I tell you one thing for certain, yonder men will win all or die. None there shall flee for fear of death.' In any case, as the Scots resumed their approach, the king could doubt his eyes no longer. 'Now so be it,' he said, 'we shall see presently.'[2]

Edward's wish for battle that day was granted, but not on the terms he had imagined and furthermore one of his ill-considered and unrestrained responses the night before came to have serious results. During the king's council of war the young Earl of Gloucester had joined with more experienced heads to recommend a further day's preparation before moving towards Stirling Castle, but Edward had not been content with rejecting Gloucester's proposal, accusing him of cowardice, the ultimate insult for a Christian knight and senior member of such a proud family.[3]

Edward's order to sound the trumpets for battle brought a frantic response. It was relatively easy for footsoldiers and bowmen to snatch up their weapons and shake themselves into their clothing, but far less so for the cavalry stationed in the forefront of the army. The knights had the painstaking task of getting into their full armour, including their helms; their horses had to be readied and their lances and other weapons brought from nearby tents before they could be helped onto their mounts. Among the cavalry the vanguard was expected to respond quickest of all and some of its members were likely to be fully arrayed but, having given the order to arm, nothing more seemed to follow in the way of commands, the king apparently gave no tactical directives beyond hastening to get into his own armour in readiness for combat. In fact, neither the king nor his commanders seemed prepared to consider anything beyond an immediate sally. Even so there was discord. Among the vanguard, Gloucester, who was still smarting from the king's slur, disputed with Hereford over who should have the honour of leading. Hereford argued that as Constable of England it was his prerogative, while Gloucester maintained his ancestors had always held the premier place in the attack.[4] Refusing to spend any more time in wrangling Gloucester called for archers to support him, although he did not wait for their arrival or even for his knight to place his surcoat, emblazoned with the De Clare coat of arms, over his head, before mounting and putting his spurs to his horse. Heading the vanguard's other knights he charged headlong across the space between the two sides, crashing against Edward Bruce's schiltron where he was killed on the wall of spears raised to meet him. A number of senior figures who followed close behind him, including Sir Robert Clifford, joint leader of a cavalry brigade the day before, Sir John Comyn, son of the Red Comyn murdered by Bruce, Sir Edward Mauley, steward of the king's household, and Sir Pain Tiptoff, engaged the Scottish spearmen and were also killed.

It was a disastrous beginning for the English. The vanguard had succeeded no better than on the previous day and such mindless acts cost them some of their most dependable and experienced commanders before the battle had properly begun. Those who so rashly charged at the forward schiltron caused an additional problem; with both men and horses lying on the ground other cavalry had the greatest difficulty in forcing a way over them to press home their assaults. In any case, when the foremost-placed horsemen found themselves checked they were not prepared to retire and allow others to attack. The spearmen who had paused to meet the horsemen's first assault now resumed their forward movement and succeeded in placing themselves against the Bannock Burn thereby anchoring the Scottish right flank. The first segment of the trap had been moved into place.

Once there Edward Bruce's men were able to hold their own against fresh cavalry attacks by jabbing their long spears through the horses' trappings and, like Moray's men the day before, when the animals reared, lunging for their hearts and entrails. At the same time the other schiltrons continued their forward movement. As Moray's schiltron came close to the forward one it clashed headlong with some of the main cavalry units moving up to threaten Edward Bruce's left flank. Such large numbers of English cavalry were despatched and so many horses milled around the schiltron that observers said it disappeared from sight 'like men plunged in the sea'.[5] With notable courage the English mounted a succession of spirited attacks, 'spurring haughtily on', but Moray's men had been through a similar experience the day before. Like Edward Bruce's spearmen they resolutely stood their ground and succeeded in bringing the forward riders crashing down. Once more the prone casualties helped to blunt the English assaults and gave Moray's schiltron the chance to move into station alongside the right-hand one. More than half the entrance was blocked. Douglas and Stewart approaching on Moray's left offered their own thicket of spearmen to the impetuous cavalry and as more men and horses were impaled, Douglas came into line and closed off the entrance.

Through lack of imagination born of overconfidence the English king and his fellow commanders had placed their army in a potential trap. With such few numbers, it was, of course, one thing for Bruce to seal the pocket, quite another to hold it shut. The interval of land between the streams was about 1200 yards wide at this point. With each spearman occupying about a yard of frontage and with only narrow intervals between the schiltrons their steel-tipped barrier was likely to have been just three or four ranks deep.

Robert Bruce, watching from a vantage point relatively near to his fourth schiltron, which he held in reserve close behind the other three, must have wondered how such flimsy human ranks, precursors of the thin red line of Scottish soldiers at Balaclava, could hold against the vastly superior numbers locked in the salient. As a gifted soldier he must also have thought it inconceivable for the English to continue to fight so disconnectedly and to leave unused so much of their actual strength but, if they did not deploy it, there seemed no reason why his spearmen should not hold the cavalry at bay as they had a few hours earlier. In the spearmen's favour, the great numbers of cavalry at the front end of the pocket were becoming so jammed together they could develop nothing like the momentum they had on the Dryfield the day before.

For a time events continued to follow the same grim pattern. The Scottish spearmen held their ground against bruising rushes of horsemen issuing from the main body of cavalry, repeated again and again with exemplary bravery. The physical demands on individual spearmen must have been enormous, for the Lanercost chronicler described the clashes as 'a great and terrible crash of spears broken and of destriers wounded to death'.[6] On the English side, some of the horses, riderless and wounded, ran amok. In their attempts to escape the terrible blood-tipped spears they not only galloped back through the cavalry squadrons scattering other horsemen, but trampled over squads of unfortunate footsoldiers as they attempted to push forward to take part in the fighting. As on the previous day the disciplined spearmen showed greater unity and control against the sporadic, if frequent, attacks from the English cavalry. They not only rebuffed the charging horses but every so often succeeded in edging their way forward further into the narrowing pocket.

More and more cavalry units eager to become involved crowded against their own forward elements, merging into what Barbour called 'one great schiltron of their own', and among its forward units the king and his escort fought as hard as anyone. Admirable as this was, it quite prevented him from seeing the overall picture and exercising the control required of a commander-in-chief, particularly over his 5000 archers who had the potential to give him victory.

In fact, so tight was the wedge of heavy horsemen locked

in desperate combat with the schiltrons that without some fundamental re-ordering neither the English bowmen nor the other infantry seemed able to tilt the balance in Edward's favour. Nor was this the case only with the footsoldiers: many cavalry units failed to come within arm's reach of the enemy and were so tightly packed that 200 knights were not even able to draw their swords.

Finally, despite the extreme difficulties, those in command of the archers ordered them to fire at the schiltrons. At first they discharged their shafts over the heads of the foremost cavalry, but with the ranks of the schiltrons being so narrow and so closely engaged they fell harmlessly beyond them. The bowmen were then ordered to fire past the cavalry directly at the spearmen. This expedient also failed for the spearmen were dwarfed by the opposing horsemen who from their horses' hooves to their helmet crests stood over seven feet high. In any case, the leaping and plunging riders repeatedly masked the archers' line of fire with the result that they hit 'few Scots in the breast but (were) striking more English in the back'.[7]

One can imagine the cavalry's rage at this but the bowmen's leaders persisted and led a considerable body of their men over the Pelstream Burn to link up with those archers who had earlier acted as skirmishers. Together they gathered on the Scottish left flank, and taking up positions some six paces apart, began to unleash a rain of deadly missiles that soon tore gaps in Douglas' lines. As Barbour reported, 'The English archers shot so fast that had their shower lasted it had gone hard with the Scots'.[8] The watching Bruce, quickly appreciating the extent of the danger, ordered up his light cavalry under Marischal Keith to try and disperse them. After crossing the burn, most probably where the bridle path forded it, they bore right and with levelled lances rode at a full gallop across the open carse. Their fierce charge against the archers' flank was so successful that the English bowmen were either killed or fled. Unlike the English heavy cavalry who had difficulty wheeling at the trot, the wiry Scottish horses with their lightly protected riders were far more difficult to elude. While no match for the English cavalry this was a task for which they were ideally suited. When the few archers who survived recrossed the stream and rejoined other English soldiers they were greeted with abuse and even blows for their failure.

Following their success the Scottish cavalry continued to patrol the Pelstream's northern bank to deter any further detachments of bowmen from crossing over. With the threat from the English archers removed – from that flank at least – the Scots continued to edge forward, particularly Edward Bruce's schiltron on the Scots' right flank. There were even reports about the few Scottish archers who survived the initial exchange enjoying an opportunity of being able to fire at the opposing cavalry from short range.[9]

The hard-fought battle had now reached its savage attrition stage, although the success of the Scottish cavalry in seeing off the English archers was an immense bonus for their side. At this point Bruce sent forward his own – and last – schiltron to bolster Douglas' weakened formation and to give additional impetus to his attacks. By doing so Bruce played his full hand, for he could not afford the situation to arrive at stalemate. Although his Scottish footsoldiers with their spears and Lochaber axes had shown they could defend themselves against mailed knights and his light cavalry had repulsed the first major English attempt to bring their bowmen into the struggle, with things so finely balanced the English could still find some opportunity for making better use of their other forces. If, despite inevitable casualties from drowning, a commander had the nerve to lead a detachment of English infantry across the treacherous Bannock Burn, then move them along its bank before recrossing at some point before the gorge he could attack the Scottish spearmen from the rear and the situation could swiftly change. As he committed his own schiltron the Scottish king emphasised the importance of their role by telling Angus Og MacDonald and its other leaders, 'My hope is constant in thee', adding, in encouragement, that if they could give some added force the day must be theirs. In response some filled the gaps made in Douglas' spear lines while others took up rearward positions among the schiltrons and, leaning with all their strength against the backs and shoulders of men whose knees were buckling and whose arms could hardly keep the tips of their long spears from sinking to the ground, attempted to impel them forward. Their presence was not lost on the English whose armoured knights experienced even greater difficulties with their spirited horses as the jabbing spearmen began a concerted forward movement.

So effective was this addition to the Scottish strength and so highly did Bruce rate the entry of Angus Og and his clansmen at the battle's climax, that he subsequently granted the MacDonalds the honour of always taking the right of the line in the royal armies. While in the absence of any fresh English initiatives the advantage appeared to be moving in the Scots' direction, where the sides came together the fighting continued with unceasing ferocity. Barbour wrote, 'Mighty was the din of blows, as weapons struck upon armour, and great was the crashing of spears with turning and thrusting, grunting and groaning . . .'[10] Within the heart of the diminishing salient conditions were worsening: men and horses were becoming so packed together that not only were they unable to fight properly, but if a knight fell or was unhorsed he became not only vulnerable to the enemy but was in the greatest danger of being trampled on by his own side.

The vital difference between the contenders at this point was that the English had still only succeeded in bringing a limited portion of their forces into contact with the enemy. However, with the commitment of Bruce's last regular formation and the resumption of some forward movement, however modest, Scottish spirits began to rise and with their growing elation signs of desperation started appearing among the English. As the Scots sensed some crumbling in the resistance they let out a triumphant shout that rolled along their battle line as each schiltron took it up. The English attempted to shout back but the Scottish cries would not be rebutted. They roared out exultantly, 'On them, on them, on them, they fail.'[11] The shouts were accompanied by attacks from all along the line and in a remarkable reversal of fortune Barbour had the Scottish short bowmen beginning to enjoy considerable success as they shot boldly 'amongst the enemy and harassed them greatly'.[12]

While at the front of the salient the fighting went on unabated, elsewhere in the English encampment events were taking a different turn. A number of the levies, who saw no chance of being involved in the action but sensed the likely outcome, began to drift off and attempt to cross the surrounding watercourses with the aim of making for the English border. Such desertions had, of course, no immediate effect on the king and his cavalry for there were more than enough horsemen to replace their casualties in the forward ranks. For outright victory the Scots needed to administer a new blow against their larger opponent, otherwise the long and costly struggle seemed destined to continue for some time and mutual exhaustion would become an increasing factor and one likely to tell against the side with fewer numbers.

At this point a fresh body entered the reckoning, namely the 'small folk', those Scottish soldiers who had arrived too late to undergo Bruce's specialised training or were without the required military equipment, together with the 'poveraill', numbers of labourers and camp servants, both men and women. This body moved forward from where Bruce had placed them below Coxet Hill and appeared at the top of the Dryfield slope in military formation, with crude banners flying and carrying all manner of improvised weapons, no doubt eager for their share of booty from the failing English. As the men amongst them began to descend the slope they roared out 'Slay, Slay. On them hastily.' To the beleaguered English struggling in their bloody-slippery pocket the sight of more than 2000 fresh men – equal in number to the king's schiltron – must have seemed like a new Scottish army entering the conflict.

Compared with the schiltrons' total strength the numerical addition was, of course, considerable but their fighting ability was quite another matter. The Scottish king himself might have had distinctly mixed feelings over such unruly elements joining his veteran fighters – men who would no doubt be ready to kill indiscriminately, whether their opponents were worthy of valuable ransoms or not. No chronicler suggested they came to the battlefield directly on Bruce's orders but it is likely they sent observers who returned and told them the Scots were getting the better of things. An English defeat meant enormous plunder and they would dearly want to be in at the death. All plunder aside there were likely to be strong patriots among them who had served this king and his followers on other fields. In Barbour's account of the battle he writes that they appointed one of their number captain saying they would help their lords to their utmost.[13] A recent writer has put forward the somewhat outlandish theory that the 'small folk' were in fact mobilised by the Knights Templar whose own war banner, the Beauseant, coming over the hill was bound to bring dismay to the English.[14] Representatives of the St Clairs, the principal Templar family in Scotland, did fight with Bruce at Bannockburn but whether they were the self-appointed leaders of the small folk remains unanswered.[15] None of the contemporary observers upon the battle supports such a theory.

Reputedly the sight of the 'small folk' coming towards him made Bruce all the more determined to try and decide things before they actually joined in. He shouted out his own battle cry and along with his spearmen pressed the English so hard that it was said more and more began to leave the ground.

With the outcome now virtually certain to go against them the English leaders determined to get their king away. His departure would seal their defeat but the Scottish spearmen were close about him; some of the Scottish knights among their ranks were even then grasping at his horses' housings and he had to clear himself with his mace.[16] No one could deny that Edward had fought bravely throughout, having had one horse killed beneath him and losing Sir Roger Northburgh, the keeper of his shield, who had been captured. At first he was unwilling to withdraw. But at all events he must be led to safety, the responsibility for which fell upon his personal escort including Aymer de Valence, Earl of Pembroke and Sir Giles d'Argentan. Both knew it would be a national disgrace if the king were killed and probably worse still if he were captured; the ransom set would be huge and the conditions for his return were bound to include the recognition of Bruce as true King of the Scots, together with a demand for his country's renewed independence.

Despite the king's protests they turned his horse's bridle and moved to the flank with no fewer than 500 knights in attendance (many of whom were doubtless glad to leave the ill-fated field).

This force was far too powerful to be checked by the Scottish light cavalry and they made a crossing place over the Pelstream Burn and galloped him northwards away from the Scots army and up the carse where he determined to find protection in Stirling Castle. To withdraw 500 knights at such a time not only guaranteed defeat, but triggered the beginning of undisciplined flight by many others causing men to start running in all directions. Understandably there were notable exceptions, like Giles d'Argentan, who, once the king was close to the castle, declared his honour would not allow him to run away and returned to the salient. There he threw himself against Edward Bruce's thicket of spearmen who killed him instantly. The Highland patriot Evan Barron went as far as to say the king's flight was followed by a panic to which there is no parallel in the history of England or Scotland.[17] This seems an overstatement when Bannockburn is compared with the chaotic aftermath that occurred among Scottish forces following later English victories such as at Flodden, and the inevitable disorder on any battlefield once cohesion is lost. However at Bannockburn the English will to fight was undoubtedly broken, a fact which the English chronicler from Lanercost acknowledged when he wrote that 'Horsemen and foot alike, noblemen, knights and squires, archers and infantry were seized with the need to escape.'[18]

Many fugitives gathered round the base of Stirling Castle while others tried to cross the River Forth where most were drowned in the attempt. Even more went southeast to cross the Bannock Burn which, particularly in places where it was non-tidal, was reckoned to have a hard base suitable for horses although where it ran across the carse the bottom was boggy.[19] It was not only the base that proved treacherous. Its banks were so slippery and liable to crumble that once committed men could not climb back, and in its gorges north of the township of Bannock horrendous casualties were suffered. Barbour reported that between its banks was so filled 'with men and horses that men could pass over dryshod upon the drowned bodies'.[20] This was agreed by all observers, including the English ones. Grey wrote that 'the troops in the English rear fell back upon the ditch of Bannockburn, tumbling one over the other'[21] and the

Lanercost chronicler underlined the effects of panic, 'there was a big ditch called the Bannockburn into which the tide flows . . . many noblemen and others with their horses fell into this ditch because of the great press of men behind them'.[22]

Once committed, Bruce succeeded at Bannockburn because he was willing to venture everything against a much superior adversary who was ill-prepared and comparatively untrained, whose knights had no respect for their own archers or footsoldiers, and who were led by a king who thought the science of tactics unnecessary. As a result the English force was closer to being an armed mob – albeit of brave men – than a dedicated force committed to defeating an enemy. In this respect it is difficult to quarrel with Professor Barrow's statement that the English army was condemned by its leadership to fight with the wrong tactics, the wrong weapons and on the wrong ground. Such English deficiencies, however, cannot take away from Bruce the credit for leading his small, highly disciplined force to a victory against all the current odds of war and one that will always rank as the premier triumph for Scotland against the English.

CHAPTER ELEVEN

≈

THE PURSUIT

'It was victory, but it was not success yet.'
Agnes Mure MacKenzie, *Robert Bruce, King of Scots*

L IKE ALL VICTORIOUS COMMANDERS the full rewards of
Bruce's success would depend upon how effectively he could
pursue the enemy's broken forces and how far he was able to
seize the chance it gave him to bring the bitter conflict between
the two countries to an end.

Bannockburn was unusual in battlefield terms for being
an absolute victory. Although the English king left the field
accompanied by a remarkably strong cavalry escort there was
no question in his mind of making it the caucus for a further
attack. Edward's one object was to free himself from Bruce's
fearsome spearmen by seeking security behind the thick walls of
a fortress still under his control. A second large body of English
horsemen which left the field intact also had nothing but escape
in mind. As for the footsoldiers they scattered in all directions.
No unit marched off under its officers in any semblance of order
or with its banners flying, although one sizeable body of men
was subsequently guided to the border and safety. The plain
fact was that the huge army which had so recently marched
into the Scottish heartland now ceased to exist. Even so, as
Professor Barrow pointed out, in one vital respect at least the
English escaped more cheaply than they deserved. While they
lost considerable numbers of noble rank, many escaped and the
biggest prize of all, the English king, got away.

In hindsight Bruce might conversely have been more single-
minded in his pursuit, yet he is not alone among gifted commanders in neglecting to take full advantage of a victory. After

breaking an army's outer shell of resistance attackers are given a signal opportunity of annihilating it but for numerous reasons, including their own exhaustion, they have often failed to do so. Few military leaders have ever come close to equalling Hannibal's great victory at Cannae in 216BC where, after surrounding and compressing a larger Roman army he broke its will and continued the slaughter until virtually the whole force was wiped out. In more modern times the Russians gained a sweeping victory at Stalingrad during World War Two, when they surrounded an army which, after a two and a half month siege, was three-quarters starved before their final attacks compelled the remainder to surrender.

At Cannae and Stalingrad no one escaped, but it is more usual for there to be comparatively large numbers of survivors. Even when the Duke of Cumberland ruthlessly hunted down the Jacobites following his victory at Culloden, sizeable remnants gathered afterwards under their commanders. Bannockburn would never be a Stalingrad or Cannae, for the English could escape by crossing the water courses encompassing their position even though this involved a relatively high level of casualties. Compared with the Duke of Cumberland at Culloden Robert Bruce had much better reasons for not pursuing his enemy to the utmost. He was most certainly deficient in cavalry, the traditional means of pursuit and exploitation quite apart from any feelings of sympathy he might have had for the defeated after his own experiences as a fugitive. His total numbers of light cavalry were no match for the 500 barded knights who accompanied the English king on his dash south nor, for that matter, did they seem capable of checking the other contingent of 600 cavalry and 1000 infantry under the Earl of Hereford which made for Bothwell Castle on the Clyde. Bruce therefore was compelled to keep his schiltrons intact in case the English decided to turn against his footsoldiers with a mixed cavalry and infantry force (such as Hereford's), and this undoubtedly reduced his capability to follow up vigorously.

In any case, with Bruce's army not much more than a third of the English strength when the battle commenced he was forced to consider mounting a full-scale attack using both cavalry and infantry upon the large numbers of English infantry who, failing to gain admittance into Stirling Castle gathered themselves on the crags at its base. In the light of his own determined and successful struggles against superior forces Bruce would expect the English to attempt some form of re-grouping and understandably he would be reluctant to risk compromising his victory. Bruce also had reason to feel himself unlucky when Edward looked for protection in Stirling Castle. The king and his powerful escort made straight for it but on their arrival its commander either told the king that if he entered the castle he would be taken by the Scots 'as none in all England . . . (will) bring you succour' or Moubray actually raised the drawbridge against him.[1] If the governor had been a less strong individual and had admitted the king, rather than pointing out his agreement to hand the castle over to the Scots, they would certainly have besieged it and in all likelihood captured the king along with all his 500 cavalry.

At Moubray's refusal Edward and his escort turned through King's Park round the rear of the Scottish army until they reached the Torwood and came onto the high road to Linlithgow. However, Bruce's chance of capturing the English king had not disappeared completely. Had he used all his cavalry to pursue the king's force he could have made things exceedingly difficult for them, for while their horses were better-armed they were also more ponderous. The Scottish horses were not only much faster but with their riders' knowledge of the country they could have been used in ambushes. However, this was not to happen.

Although Douglas, with the anticipation and swiftness of thought that so distinguished him as a soldier, left his schiltron as soon as he saw the English king move northwards and asked for Bruce's permission to lead the Scottish cavalry in pursuit, Bruce refused. Quite apart from Edward's large cavalry escort and the numbers of footsoldiers that began following their king to Stirling Castle the remainder of the English cavalry force still heavily outnumbered Bruce's horsemen and he felt it too great a risk to use all his cavalry on a single mission, however important. In fact the move away by the king's escort caused the other large group of cavalry and infantry to start moving south and Barbour was sure the large numbers around the castle were the chief reason 'that the King of England escaped to his own country'.[2] Bruce eventually compromised by allocating Douglas just sixty horse for the pursuit. Undeterred by the uneven odds he set off after the English king. On the road he was fortunate to meet with a fellow Scot, the young Sir Lawrence Abernethy who, with eighty horse, had come to join the English. On being told the result of the battle, Abernethy was persuaded to change allegiance and join Douglas. Pausing briefly to take public pledges of loyalty from Abernethy and his men, Douglas set off with a force more than double in size, although it was still heavily outnumbered by the English.

He caught up with Edward and his party just after Linlithgow, but instead of taking the expected route over the Lammermuir hills to Berwick, the king turned due east along the shorter coast road to Dunbar. Douglas was thus deprived of many favourable ambush points along the Roman road but so urgently did he shadow the party that, as Barbour remarked, no Englishman could stop even to make water and any whose horses broke down were swiftly captured. Aymer de Valence's biographer believed that Valence and his followers were responsible for defending the party and fighting a prolonged rearguard action against Douglas' attacks. If this is so, their heavy casualties were equally or more likely to have been caused by this action than during the main battle; from Valence's retinue of twenty-two knights and fifty-nine men at arms, four knights were killed and ten taken prisoner with a similar proportion of losses among the men at arms. It is known for certain that just one knight, John Comyn (son of John Comyn of Badenoch), had already been killed on the field of Bannockburn and if just a proportion of these casualties occurred later it points to the determination of Douglas' pursuit.[3]

When the king and his knights reached Dunbar Castle, owned by the sympathetic Earl Patrick of Dunbar, they jumped off their horses and ran in leaving them unattended outside. The king and a few chosen knights sailed to Bamburgh in an open boat and from there went by land to Berwick but the main body who followed him by land had a far more difficult journey. They were chased for a full fifty miles by Douglas and Abernethy and although they shed their armour to help increase their horses' speed some still fell into their pursuers' hands.[4] If Douglas had commanded the whole complement of Scottish cavalry it is more than possible he could have captured the king. Even with Douglas' restricted number of pursuers Edward had no doubt about the good luck associated with his escape, for in thanksgiving this less than religious monarch subsequently founded the Carmelite college of Oriel at Oxford.[5]

Bruce enjoyed better luck with the other contingent of more than 600 mounted men and 1000 foot under the Earl of Hereford. They made their way to the stronghold of Bothwell Castle lying about twenty-five miles southwest of Stirling, where its constable admitted the party's leading commanders who, along with the two senior earls of Hereford and Angus, had included Sir John Seagrave, Sir Anthony Lucy, Ingram Unfraville and Maurice, Lord of Berkeley amounting to fifty in all. The castle's constable was a Scot, Sir Walter FitzGilbert, who hitherto had inclined to the stronger side which up to this time had been the English. When however he learned the reason for his having so many distinguished guests and, even more importantly, the extent of the Scottish victory, he promptly removed their weapons and made them prisoners.[6] On the arrival of Edward Bruce, whom the king had sent in pursuit, FitzGilbert handed them over.

After Edward II himself, the Earl of Hereford was the greatest single prize from the battle: in return for his release Bruce was granted fifteen Scottish captives among whom he specified his wife, Elizabeth, his daughter Marjorie, his sister Christiana and that great patriot from the time of William Wallace, Robert Wishart, Bishop of Glasgow, now blind and sick after eight years of harsh captivity. In return for Hereford Robert Bruce's nephew, the Earl of Mar, was also given release but as he had formed a warm friendship with the English king he opted to remain in England. Deprived of their senior leaders few men from the rest of Hereford's large force reached England safely: some were killed close to Bothwell Castle while many others were killed by common folk as they made their way to the border.[7] Any who escaped apparently only did so in abject confusion.[8] In their flight it was every man for himself, for even if the nobles avoided injury, in the event of their being captured they became liable to pay a ransom. This could have grave results. In 1317, for instance, when Aymer de Valence himself was on a later mission to France on behalf of the king he suffered the misfortune not only of being captured but having a huge ransom of £10,400 set on his head. Although the king paid the first £2,500 the ransom caused Valence serious financial problems for the rest of his life and was the reason for his dying in debt in 1324.[9]

The large numbers of ordinary English soldiers who escaped the battlefield and congregated in large numbers at the base of Stirling Castle did not give Bruce the trouble he expected. They soon tamely surrendered.

Only one sizeable group of men – all footsoldiers – made good their escape to England. There is some doubt who was responsible for their delivery. The *Lanercost Chronicle* reported a large body of fugitives fleeing to Carlisle and it has been suggested that Aymer de Valence, after leading the king towards Stirling Castle, was responsible for shepherding the half-naked Welsh levies recruited from within his earldom to the border city. Certainly the greater part of one organised party, possible several thousands strong, safely crossed the border despite being harried all along the 100-mile route to Carlisle.[10] No chronicler, however, actually mentions Valence by name and Barbour is quite specific in saying that Sir Maurice de Barclay set forth from the battle with a great host of Welshmen.[11] Barclay was certainly in Valence's retinue of knights and Valence may have ordered him to take charge of the Welsh levies or, after leading them off, handed over responsibility to Barclay. J R S Phillips, Valence's biographer, cites evidence supporting the presence of Valence with the king on his flight to Dunbar and sailing to Berwick from there.[12] Whether Valence was responsible or not for leading off and then handing his Welsh levies over to Barclay before subsequently fighting off Douglas and his pursuers on the road to Dunbar, he emerged from Bannockburn with more credit than most of his contemporaries.

From the nature of the battle it was inevitable a sizeable proportion of the vast English army would leave the field quite apart from those who negotiated the Pelstream Burn and made northwards for Stirling Castle. How many other footsoldiers actually succeeded in escaping to England is far more difficult to say. While the archers had only briefly been in action and the foot virtually not at all, both faced the initial problem of crossing the fast-flowing and deep Bannock Burn before moving south towards the English border over 100 miles away. After the burn had claimed its proportion of victims, for the survivors, demoralised, frightened, with little or no food, the journey to Carlisle across barren border country must have seemed endless and it was indeed beyond the capability of many. With only one organised group coming off the battlefield it is certain a large proportion fell to the avenging Scots. If two-thirds of the horsemen and infantry who did not gain admittance to Bothwell Castle failed to reach the border it is not likely that many others would do much better. It seems doubtful if even a third of the footsoldiers returned to England. But in contemporary eyes such ordinary soldiers (the poor bloody infantry of later centuries) counted for less than men of noble blood: fresh levies could be raised fairly easily and such men earned no bonuses for their captors. Some of those who succeeded in crossing the border still had some weeks' walking before they returned to their home villages.

As for the nobility, if their casualties were not as high as they might have been they were still undoubtedly high compared with most medieval battles, partly because many nobles were killed in the savage early encounters. Gloucester died together with thirty-four barons and several hundred knights, but every knight was accompanied by one or more squires, and other members of their personal household, many of whom would have been killed along with their masters. While he might be guilty of some exaggeration in this respect, Barbour relates how on the battlefield 200 golden spurs – the spurs of knighthood – were taken from the bodies of the dead knights, a total which exceeded Scottish losses at Flodden two centuries later, although in that battle it included their king. At Bannockburn all such knights were buried in sanctified ground, while dead soldiers were placed in great pits acting as communal graves.[13]

On the Scottish side the casualties were very light. Barbour wrote that two knights were killed, Sir William Vipont and Sir Walter Ross (much mourned by Edward Bruce), while Sir William Airth was killed as he guarded the Scots baggage. As for the private soldiers, if the one death suffered by Moray's schiltron on the first day of the battle is any guide, then their casualties would also have been relatively light, as they kept their cohesion throughout. Although Douglas' schiltron found itself a target for the dreaded archers it was only for a comparatively short time before these were successfully dispersed, and the phalanx was unlikely to have suffered more than 200 casualties for this reason.

As in other medieval battles, equally or more important for the victors than those killed were those they captured: after Bannockburn there were probably 500 or so men of rank, nobles, knights and squires, who were worth ransoming. The barons, baronets and knights among them amounted to more than 100, much the most important being Humphrey de Bohun, Earl of Hereford. After his victory Bruce could afford to be magnanimous, but while the details of their ransoms were being discussed the Scottish king apparently treated his prisoners with so much kindness and courtesy that even the English witnesses acknowledged he went far to winning their hearts.[14]

In certain cases he also showed a willingness to waive their ransom. One such case was that of Sir Marmaduke Twenge, the English hero of Stirling Bridge. Twenge found himself surrounded and after discarding his arms and armour hid himself all night, appearing before Bruce next morning dressed only in his shirt. His humiliation and state of undress would have amused many a victorious monarch but Barbour related how the king greeted him. 'Welcome, Sir Marmaduke, to what man art thou prisoner?'

'To none,' he said, 'but here to you I yield to be at your pleasure.'

'"And I receive thee, sir," said the King.'[15] Bruce much valued bravery; he granted Twenge freedom without ransom and gave the veteran soldier gifts to take back with him. Another prisoner who understandably enjoyed Bruce's special favour was Ralph de Monthermer, stepfather of the young Earl of Gloucester who was killed in the battle's early stages. It was Monthermer who, when Bruce was at the court of Edward I, reputedly sent him a pair of spurs, a hint that Bruce acknowledged by escaping from Edward's vengeance. Bruce repaid the debt by both entertaining Monthermer and releasing him without ransom which as Edward II's brother-in-law would have been set at a very high level.

Although such conspicuous courtesy towards the defeated enhanced Bruce's cause there seems no reason to doubt his sincerity towards such victims of war. He mourned the death of the young Earl of Gloucester as a cousin. After having Gloucester's body laid out in a nearby church he kept a night's vigil over it, before sending the corpse to King Edward at Berwick together with that of the next highest-ranking magnate, Robert Clifford.[16]

In addition to the material benefits from the ransoms Scotland profited from the proceeds of the English baggage train which the Scots captured in its entirety. As well as money to pay the soldiers, it carried large quantities of gold and silver vessels, armour, cloths, wine, hay and the family plate of those nobles who had been promised estates in Scotland. At the time it was said to be worth £200,000.[17] Some idea of its modern value can be gauged from a comparison between the pay of a soldier then and now. J E Morris set the average wage for soldiers in the Welsh Wars at 2d a day,[18] a figure that remained constant until 1333 when Edward III had great difficulties raising men to fight in Scotland and increased it to an inflationary 3d a day. Working on the figure of 2d a day, a soldier's annual pay was about £3.00. Compared with the wages of a trained British soldier in 1998 of £13,000 a year the baggage train would be worth roughly £866,000,000. The material rewards to Scotland from Bannockburn would, therefore, certainly be more than a billion pounds in modern figures and, with the relative scarcity of monetary transactions in the fourteenth century, in practical terms it would certainly be much higher. The value of the baggage train was supplemented by the considerable spoils taken by individual soldiers from both the dead and captured. In addition to such material benefits the battle allowed Bruce to be reunited with the female members of his family after an interval of eight years or more and for the possibility of a male heir to be revived. Even then they were not actually released until the autumn. The outcome also brought the transfer of the two great castles of Stirling and Dunbar into Scottish hands. On the day following the battle both Sir Philip Moubray and Patrick, Earl of Dunbar surrendered and swore allegiance to Bruce.

Bannockburn was unquestionably the greatest victory Scotland ever achieved against the English and by the same reasoning England's worst defeat since the battle of Hastings. The immediate benefits of the battle to the victors were enormous: the challenge mounted by a fearsome army led by an English king had been eliminated; long-held Scottish captives, including Bruce's immediate family, were released; and the material advantages from ransoms and booty were felt throughout Scotland. Bruce's hereditary right to the throne of Scotland and his country's claim for a separate existence had now been justified by success in battle, along with the support given him by the majority of Scotland's people. The English were by no means ready to acknowledge officially Bruce's right to the throne of Scotland, but whatever subsequent machinations were pursued by the English king and the English church against the northern kingdom's legal and religious position, Bannockburn enabled Scotland to regain its confidence as an independent country which it was to express in a most memorable way in 1320.

If only the Scots had succeeded in capturing Edward II then peace and England's full recognition of Scotland as a sovereign power under Robert Bruce must have followed quickly, but this was not to be. While the battle was undoubtedly a great triumph its results were not as beneficial as Scotland could reasonably have hoped. Like Wallace's triumph at Stirling Bridge and Edward I's victory against him a year later, Bannockburn did not succeed in bringing about an immediate end to such a bitter war, although, as the next chapter reveals, it gave Scotland a powerful platform upon which to pursue her campaign for peace and so deploy her forces that England would eventually be forced to recognise her independence. Conversely, in the years following, the battle's military lessons would be taken more to heart by the defeated than by subsequent generations of Scottish soldiers.

AFTERMATH

'We make war that we may live in peace'

Aristotle

O NCE EDWARD II HAD eluded his pursuers, the chances that a single victory, however conclusive, would bring hostilities between England and Scotland to an end became minimal for, while he was regarded as indecisive and incompetent where his father was feared and respected, he was equally arrogant and obstinate towards Scotland. The English king's great seal and royal shield were captured by the Scots along with the other spoils of battle, but if Bruce ever really hoped his conciliatory gesture of returning them would bring a positive response regarding peace he was disappointed. English aims towards Scotland remained the same, namely to prevent the recognition of Robert Bruce as legitimate king and to continue their claims of suzerainty over the country.

In spite of this Bannockburn was significant in many ways. It undoubtedly strengthened Bruce's position and marked the end of earlier Comyn dominance within the kingdom, although it should not be forgotten that he still faced continued external opposition from the Balliol faction where 'In Argyll and Ireland John of Argyll and other émigrés continued to whip up bitter resistance'.[1] As with Stirling Bridge sixteen years before, the battle caused people from across the land, the so-called 'community of the realm of Scotland', to feel a stronger sense of identity and pride for their nation and, in the case of Bannockburn, for their warrior king as well. As Evan Barron expressed it, after Bannockburn Scotland had 'an unconquerable confidence in her ability to hold her own at all times, and under any conditions against the whole might of England'.[2]

An immediate and tangible result, of course, was the passing of the military initiative into the hands of the northern kingdom. After Bruce found his initial attempt at making peace rebuffed he returned to military persuasion, resuming and extending the tactics that had succeeded before the great battle: the raids into northern England were continued and major new initiatives undertaken. He set out, for instance, to capture Berwick, the last Scottish stronghold still in English hands (together with the English border fortress of Carlisle) and, in response to a request from the sub king of Tyrone, undertook a campaign to conquer Ireland. The raids continued to hold a central place in his attempts to compel England to agree peace terms, for they not only challenged English sovereignty across the northern counties but highlighted the crown's inability to defend its people. In addition, the regular supplies of booty accruing from them, together with the financial contributions made by areas seeking to buy immunity, were of considerable benefit to his impoverished country. In the battle's immediate aftermath and before their coming difficulties in Ireland, those conducting such raids were likely to feel such assurance in each other that defeat at the hands of the defenders seemed virtually inconceivable. As long as Douglas retained a pivotal role, however, they were never likely to develop the same attitude of mindless overconfidence exhibited by the English prior to Bannockburn.

Bruce's motives for a conquest of Ireland were far less clear, but in all probability they included some ideal of a pan-Celtic brotherhood between the kings of Scotland and Ireland (and also his wish to remove his over-ambitious brother, Edward, from Scotland). Military success there could also eliminate Ulster as a source of supply for any new English invasions of Scotland and provide a base from where Bruce could conceivably attack Wales and Middle England.

All such military actions could also justly be viewed as a powerful platform for fresh diplomatic and constitutional initiatives. Just two months after the great battle following a particularly devastating raid into northern England by Edward

Bruce, James Douglas and John de Soules (grand nephew of the one-time guardian), Bruce wrote to Edward offering peace. This was discussed at an English parliament held at York but, although the English king was willing to accept an armistice, he refused outright any recognition of Scottish autonomy. In November 1314 Bruce held a parliament at Cambuskenneth where with a confidence buoyed by military success he both tightened his control over Scotland and distinguished further between the two countries by confirming his earlier threat that all those holding land in Scotland who refused to pledge loyalty to him should be disinherited – although he subsequently gave them a further year in which to make up their minds. In December 1314 Bruce again demonstrated his ability to invade the English northern counties virtually at will by leading a major raid along the Tyne valley and afterwards received payment for a truce until midsummer 1315. Even less to the English king's liking, he accepted the feudal homage of the inhabitants there.[3]

However able their leader, such incursions could not have been pursued so successfully without good subordinate commanders. Douglas and Moray in particular developed their raiding techniques into a form resembling those of the Vikings in the ninth century.[4] They developed a high degree of mobility: mounted on their wiry, sure-footed horses called 'hobins' (from which they took the name of 'hobelars'), they travelled light, each attacker carrying an iron plate under his saddle upon which he could bake oatcakes – bannocks – on the camp fires at the end of the day to be eaten with steaks of beef from stolen cattle. Their return journeys were inevitably slower since together with horses, cattle and prisoners for ransom, their pack horses would be burdened by coin and other booty, but such was their reputation that they usually came back unchallenged. So regular and damaging did these raids become that Northumberland, for instance, suffered from considerable depopulation and lawlessness. Equally serious for English morale, there seemed no effective counter measures against them. Capable of travelling more than twenty-five miles a day such redoubtable raiders appeared able to pick their targets at random. With the breakdown of local administration the situation was made worse by bands of mounted freebooters called 'schevaldores' whose excesses were often blamed on Bruce's raiders.

Under Bruce's direction the skills and daring of his commanders enabled him to maintain the military dominance gained at Bannockburn, first over Edward II, seriously hampered as he was by continuing conflict with his nobles, and then over the young Edward III before his own development into an outstanding king commander. This was all the more noteworthy in the light of England's far superior resources and its military and diplomatic support from other countries, particularly from the Vatican. With relatively little scope politically Bruce knew well enough that it was only by keeping up, or increasing, the military pressure over a protracted period if necessary, that England could finally be compelled to recognise Scotland's right to full independence. The very size of the task became evident when, despite continued English disunity, this took fourteen further years, and success did not come until Bruce was sick and near death.

That it took so long owed as much to Scotland's limited military resources as to England's resoluteness. Their brilliant commander also committed what turned out to be a major strategical blunder by allowing his Irish adventure to drain off forces that, in the period immediately after Bannockburn, could surely have been used to far better effect on the mainland. Yet when the Irish campaign was behind him, while he understandably lacked the ability to deal his opponent a conclusive final blow, Bruce showed an unwillingness to hazard his forces against English armies invading Scotland.

Geographical factors weighed heavily against offensive operations mounted by either country. England's problems were primarily concerned with supplying its armies as they marched through the desolate regions of the borders before reaching the Scottish heartland. Scotland on the other hand was not capable of sending a sufficiently large force far enough into England to damage it severely. Effective as they were, Scottish raids had a relatively limited effect, as England's true strength lay a long way from its northern border. Not only was its seat of government in the south, but also most of its shipping, the greater bulk of its industry, its main centre of population, and the bulk of its food production. Even relatively deep raids into England's northern counties could, therefore, never threaten the country's vitals.

Scotland's military limitations were probably most clearly apparent during 1316–18 when their border raids were seriously affected by the demands of Edward Bruce's Irish campaign, as were other initiatives that met with disappointing results. In July 1315 the Scottish king attempted to capture Carlisle but was driven back for want of adequate siege equipment, together with a most efficient defence of the city conducted by the sheriff of Cumberland, Sir Andrew Harcla. In December of the same year Bruce and Douglas made a second attempt to capture Berwick, again without success. In Ireland, too, their forces were thinly spread. Although the Scots' invaders enjoyed initial victories in Ulster and Edward Bruce was crowned King of Ireland at Dundalk in May 1316, the campaign was soon to go badly wrong. A combined expedition led by Robert and Edward Bruce during the winter of 1316–17 was seriously affected by famine conditions, together with unexpectedly determined opposition. In the spring of 1317 Robert Bruce was compelled to return home and at the end of 1318 the Irish campaign ended in defeat with Edward Bruce's death in battle.

During 1316 and 1317, with so many troops away, much of the border raiding depended on the skill and energy of James Douglas, who heavily defeated a strong group of English and Gascon knights venturing out from Berwick. Soon afterwards he met two other cavalry detachments, one sent from Jedburgh by the Earl of Arundel, the other from near Berwick under Robert Neville of Raby, the so-called 'Peacock of the North', whom Douglas killed. In recognition, during 1317 Bruce appointed him Warden or Lieutenant of Scotland. In the spring of 1318 Douglas succeeded at last in capturing Berwick and followed this up in the autumn of 1319 by carrying out his most destructive and penetrating raid yet, burning all the gathered harvest and seizing large numbers of men and animals from Gilsland and Westmorland.[5] If all Scottish military resources had been used as effectively and the raids had penetrated deeper still, there would have been such a continued and increasing outcry from northern England that the war might not have continued for so long.

Another reason for its length was the obduracy and capacity for intrigue shown by Edward II. Although his military ineptitude had caused such humiliation, he was more successful in other ways. Through his close relations with the papacy he conducted a religious (and diplomatic) offensive against Bruce to prevent him gaining Scottish independence. In a deeply religious age this was a powerful card to play. Since Bruce's sacrilegious murder of John Comyn in 1306 and the subsequent support he received from the Scottish bishops, the Gascon Pope Clement V, whether or not favourably inclined towards the English, was understandably not well disposed towards him. Clement not only served sentence of excommunication upon both Bruce and the Scottish church but repeated it time after time.

After Clement's death in 1316 the new Pope, John XXII, sought an end to hostilities in Europe so that its monarchs could join him on a projected crusade against the Turks. This, of course, required peace between England and Scotland and in 1317 he attempted to force the Scots into a two-year truce. Bruce received the Pope's two cardinals courteously but refused to consider their peace proposals as long as they addressed him as 'Governor of Scotland' and not as its true king. Continuing in the same ironic vein he told them he could not open their sealed letters as they might be intended for another Robert Bruce. The Scottish king was able to adopt such a stance partly because the English appeared incapable of gaining the military advantage their greater resources warranted. In fact, the Scots showed they had no intention of observing the Pope's proposed truce when Douglas besieged and succeeded in capturing Berwick during the two-year period. This provoked the Pope into ordering the four senior Scottish bishops, of St Andrews, Aberdeen, Dunkeld and Moray, to appear before him at the papal curia, and when they refused he excommunicated them together with Bruce; while this was not an uncommon occurrence for any of them, in a religious age its seriousness could not be doubted.

In response, during April 1320 the Scots sent a remarkable document to the Pope justifying their country's independence and their own love of liberty. William Wallace had expressed the same sentiments in earlier years but the confidence behind this elegant and remarkable document could only have come after Bruce's success at Bannockburn with its unifying effect upon Scotsmen of all classes. The letter, known as the Declaration of Arbroath because it was dated at the abbey there, was, in the opinion of Professor Barrow, likely to have been first sent as a round robin to be seen by as many earls, barons and other people as possible. Probably drafted by Bernard of Linton, Abbot of Arbroath and Scotland's Chancellor, it was signed by eight earls and forty-four other senior laymen, many of them previous supporters of John Balliol and the Comyns, and also by a relatively large number of modest freeholders, collectively representing 'the whole community of the realm of Scotland'.

The declaration was a tour de force written in an elegant but restrained style and purporting to represent the Scottish nation rather than any current royal power. It asserted the country's independence since ancient times, condemned the aggression of the two Edwards and begged the Pope to help bring such aggression to an end by persuading the King of England to be content with his own country and 'suffer us to live in that narrow spot of Scotland, beyond which is no habitation, since we desire nothing but our own'. Approaching the end of the letter the language rose to a climax: 'for as long as a hundred of us remain alive, we intend never to be subjected to the lordship of the English in any way. For it is not for glory in War, riches or honours that we fight but only for the laws of our fathers and for freedom, which no good man loses except along with his life'. It concluded with the admonition, 'But if your holiness too credulously trusts the tales of the English fully or does not leave off favouring the English to our confusion then we believe that the Most High will blame you for the slaughter of bodies, the destruction of souls and other misfortunes that follow, inflicted by them on us and by us on them'.[6]

However far it was orchestrated by Robert Bruce and his ministers such a patriotic claim for national independence was remarkable in the early part of the fourteenth century. Its sentiments were to be mirrored in the United States Declaration of Independence, directed against the British over four centuries later. But however powerful, neither the Pope nor the English king was as yet willing to heed the message. Admittedly the Pope did ask the English to justify their claim to Scotland but by 1325, after renewed English pressure, he still had not raised his interdict on the northern kingdom, although by now he at least addressed Bruce by his royal title.

In reality Scotland was not nearly so united as the Declaration pretended: indeed while it was being considered by the papacy charges of treason were being prepared against several who had actually placed their signatures on it. The reluctance of men like Roger Moubray, William Olifant and William Mowat to sign was demonstrated by their names not appearing in the main draft but being added last of all. Such men were supporters of Balliol and the Comyns who, according to the three chroniclers, Barbour, Fordun and Grey, during 1320 plotted to kill the king. With Bruce's success against the English seemingly so close they probably felt forced to reveal their hands in a desperate bid to seize power by assassinating Robert Bruce and placing their own candidate on the throne, in this case William de Soules, grandson of Alexander Comyn, Earl of Buchan. De Soules, who had also signed the Declaration, was the hereditary Seneschal (or butler) of Scotland. During the previous year he had helped to negotiate the truce with England but he was by no means a strong or charismatic figure. On the plot being discovered David Brechin, Gilbert Malherbe, John Logie and a squire, Richard Brown, were condemned to be executed by a parliament held at Scone on 4 August 1320. Gilbert Malherbe, John Logie and Richard Brown were accordingly drawn, hanged and beheaded while David Brechin was hanged and beheaded. Although another conspirator, Roger Moubray, died before being convicted, his body was brought before the judges to be quartered as a traitor. However on Bruce's intervention the body was spared and given decent burial. De Soules was treated comparatively leniently being condemned to perpetual imprisonment. He was confined in Dumbarton Castle where he was said to have died in a tower of stone. The same sentence was passed on the Countess of Strathearn, widow of the pro-Comyn Earl Malise, who was also involved in the plot.

With the conspiracy firmly suppressed, Bruce's position became stronger than ever. Although evidence of a less than united community within Scotland so soon after the Declaration was submitted must have caused a degree of embarrassment, none of the conspirators, except De Soules, had held high rank or belonged to the king's inner circle of councillors. Such a short, limited and unsuccessful uprising could not compromise Scotland's clarion call for independence.

However the Scottish military initiatives were continued, and by Christmas 1319 their superiority in the border areas was such that the English were compelled to ask for a truce of two years. This was accepted at a meeting between the two sides at Newcastle, where Scotland was represented by a deliberately restrained Scottish delegation led by William de Soules. Although the English delegates were given the authority to discuss a longer term peace they were still not allowed to recognise Scottish sovereignty, and this was not pursued. During 1321, as a result of new papal pressure, envoys from both countries met again to discuss a more permanent peace – but were no nearer to reaching an agreement.

On 6 January 1322, six days after the two-year truce ended, Douglas and Moray resumed the military pressure and restarted raiding. For the first two months the English were as divided among themselves as ever until under the command of Andrew Harcla (who had already distinguished himself against the Scots at Carlisle) the king's levies from Cumberland and Westmorland, clearly imitating Bruce's tactics at Bannockburn, defeated Edward II's bitter enemies the earls of Hereford and Lancaster. Hereford was killed and Lancaster, who had been secretly corresponding with Douglas, was taken prisoner before being executed.

As a result, in July 1322 Edward was able to lead his last expedition into Scotland. Bruce responded by refusing to be drawn into a major battle and reverting to his scorched earth tactics. Apparently, in the whole of the normally fertile Lothian region they found just one lame cow that could not be driven off. Seeing it, the Earl of Surrey remarked, 'This is the dearest beef that I yet beheld; for of a certainty it has cost a thousand pounds and more'.[7] As Bruce intended, the English army was soon brought close to starving and the king had no option but to withdraw. The initiative passed to his opponents who were not likely to miss such an opportunity.

After Edward II and his forces re-entered England many of them dispersed, and Bruce seized the chance of leading a powerful contingent in pursuit of the English king. Edward fled from Byland Abbey in Yorkshire to Rievaulx Abbey near Malton. Douglas and Moray, who were characteristically in the forefront of the Scottish forces, found their direct route to Rievaulx blocked by Edward's household knights under the Earl of Richmond, John of Brittany. Without hesitation the Scots attacked the powerful position, with Douglas and Moray leading the assault uphill while Highlanders charged along the even higher ground to its flank. Faced with a twin assault the English broke and ran, although they delayed Bruce long enough for Edward to escape. He rode to Bridlington where he took ship to York, but again suffered the humiliation of defeat, this time in his own country, and of having to abandon his personal equipment, including silver plate and jewellery, even his horse trappings and harness. Richmond himself was captured together with other nobility including a French lord, Henry de Sully, whom Bruce, unwilling to antagonise France, ordered to be released without ransom. Sully however developed such an admiration and liking for the Scottish king that, before his return to France, he offered to take part in negotiations between England and Scotland for a new and long-standing truce. Whatever approaches were being considered by the countries' two governments, from early 1323 many northern nobles made private treaties of immunity with the Scots in an effort to protect their communities. By far the most serious was made by Andrew Harcla, now Earl of Carlisle, who concluded that 'the King of England neither knew how to rule his realm nor was able to defend it against the Scots, who year by year laid it more and more waste, [and] he feared lest at last the King should lose the entire kingdom'.[8] Harcla entered into secret negotiation with Bruce and on 3 January 1324 negotiated a draft peace treaty which he openly proclaimed within his earldom. Edward II was enraged, proclaiming Harcla a traitor, and when a friend, Sir Anthony de Lucy, betrayed Harcla, Edward II had him taken prisoner and, after a summary trial, inflicted on him the traitor's fate of being hanged, disembowelled and quartered.

Carlisle no longer had a strong leader to defend it against the northern raiders and the likelihood of its capture gave the English a particularly strong reason to propose a new truce, this time for the remarkable period of thirteen years. It was accepted and ratified by Bruce at Berwick on 7 June 1324. A truce of such a length went far towards the English acceptance of Scottish independence and Bruce made his ratification as King of Scotland. By his acceptance Bruce must have believed a full-scale peace treaty was sure to follow long before the thirteen years elapsed. In the short term the truce's most important outcome was that England agreed not to oppose the Scottish supplication to the Pope requesting the removal of his interdict against their country. Moray was sent to Rome as Bruce's representative supported there by Henry de Sully. Despite Edward II's promise not to interfere, in 1324 he also sent a powerful delegation to press the Pope to continue with his interdict and, as a result, the only concession made by the papacy was the formal recognition of Bruce as King of Scots. In the same year the English king commanded Edward Balliol, son of king John, to come to England from Picardy where he had been living on the ancestral estates. The motive was plainly to run Edward Balliol as a contender for the Scottish throne. Despite Edward II's continued machinations, the truce succeeded in bringing a cessation of hostilities between the two countries and laid the foundation for genuine peace talks to commence at York in 1324, although Scottish hopes here broke down upon Edward II's continued intransigence. Earlier in the year, however, Scotland had been able to celebrate the long-awaited birth of an heir to Robert Bruce and his queen.

In 1326 Scotland's reacceptance as a sovereign European state moved a stage closer when relations between England and France declined and the 'auld alliance' was officially renewed with Scotland and France signing a defensive treaty whereby each country would come to the other's aid if they were attacked by

England. Whatever these developments in Europe might herald, it was England's recognition that remained all-important. The convulsions therefore in the English court which led to Edward II's deposition in favour of his fourteen-year-old son, and the king's subsequent murder by his wife Isabella and her lover, Sir Roger Mortimer, brought a new and dangerous situation for Scotland, especially as Edward's loss of Scotland had been cited as an important reason for his deposition.

Bruce was no longer robust physically and a seemingly endless truce while England regathered its military strength appeared to be neither in his nor Scotland's best interests. He therefore decided to remind the new English ruler of his military presence by attacking the castle of Norham on 1 February 1327, the very day of Edward III's crowning. The attack failed when the castle's commander received warning of it, and Bruce did not follow it up with further hostile acts. On 6 March the English Council of Regency under Henry, Earl of Lancaster, confirmed their desire for a renewal of the truce between the two countries, but although Scottish envoys went to York avowedly to negotiate its renewal, what both countries now wanted, in fact, was a resumption of warlike operations. On the Scottish side it was hoped that new military successes would at last force England to acknowledge their country's independence, and on England's part there was a new determination to re-exert their hold over what they saw as a rebellious Scotland and to inflict punishment for its destructive raiding. There could be no better fillip for the new regime than a victory over the Scots. From early April the English issued writs to commence military preparations and sent troops under the command of two earls, Lancaster and Kent, to Newcastle.

Following the inevitable breakdown of negotiations at York James Douglas wasted no time in making a raid into the English northern counties, thus marking the beginning of a fresh Scottish campaign. In early July, Douglas, Moray and Earl Donald of Mar led a far more considerable force into northern England, through the Kelder gap and down the North Tyne, with Wearsdale as their objective. Despite poor health, Bruce himself went to Ireland where he obtained a truce from the Ulster seneschal, Sir Henry Mandeville, that stopped him helping the anticipated

English invasion of Scotland. Bruce also brought away a promise of much-needed food supplies for the northern kingdom.

As Bruce had rightly anticipated, the new English government showed its own eagerness for military action by sending a large army to seek out and crush the Scottish forces. In support were many Hainaulters under command of John of Hainault to whose niece the young English king was betrothed. These included 700 mounted men at arms.[9] The English also brought a frightening new weapon in the shape of small cannons but during this campaign they remained impotent, as it rained so much that their gunpowder was rendered useless. The fifteen-year-old Edward III was the army's nominal commander, although in practice the direction came from the earls of Lancaster and Kent, with John of Hainault leading the cavalry. James Douglas was the overall Scottish commander and, in Bruce's absence, Douglas' remarkable leadership skills, clearly evident before and during the great battle of Bannockburn, came into their own.

The success of Scottish tactics during the campaign of July and early August 1327 and the corresponding bafflement and misery of the English have been described in graphic fashion by a Hainaulter, Le Bel. From the outset Douglas' lightly armed force, burning and pillaging as they went, led the English a rare dance through Wearsdale and Teesdale. The English were determined enough but their pursuit was impeded by their cumbersome train of waggons and the other equipment required by an orthodox force. As Le Bel described it, Douglas led them 'through woods and swamps and wildernesses and evil mountains and valleys'.[10]

At length Douglas chose a good defensive position south of the Wear and waited for his pursuers. The next day it started raining heavily and it continued to rain for a further eight days. On the ninth day the Scottish scouts captured an English squire, Thomas of Rokebury, but Douglas released him so that he could brief the English about the whereabouts of the Scottish camp. There was much manoeuvring as the English moved up and the Scots exchanged one good defensive position for another, but although Douglas was far better placed as a master of speed and surprise commanding a smaller and handier force, he determined to take no risks. At one point he and his fellow commanders refused Edward III's naïve request (in some ways reminiscent of the young Bruce's at Methven against Valence) that the Scottish forces leave their strong defensive position and fight superior numbers of English on the plain. As Le Bel reported, 'They said they would do neither the one nor the other. They said that, as the King and his staff could see, they were in his realm and had burned it and wasted it; and if this vexed him he could come and stop them, for they would stay where they were for as long as they pleased'.[11]

In such a situation Douglas' cunning came into its own, as he played on the enthusiasm of the English to pursue him and bring him to battle. On the night of 3 August Douglas suddenly decamped, but kept his camp fires burning to deceive his opponents. Moving across the Wear to Stanhope Park, one of the Bishop of Durham's hunting demesnes, he took up a strong position, with a river before it and an impassable marsh to its rear. The next day the English duly resumed their pursuit, and made camp on the river's opposite bank, from where they planned to surround Douglas' position and then starve the Scots out. However, the English were so tired after their move and the labour involved in setting up their tents that they neglected to put out an adequate number of picquets. That night Douglas led a raiding party into the opposing camp, cutting down large numbers of sleeping and bewildered men as he went. Spurring into the centre of the encampment he slashed the guy ropes of the royal tent and attempted to seize the young monarch, but despite inflicting many casualties on the king's household, including its chaplain, he failed. In fact, the tables were almost turned for as he waited to shepherd his men out of the camp, he only narrowly avoided capture.

The next day the English set about investing Stanhope Park, certain that Douglas would be forced eventually to attempt a break-out and suffer defeat in the process. Douglas' co-commander Moray also saw no other option than to fight. But the Scottish commander knew differently: on 6 August he arranged for a Scottish knight to be 'captured' who told the English that Douglas was planning a break-out attempt that evening. In expectation the English stood to arms all through the night as Douglas' heralds blew their horns in an endless series of commands and his camp fires continued to burn brightly. Under cover of this activity the Scottish army stole away over the seemingly impassable marsh, which they crossed by laying down wooden hurdles that they afterwards retrieved. When dawn came and the English could make out the empty camp on the opposite hillside, their opponents were four or five miles north on their way to Scotland.

During the campaign Douglas gave the English a classic lesson in waging war. If his despoiling tactics and avoidance of battle appeared unchivalric to both his opponents and possibly to many young bloods in his own force, they were the result of his long experience of warfare against the English, both before and during the great battle at Bannockburn. Like his master Bruce, he knew how much that victory had owed to shortcomings in English leadership. During the Wearside campaign he realised the only hope for the English was to pin him down and destroy his forces. He was determined to deny them that and in the process to demoralise the large army they had assembled at such cost: this achieved, northern England would be open to further destructive raids.

Meanwhile gazing across at the guttering campfires in the Scottish camp the English leadership knew only too well they had no further military options. Their army was utterly worn out, their horses ruined and the men's personal equipment rotted by the rain. Their only course of action was to return south, baffled and empty-handed. Faced with such humiliation the young Edward III burst into tears in his disappointment and frustration. Back in York it became clear that although the English might issue further writs for military service, their offensive capability had been temporarily destroyed. With the exchequer empty (the crown jewels had been pawned to pay for the mercenaries) and the Hainaulters dismissed, Douglas' skills had made sure the military initiative stayed in Bruce's hands. Once the Scottish army had rested and been given new horses the destructive raids were resumed across Northumberland together with attacks upon its castles, and Bruce now began openly to grant lands to his supporters there as a clear signal that he intended to incorporate the county into Scotland, to be followed no doubt by others.[12]

As intended, the English now seriously entered into peace negotiations and their delegates arrived in Edinburgh on 10 March 1328. Agreement between the two nations, including a dynastic union between Bruce's son, David Bruce, and King Edward's sister, Joan, was reached within seven days to be ratified by an English parliament at Northampton on 4 May. The thirty-two-year war had finally ended and with it Bruce achieved his lifelong aim.

Bannockburn provided the martial platform that led to Scotland's eventual re-emergence as a sovereign state free from English suzerainty and to the recognition of Robert Bruce, the usurper claimant, as her legitimate king. It gave Scotland a military ascendancy over England which under Bruce it never lost, and an increased pride and confidence that led the Scottish leaders to address, even to chide, the Pope not just on behalf of their king but the whole community of the realm to remove his interdict over the country. Without the outstanding personal qualities of Robert Bruce, the rare skills and commitment of his commanders, and the constancy of the Scottish church it is extremely doubtful whether the English would have finally been forced to sign the Treaty of Northampton. Without their defeat at Bannockburn they would certainly not have done so.

No later consideration can invalidate the primary contribution of Bannockburn towards the regaining of Scottish independence. However, Bruce's death a year later was followed by those of his leading commanders in the battle, Douglas in 1330 and both Moray and Keith in 1332, the latter in battle at Dupplin Moor. With the passing of the men who fully understood the grave risks Bruce had taken at Bannockburn and knew the true extent of English military incompetence there, later Scottish commanders were liable to be less circumspect. Raymond Campbell Paterson condemned subsequent Scottish military leaders for having 'an illusory sense of invulnerability': this may be too harsh, but they certainly deserve to be criticised for a disastrous lack of imagination.[13]

Traditionally, serious defeats cause nations to rethink their military options; from Wallace's defeat at Falkirk Bruce realised his schiltrons had to be trained in mobility, and following their defeat at Bannockburn the English realised the need to co-ordinate their different arms in battle. The fractious English knights, who in 1314 decried both archers and spearmen, were soon to fight dismounted shoulder to shoulder with ordinary soldiers, and with longbowmen on their flanks. This deadly combination was to give them victories over Scotland at Dupplin Moor (1332), at Halidon Hill (1333), Neville's Cross (1346) and at Flodden Field (1513). It also gave them ascendancy over France at Crécy in 1346 and Poitiers in 1356, despite being heavily outnumbered. At Crécy all the English infantry were bow-armed, but while it was primarily a victory for the English longbow, Edward III also adopted earlier Scottish tactics to reinforce his success by, for instance, digging pits to slow the advance of the opposing cavalry.[14] Significantly Crécy, like Bannockburn, was a victory for a smaller, well-disciplined army against a much more powerful adversary who failed to make his numerical superiority count.

Bannockburn had a quite different effect upon Scottish commanders. It established a tradition, or at least re-emphasised the favoured Scottish characteristic of taking the offensive, but in doing so at Dupplin Moor, Halidon Hill and Neville's Cross – against English archers supported by dismounted knights – they suffered terrible casualties in the process. There also came into being an enduring faith in the schiltron, the thicket of yeoman spearmen who had proved so formidable under Bruce's direction. This faith persisted into the mid-sixteenth century with the disastrous battle of Pinkie Cleuch (1547) where the Scottish schiltrons, unsupported by cavalry or archers, were assailed from all sides by heavy English cavalry, supported by long and shortbowmen together with mounted arqubusiers, and most deadly of all by massed guns firing at short range, whose shot tore bloody corridors in their massed ranks. With their dedication both to the offensive and the schiltron Scottish commanders forgot what was arguably Bruce's greatest legacy to Scottish arms, the ability to switch their formations from the offensive to the defensive. Weaker leadership would allow fatal divisions to appear in the command structure as at Dupplin Moor, when the rivalry between Lord Robert Bruce and his overall commander, Donald of Mar, led to them disputing who would be first to charge the enemy, with the result that both were killed.

It might seem all too simple to attribute the Scottish defeat at Pinkie Cleuch to their victory at Bannockburn over two centuries before, although the Scottish commander there, James Hamilton, Earl of Arran, ordered his army to leave a strong defensive position and attack in a tragic parody of Bruce's initiative. At Pinkie, unlike Bannockburn, Arran was fighting an enemy who had gained greater military experience from fighting on the continent. It is also true that Scottish tactics had remained static and unimaginative, with too little appreciation of the fact that cavalry would re-emerge as the arbiter of war supported by a new military arm. This could in part have been due to Scotland's lack of involvement in European wars, but not entirely since many Scottish mercenaries had taken prominent roles in the continuing conflicts abroad. Victory at Bannockburn was undoubtedly a factor, and an important one at that, in Scottish over-confidence that led to costly and repeated defeats.

Even still, Bannockburn's positive attributes are incomparably greater. However many times Scottish armies might have been subsequently beaten by the English, however weak the country's monarchs or divided its national councils, even with their king a captive in English hands, Scots still remembered that they had succeeded in checking English ambitions to incorporate their country into a greater England. By the Treaty of Northampton, Edward, grandson of Edward Longshanks, Hammer of the Scots, whose aim was nothing short of full conquest, 'willed and consented that the said Kingdom, according to its ancient boundaries, observed in the days of Alexander III should remain unto Robert King of Scots, his heirs and successors, free and divided from the Kingdom of England, without any subjection, right of service, claim or demand whatever; and that all writings which might have been executed at any time to the contrary should be held as void and of no effect'.[15]

This remains the true measure of Robert Bruce's victory at Bannockburn.

NOTES

INTRODUCTION TO THE 700TH ANNIVERSARY EDITION

1 Letter from Robert the Bruce to Edward II (London, British Library, MS Cotton Titus A XIX, f. 87r).
2 As a result the crest subsequently adopted by the Grey family took the form of a scaling ladder.

INTRODUCTION

1 As a result the crest subsequently adopted by the Grey family took the form of a scaling ladder.
2 *Chronicle of Lanercost*, 208.

PROLOGUE

1 Murison, A F, *Sir William Wallace*, 105.

CHAPTER ONE

1 Fergusson, J, *William Wallace*, 9.
2 Barrow, G W S, *Robert Bruce and the Community of Scotland*, 12.
3 Traquair, Peter, *Freedom's Sword*, 31.
4 *Chronicle of Lanercost*, 145.
5 *Andrew of Wyntoun's Orygynale Cronykil of Scotland*, Book vii, ch. xi.
6 Paterson, Raymond Campbell, *For the Lion*, 9.
7 Morris, J E, *The Welsh Wars of Edward I*, 283.
8 Fergusson, J, *op. cit.*, 39.
9 Neither Agnes Mure MacKenzie in her *Robert Bruce, King of Scots*, nor the authoritative Professor Barrow pointed to the

presence of the nobles with Wallace's cavalry at Falkirk as a potent factor in his choosing to fight where he did.

10 Murison, A F, *Sir William Wallace*, 35–6.

11 Morris, J E, *op. cit.*, 286–92.

CHAPTER TWO

1 Barrow, G W S, *Robert Bruce and the Community of the Realm of Scotland*, 84.

2 *ibid.*, 123; Stones, E L G, *Anglo-Scottish Relations, 1174–1328*, No. 32, 120.

3 Barrow, G W S, *op. cit.*, 124.

4 Calendar of Documents Relating to Scotland, Vol. ii, 1420, 1437, 1653.

5 *ibid.*, 1071.

6 *ibid.*, 1978.

7 *ibid.*, 1092, 1111.

8 Barbour, John, *The Bruce*, 13.

9 *Chronicle Guisborough*, 366–7.

10 Bower, Walter, *Scoticronicon*, Vol. 7, Book vi, 309–13; Scott, Ronald McNair, *Robert the Bruce*, 72.

11 *Liber Pluscardensis*, Book ix, 229.

12 Barrow, G W S, *op. cit.*, 148.

CHAPTER THREE

1 Wright, Thomas (ed.), *Chronicle of Pierre de Langtoft*, 367.

2 Stones, *Anglo-Scottish Relations*, No 34, 237–9.

3 *Chronicle Rishanger*, 211.

4 Barbour, John, *The Bruce*, 24.

5 Scott, Ronald McNair, *Robert the Bruce*, 87 (Sampson, Official Guide, Kildrummy Castle).

6 Barbour, John, *op. cit.*, 54; Bingham, Caroline, *Robert the Bruce*, 141.

7 Palgrave, F, (ed.), *Documents and Records Illustrating the History of Scotland*, 358.

8 Barbour, John, *op. cit.*, 50.

9 *ibid.*, 76, 77.

10 *Chronicle Lanercost*, 182.

11 Scott, Ronald McNair, *op. cit.*, 242 (King Robert's Testament).
12 Gough, Henry (ed.), *Itinerary of King Edward I*, Vol. ii, 266–275.
13 Calendar of Documents Relating to Scotland, Vol. iii, 80.
14 According to Barbour the date of the battle was 31 December 1307. This is plainly wrong and Professor Barrow inclines to a later date, likely to have been 23 May 1308.
15 Barbour, John, *op. cit.*, 148; Young, Alan, *Robert the Bruce's Rivals*, 14.
16 Acts of Parliaments of Scotland, Vol. I, 1124–1423, 289.
17 *Chronicle Lanercost*, 190.
18 *Vita Edwardi Secundi*, 12.
19 *ibid.*, 48.
20 Barbour, John, *op. cit.*, 182.
21 *ibid.*, 184.

CHAPTER FOUR

1 *Rotuli Scotiae*, I, 86.
2 Morris, J E, *The Welsh Wars of Edward I*, 286–93; Calendar of Documents Relating to Scotland, Vol. ii, 956.
3 Morris, J E, *Bannockburn*, 40.
4 Powicke, Michael, *Military Obligation in Medieval England*, Oxford, 1962, 135.
5 Morris, J E, *op. cit.*, 82–3.
6 MacNamee, Colm, *The Wars of the Bruces*, 23.
7 Hyland, Ann, *The Warhorse, 1250–1600*, 7.
8 *New Foedera*, ii, 203.
9 Hyland, Ann, *op. cit.*, 31.
10 Davidson, Martin and Levy, Adam, *Decisive Weapons*, 33–6.
11 Caldwell, David H, *Scottish Weapons and Fortifications 1100–1800* (Edinburgh 1981), 254.
12 Morris, J E, *Bannockburn*; MacKenzie, William Mackay, *Bannockburn*.
13 Traquair, Peter, *Freedom's Sword*.
14 Round, J H, *Feudal England*, 292; Morris, J E, *Welsh Wars of Edward I*, 41.
15 Barrow, G W S, *Robert Bruce*, 207.
16 *Vita Edwardi Secundi*, 201.
17 Barbour, John, *The Bruce*, 186.
18 Morris, J E, *Bannockburn*, 292.

19 Calendar of Documents Relating to Scotland, Vol. ii, 1882; Vol. iii, 190.
20 Traquair, Peter, *op. cit.*, 183.
21 General Christison is the author of *Bannockburn: The Story of a Battle*, National Trust for Scotland, 1962.
22 Becke, Major A F, 'The Battle of Bannockburn' in *The Complete Peerage* 1949, Vol. xi, Appendix 13, 15.
23 *Scoticronicon* (1759 edition) ii, xxi, 248.
24 MacKenzie, W M, *op cit.*, 23.
25 Barbour, *op. cit.*, I, 426.
26 Calendar of Chancery Warrants, I, 436.
27 Barbour, *op. cit.*, 191–2.
28 Barrow, *op. cit.*, 210.
29 Scott, Ronald McNair, *Robert the Bruce*, 146, 7.
30 *Rotuli Scotiae*, I, 120a.
31 MacNamee, *op. cit.*, 125.
32 Scott, Ronald McNair, *op. cit.*, 144.

CHAPTER FIVE

1 *Documents and Records Illustrating the History of Scotland*, 19–20, 29–31.
2 *Chronicle Lanercost*, 111–112.
3 Scott, Ronald McNair, *Robert the Bruce*, 23.
4 *The Scots Peerage*, edited by Sir James Balfour Paul, ii, 432.
5 Barrow, G W S, *Robert Bruce*, 124.
6 Ranald Nicholson, for instance, has written caustically that by 1306 Bruce 'seemed to have purged himself of any excessive Scottishness'. [Nicholson, R, *Scotland: the later Middle Ages* (Edinburgh 1974), 70.]
7 Calendar of Documents Relating to Scotland, Vol. ii, 1807.
8 Barbour, John, *The Bruce*, 160.
9 Calendar of Documents Relating to Scotland, Vol. iii, 76 and 362.
10 Barbour, John, *op. cit.*, 169.
11 Barrow, G W S, *op. cit.*, 293.
12 Barbour, *op. cit.*, 237.
13 Barrow, G W S, *op. cit.*, 436.
14 Scott, Ronald McNair, *op. cit.*, 188.
15 *ibid.*, 173.

16 Barbour, John, *op. cit.*, 9.
17 Taking full advantage of Lamberton's secret agreement Douglas struck down the Bishop's groom who tried to prevent him from taking the horse.
18 Barbour, *op. cit.*, 21.
19 This was the case at Weardale in 1327 when the English fought against Scottish forces led by Douglas and Moray.
20 Acts of the Parliaments of Scotland, I, 119.
21 Royal Commission on Historical Manuscripts, 5th Rep. Appendix, 626.

CHAPTER SIX

1 Prestwich, Michael, *The Three Edwards*, 79.
2 After he had become king one household account still included quantities of iron and plaster for his private works. Cottonian MS, 57.
3 *Chronicle Lanercost*, 206.
4 Cottonian MS, 84.
5 Wright, Thomas, *The Roll of Arms of the princes, barons and knights who attended King Edward I to the siege of Caerlaverock*, 1864.
6 Calendar of Documents Relating to Scotland Vol. ii, 1191.
7 *Foedera Conventiones, Litterae*, I, ii, 983.
8 Calendar of Documents Relating to Scotland, Vol. ii, 1909.
9 Hamilton, J S, *Piers Gaveston, Earl of Cornwall 1307–1312* (Wayne State University Press, 1988), 35.
10 Skene, W (ed.), *Johannis de Fordun, Chronica Gentis Scotorum* (Edinburgh 1871), 346.
11 Edward's remarkable devotion to Gaveston went beyond the grave; the king's outlay on his burial and for devotion to be paid to his memory amounted to £850, apart from his subsequent grants to Gaveston's family and servants. [Hamilton, *op. cit.*, 100.]
12 Phillips, J R S, *Aymer de Valence*, 21.
13 Barbour, John, *The Bruce*, 24–5.
14 *Vita Edwardi Secundi*, 11.
15 *Chronicles of the Reigns of Edward I and Edward II*, ii, 183, 195.
16 Phillips, J R S, *op. cit.*, 61, 62.

17 *ibid.*, 280–1.

18 Thompson, Edward Maunde, *Dictionary of National Biography* (OUP, 1995).

19 *Chronicle of Walter of Guisborough*, 274.

20 Parliamentary Writs, Vol. ii, 676.

21 *Chronicles of the Reigns of Edward I and Edward II*, ii, 191.

22 Turner, T H, 'The Will of Humphrey de Bohun, Earl of Hereford and Essex', *Archaeological Journal*, Vol. 2, 1845, 346.

23 Chron. Knyghton, 2480.

24 *Chronicles of the Reigns of Edward I and Edward II*, i, 171.

25 Barbour, John, *op. cit.*, 224.

26 *Foedera Conventiones, Litterae*, I, 974–5.

CHAPTER SEVEN

1   Calendar of Documents Relating to Scotland, Vol. iii, 365.

2   *Vita Edwardi Secundi*, 50.

3   *Rotuli Scotiae*, I, 127.

4   Calendar of Documents Relating to Scotland, Vol. ii, 1168.

5   Hyland, Ann, *The War Horse*, 34.

6   Calendar of Documents Relating to Scotland, Vol. iii, 361.

7   MacKenzie, W M, *The Battle of Bannockburn*, 41 (note).

8   Some of the old cuttings are still clearly evident today.

9   Barrow, G W S, *Robert Bruce*, 302.

10 Earlier commentators, including W M MacKenzie interpreted the pows as pools, MacKenzie calling them 'great blobs or lagoons of water' but Professor Barrow has effectively demolished this explanation by establishing them as streams, whether slow-running or not.

11 Barbour, John, *The Bruce*, 190–191.

12 *ibid.*, 192.

13 Christison, General Sir Philip, *Bannockburn National Trust Guidebook* 1997, 15; Traquair, Peter, *Freedom's Sword*, 185.

14 Barbour, John, *op. cit.*, 193.

15 *ibid.*, 195.

16 Barrow, G W S, *op. cit.*, 217.

17 *Chronicle Lanercost*, 225.

18 Barbour, John, *op. cit.*, 200.

19 *ibid.*, 200.

CHAPTER EIGHT

1 *Vita Edwardi Secundi*, 51.
2 Barbour, John, *The Bruce*, 202.
3 *Scalacronica*, 54.
4 Barrow, G W S, *Robert Bruce*, 221.
5 *Chronicle Lanercost*, 225.

CHAPTER NINE

1 *Vita Edwardi Secundi*, 51–2.
2 Barbour, John, *The Bruce*, 209.
3 Morris, J E, *Bannockburn*, 39.
4 Barbour, John, *op. cit.*, 209.
5 *ibid.*, 210.
6 *Scalacronica*, 54–5.
7 *Vita Edwardi Secundi*, 51; *Chronicle Lanercost*, 206.
8 Barbour, John, *op. cit.*, 204–5.
9 *Scalacronica*, 55.
10 Barrow, G W S, *op. cit.*, 319 (*Chronicon Galfridi le Baker*, Thompson (ed.), 7).
11 Morris, J E, *op. cit.*, 72.
12 *Scoticronicon*, Vol. VI, Bk 12, Ch. 22, 365.
13 *Chronicle Bower*, ii, 249–50.
14 Barrow, G W S, *op. cit.*, 215.
15 Ramsay, Sir James of Bamff. *Genesis of Lancaster*, Vol. i, 1307–1368 (Oxford 1913), 65.
16 MacKenzie, W M, *The Battle of Bannockburn*, 92 (MS held in Corpus Christi College, Cambridge).
17 *Chronica Monasterii de Melsa*, Bond, E A (ed.), 1867, Vol. II, 331.
18 Miller, T, *The Site of the Battle of Bannockburn*, Historical Association 1931.
19 His arguments here are contained in Christison's *Bannockburn: the Story of a Battle* (National Trust for Scotland, 1962 edition).
20 Scott, Ronald McNair, *Robert the Bruce*, 150–151.
21 Traquair, Peter, *Freedom's Sword*, 90.
22 Letter of General Christison to Hugo Millar in the *Scotsman* of 5 July 1960.

CHAPTER TEN

1 *Chronicle Lanercost*, 225.
2 Barbour, John, *The Bruce*, 212.
3 Traquair, Peter, *Freedom's Sword*, 192.
4 *Vita Edwardi Secundi*, 204.
5 Barbour, John, *op. cit.*, 214.
6 *Chronicle Lanercost*, 225.
7 *Chronicle, Baker of Swinbroke* (edited with notes by Edward Maunde Thompson) (Oxford, 1889), 8.
8 Barbour, John, *op. cit.*, 217.
9 MacKenzie, W M, *The Battle of Bannockburn*, 79.
10 *ibid.*, 220.
11 *ibid.*, 221.
12 *ibid.*, 222.
13 *ibid.*, 223.
14 Sinclair, Andrew, *The Sword and the Grail* (1993), 46–7.
15 On the anniversary of the battle Scottish Templars still pay tribute to their predecessors who fought there.
16 *Scalacronica*, 142.
17 Barron, Evan, *The Scottish War of Independence*, 472.
18 *Chronicle Lanercost*, 228.
19 Becke, Major A F, *The Complete Peerage*, Vol. xi 1949, Appendix B.
20 Barbour, *op. cit.*, 225.
21 *Scalacronica*, 56.
22 *Chronicle Lanercost*, 226.

CHAPTER ELEVEN

1 Barbour, John, *The Bruce*, 255; *Vita Edwardi Secundi*, 54.
2 Barbour, John, *op. cit.*, 227.
3 Phillips, J R S, *Aymer de Valence, Earl of Pembroke 1307–1324*, 75.
4 *Vita Edwardi Secundi*, 55.
5 *Chronicle, Baker of Swinbroke*, 9.
6 Barron, Evan, *The Scottish War of Independence*, 473.
7 Barbour, John, *op. cit.*, 227.
8 Phillips, J R S, *op. cit.*, 116–17.

9 *Chronicles of the Reigns of Edward I and II*, iii, 231.

10 Phillips, J R S, *op. cit.*, 116, 7.

11 Barbour, John, *op. cit.*, 227.

12 *Chronicle Lanercost*, 209; *Vita Edwardi Secundi*, 55; *Scala-cronica*, 143.

13 Barbour, John, *op. cit.*, 234.

14 Riley, HT (ed.), *Historia Anglicani of Thomas Walsingham*, 2 vols, Rolls Series (London 1863–4) Vol. i, 141–2.

15 Barbour, John, *op. cit.*, 230.

16 Barrow, G W S, *Robert Bruce*, 230.

17 Mackenzie, Agnes Mure, *Robert Bruce King of Scots*, 282.

18 Morris, E J, *The Welsh Wars of Edward I*, 88, 98.

AFTERMATH

1 McNamee, Colm, *The Wars of the Bruces, 1306–1328*, 66.

2 Barron, Evan, *The Scottish War of Independence*, 479.

3 *Chronicle Lanercost*, 229.

4 Barrow, G W S, *Robert Bruce and the Community of the Realm*, 337.

5 *ibid.*, 342.

6 *Scoticronicon*, Vol. vii, Book 13, 3.

7 Barbour, John, *The Bruce*, 318.

8 Paterson, Raymond Campbell, *For the Lion*, 82.

9 Fryde, N, *Tyranny and Fall* (Cambridge 1979), 185–92.

10 *Chronique de Jean le Bel* (Paris 1894), 55/6.

11 Davis, I M, *The Black Douglas*, 138.

12 *Rotuli Scotiae*, 2216.

13 Paterson, Raymond Campbell, *op. cit.*, 104.

14 Wailly, Henri de, *Crécy: Anatomy of a Battle* (1987), 51.

15 Ramsay, Sir J H, *The Dawn of the Constitution* (1908), 196.

SELECT BIBLIOGRAPHY

Acts of Parliament of Scotland 1124–1423.

Barbour, John, *The Bruce*, translated by George Eyre-Todd, Edinburgh, 1907.

Barron, Evan McLeod, *The Scottish War of Independence*, 1914.

Barrow, G W S, *Robert Bruce and the Community of the Realm of Scotland*, Edinburgh, 1988.

Bingham, Caroline, *Robert the Bruce*, 1998.

Bower, Walter, *Scoticronicon*, edited and translated by D E R Watt, Aberdeen, 1991.

Brooke, Daphne, *Wild Men and Holy Places*, Edinburgh, 1998.

Calendar of Documents Relating to Scotland, Joseph Bain, Vol. 3, 1307–57, Edinburgh, 1887.

Caldwell, David H, *Scotland's Wars and Warriors*, The Stationery Office, 1998.

Chronica Majora Matthew Paris, 1880.

Chronica Monasterii S. Albani, edited by H T Riley, London, 1863.

Chronicles of the Reigns of Edward I and Edward II, edited by W Stubbs, Rolls Series, London, 1882.

The Complete Peerage, Vol. xi Rickerton to Sisonby, 1949.

Bartholomaei de Cotton, Historia Anglicana, 1859.

Christison, Philip, *Bannockburn: A Study in Military History*. Proceedings of the Society of Antiquaries in Scotland, Vol XC, 1959.

Davis, I M, *The Black Douglas*, 1974.

Documents and Records Illustrating the History of Scotland, edited by F Palgrave, 1837.

Dodge, W P, *Piers Gaveston*, 1899.

English Historical Review, Article by J G Edwards, xxxix.

Fergusson, J, *William Wallace, Guardian of Scotland*, Stirling, 1938.

Fergusson, Sir James, *The Declaration of Arbroath*, Edinburgh University Press, 1970.

Flores Historiarum of Matthew Paris, edited by H R Luard Lord, 1890.

Foedera, Conventiones, Litterae, edited by Thomas Rymer, London 1816–18.

Gough, H, *Itinerary of Edward I*, 1900.

The Chronicle of Walter of *Guisborough*, edited by H Rothwell, Camden 3rd Series Ixxxix.

Royal Commission on *Historical Manuscripts*, 5th Rep, Appendix.

Chronicon Walteri de Heminburgh, Vol. II.

Itinerary of King Edward I, edited by Henry Gough, 1900.

Johnstone, Hilda, *Edward of Carnarvon*, Manchester, 1946.

Chronicle of Lanercost, edited and translated by Sir Herbert Maxwell, Glasgow, 1913.

Chronicle of Pierre de Langtoft, edited by Thomas Wright, 1866.

Mackenzie, Agnes Mure, *Robert Bruce, King of Scots*, 1934.

MacKenzie, W M, *The Battle of Bannockburn*, Glasgow, 1913.

McKisack, M, *The Fourteenth Century 1307–99*, Oxford, 1959.

McNamee, Colm, *The Wars of the Bruces*, Tuckwell Press, 1997.

Morris, J E, *The Welsh Wars of Edward I*, Oxford 1968.

Murison, A F, *Sir William Wallace*, 1818.

Nicolas, N H, *The Siege of Caerlaverock*, 1818.

Palgrave, F. *Documents and Records Illustrating the History of Scotland*, 2 vols.

Paterson, Raymond Campbell, *For the Lion*, Edinburgh, 1996.

Paterson, Raymond Campbell, *My Wound is Deep*, Edinburgh, 1997.

Liber Pluscardensis, edited by F S H Skene, Edinburgh, 1877.

Powicke, M, *Military Obligations in Medieval England*, Oxford, 1962.

Prestwich, M, *Edward I*, 1988.

Prestwich, M, *The Three Edwards*, 1996.

The Scots Peerage, edited by Sir James Balfour Paul, Vol. 2.

Phillips, J R S, *Aymer de Valence, Earl of Pembroke 1307–1324*, Oxford 1972.

Ramsay, J H, *Genesis of Lancaster*, Vol. I, Oxford, 1913.

Reese, Peter, *William Wallace*, Edinburgh, 1996.

Chronica Willelms Rishanger, edited by H T Riley, Rolls Series, 1865.

Rotuli Scotiae, edited by D Macpherson, 1814–19.

Scalacronica of Sir Thomas Gray of Heton, translated by Sir Herbert Maxwell, Glasgow, 1907.

Scott, Ronald McNair, *Robert the Bruce*, Edinburgh, 1993.

Stones, E L G, *Anglo Scottish Relations 1174–1324*, 1965.

Traquair, Peter, *Freedom's Sword*, 1998.

Tout, T F, *The Place of the Reign of Edward II*, Manchester, 1914, 1936.

Vita Edwardi Secundi, notes and introduction by N Denholm-Young, 1957.

Walsingham, Thomas, *Historia Anglicani*, 1863.

Watson, Fiona, *Under the Hammer: Edward I and Scotland*

1286–1307, Tuckwell Press, 1998.

Andrew of Wyntoun's Orygynale Cronylcil of Scotland, edited by David Lang, Edinburgh, 1872.

Young, Alan, *Robert the Bruce's Rivals: The Comyns, 1212–1314*, Tuckwell Press, 1997.

INDEX

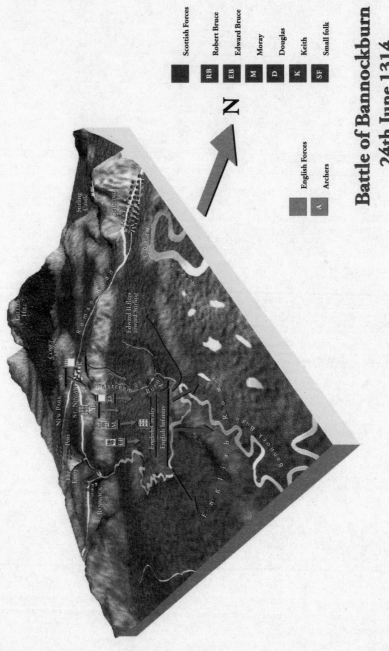

Battle of Bannockburn 24th June 1314

N

	Scottish Forces
RB	Robert Bruce
EB	Edward Bruce
M	Moray
D	Douglas
K	Keith
SF	Small folk

	English Forces
A	Archers

Stirling Castle

STIRLING

River Forth

Gillies Hill

Roman Road

CONEY HILL

New Park

St Ninians

Halbstream Burn

Edward II flies toward Stirling

English Cavalry

English Infantry

Bannock Burn

BANNOCK

The Entry

The Poss

English Road

ROBERT THE BRUCE: KING OF SCOTS

RONALD MCNAIR SCOTT

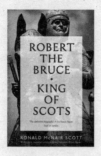

The definitive biography of Scotland's legendary leader by British novelist and former Sunday Times literary critic, Ronald McNair Scott

Robert the Bruce had himself crowned King of Scots at Scone on a frozen March morning in 1306. After years of struggle, Scotland had been reduced to a vassal state by Edward I of England and its people lived in poverty. On the day he seized the crown Bruce renewed the fight for Scotland's freedom, and let forth a battle cry that would echo through the centuries.

Using contemporary accounts, Ronald McNair Scott tells the story of Scotland's legendary leader, and one of Europe's most remarkable medieval kings. It is a story with episodes as romantic as those of King Arthur, but also one which belongs in the annals of Scottish History, and has shaped a nation.

'The definitive biography of this heroic figure' *Mail on Sunday*

'A thundering good narrative . . . splendidly told'
Sunday Telegraph

£9.99

978 1 78211 177 1

www.canongate.tv

WALLACE: A Biography

PETER REESE

'I have brought you to the ring, now hop if you can.'

Wallace's famous injunction before the battle of Falkirk is still remembered today. The first section of this major biography deals with the history of Wallace and his time. Wallace's courage and heroism during Scotland's darkest days were instrumental in creating a sense of national identity. From the early killing of the Sheriff of Lanark, Sir William Haslerigg, through his crowning triumph at Stirling Bridge to his terrible end, Wallace was unswerving in his devotion to the cause of Scottish freedom. The brutality of his end is a testament to the fear and humiliation his name inspired in Edward I.

The second section of the book studies the impact of the man and the myth on later generations. The guerrilla tactics initiated by Wallace were later used by Robert the Bruce to great success. Blind Harry's epic poem (1478) personifies the will and desire of Scottish people for independence in the figure of Wallace. Over 200 years after his death Scotland's greatest knight continues to inspire nationalists in this country and throughout the world.

£9.99

978 0 86241 607 2

www.canongate.tv

CANON‖GATE.tv

CHANNELLING GREAT CONTENT

WATCH

INTERVIEWS, TRAILERS, ANIMATIONS, READINGS, GIGS

LISTEN

AUDIO BOOKS, PODCASTS, MUSIC, PLAYLISTS

READ

CHAPTERS, EXCERPTS, SNEAK PEEKS, RECOMMENDATIONS

DISCOVER

BLOGS, EVENTS, NEWS, CREATIVE PARTNERS

SHOP

LIMITED EDITIONS, BUNDLES, SECRET SALES